Spa-Finders® Guide to Spa Vacations

Spa-Finders® Guide to Spa Vacations

AT HOME AND ABROAD

Jeffrey Joseph

*President, Spa-Finders Travel
Arrangements Ltd.*

with Dari Giles

Produced by The Philip Lief Group, Inc.

WILEY

John Wiley & Sons, Inc.

New York • Chichester • Brisbane • Toronto • Singapore

This book contains descriptions of many spas and the numerous treatments they offer. Material on treatments, diets, and exercise regimens is presented for informative purposes only. The author does not endorse any particular spa or treatments. Readers should consult with their personal physician to determine whether a particular treatment, diet, or exercise program is compatible with their medical and physical status.

Library of Congress Cataloging-in-Publication Data

Joseph, Jeffrey.
    Spa-Finders guide to spa vacations : at home and abroad / Jeffrey
  Joseph, with Dari Giles.
        p. cm.
      "Produced by the Philip Lief Group, Inc."
      Includes bibliographical references.
      ISBN 0-471-51555-8
      1. Health resorts, water-places, etc.—Directories. I. Giles,
  Dari. II. Spa-Finders Travel Arrangements, Ltd. III. Philip Lief
  Group.
  RA794.J67   1990
  613'.122'025—dc20   89-48992
                                                                CIP

Printed in the United States of America

    10   9

Spa-Finders Guide to Spa Vacations describes, in depth, some of the best spas in the United States and around the world. Jeffrey Joseph, President and founder of Spa-Finders Travel Arrangements, Ltd., has surveyed thousands of his clients in order to get the most complete and specific information and feedback about each spa. The unique guest feedback sections included with almost every spa entry relay the actual sentiments of Spa-Finders clients, offering the reader first-hand knowledge of what to expect at specific spas.

ACKNOWLEDGMENTS

My thanks go to the wonderful people who lent their kind support and assistance in making this book a reality—Arthur Black, Hannelore Leavy, Mark Dmytryk, Frank van Putten, Maggie Marshall, Robinson Rea, and Larry Cannon.

DEDICATION

My family, who provided the financial and moral support that has made Spa-Finders possible—

my parents, Ben and Gloria Joseph;
my brother, Leslie Joseph;
and my sister and brother-in-law, Corrine and Moshe Shukartsi.

—Jeffrey Joseph

How This Book Is Organized

The *Spa-Finders Guide to Spa Vacations* is designed to help you find the perfect spa for you. It explains how to locate the specific information you want quickly and easily. The introduction and the four chapters that follow give you a good indication of what the spa experience is like and what you should look for when choosing a spa vacation to meet your individual needs.

Chapter 4 begins with a health profile questionnaire that is designed to pinpoint your spa vacation needs. It covers diet, exercise, and pampering, as well as other life-style considerations. The questionnaire is followed by the "Spas-at-a-Glance Handy Reference Guide," which presents a geographical listing of the spas described in this book. The listing begins with an explanation of the symbols used throughout the book. The letter symbols indicate types of spas (e.g., FB-SC stands for Fitness/Beauty Spas—Self-Contained), and the dollar signs refer to the price range of a week-long spa visit.

Chapter 4 is then divided into separate sections for each spa type, including a section on spas abroad. Entries are listed alphabetically within each section. Some spas belong to more than one category; complete listings appear once, and cross-reference symbols are supplied where appropriat .

At the back of the book, the Spa Almanac lists spas by specific categories, such as "The Best Workout Spas." "Spas on the Beach," and "Spas with Supreme Pampering." Finally, the Beauty and Pampering Glossary provides definitions or descriptions of many of the terms and treatments described in the book.

Contents

Introduction: The Joy of Spa-ing   1

1 Spa Exercise   15

2 Spa Pampering for Men and Women   25

3 Spa Cuisine and Nutrition   31

4 Finding the Perfect Spa for You   39

Your Health Profile   41

Spas-at-a-Glance Handy Reference Guide   52

Fitness and Beauty Spas (Self-Contained)   58

Fitness and Beauty Spas (at a Hotel or Resort)   97

Luxury Spas   183

Weight-Loss Spas   207

New Age Retreats   235

Spas Abroad   245

Spa Almanac   273

Beauty and Pampering Glossary   281

Index   285

Introduction:
The Joy of Spa-ing

Ah, spas . . . for slimming, soothing, pampering, and renewing, spas to change the way we live, eat, move, and even the way we breathe.

"Spa" is the name of a town with a celebrated watering place in Belgium's Ardennes Forest. The ancient Romans first discovered Spa's natural springs, and the iron-rich waters that flow from them have been recognized as lowest in salt or mineral impurities—the purest water in the world. Today, the term "spa" is a generic term used to describe an amazing array of health-oriented vacation opportunities, with choices in everything from geographic location to nutritional philosophy.

As recently as five years ago, most people's idea of a health spa was a place for the rich and famous to slim down or dry out. But as five million people visit spas each year, these misconceptions are quickly dispelled. Who really goes to spas? *Time* magazine noted that the profile of the typical American spa-goer has radically changed: "Middle-class baby-boomers are overtaking the rich and elderly as primary spa clients."

And why not? These days a spa vacation can be one of your best travel buys, with a great variety of options, values, and discount packages available for the price-conscious. Some cater to women, sprinkled with "men only" and "couples only" weeks, while others welcome men and women working out together. Low-key and low-maintenance, a spa vacation is generally devoid of glitz and glamour, and it doesn't require an expensive wardrobe. But the real appeal of a spa vacation is that it is actually an investment in yourself—your chance to rethink, reevaluate, and relearn the way you live in this fast-paced world.

For smart people concerned about the quality of their lives, I believe that regular spa visits are as important as appointments with the dentist and the doctor. Vacationing at a spa renews our commitment to becoming the best that we can be—fitter, stronger, trimmer, and more centered—ready to deal with all the dilemmas of daily life without overloading on stress. After all, good health and physical fitness are a process of evolving. A spa vacation speeds up the process and makes it a whole lot more fun. Thousands of my clients agree, and you will, too.

Whatever your fitness goals or pampering desires, whatever your financial resources, you can find a spa to fit your needs. We're here to help, so let's get started.

Different Types of Spas

Choosing the right spa is crucial, but I've made that easy by describing the seven most popular types of spas—by which this book is organized. And in Chapter 4 you'll find a detailed self-discovery questionnaire to help you narrow down your choices and tailor your spa vacation to fit your personal "wish list," making sure that your spa experience is satisfying in every way. You can also use the handy spas-at-a-glance chart found on page 52 to cross-reference your choices.

CLASSIC (SELF-CONTAINED) SPAS

Classic spas—such as The Oaks at Ojai in California—are the places we picture celebrities visiting. The entire facility is dedicated to fitness and relaxation, weight loss or weight management, and body pampering. Not just for the rich and famous, there are many spas in this category that are nonexclusive and surprisingly affordable.

If you want to explore all of your fitness and health options while enjoying equally healthy doses of self-indulgence, the classic spa may be your best bet. Self-contained spas tend to take a very focused view of fitness and health. They emphasize diet and exercise, and usually ban the use of tobacco and alcohol on their premises. The people who go to these spas (mostly women) do so because the environment offers them total support in their efforts to lose weight, manage stress, and to change and improve their life styles. And you'll be happy to find that spa-goers who share similar goals tend to draw together like members of a club.

Even if you've never taken a spa vacation, you probably have a fairly accurate idea of what such a stay involves: aerobic dance, elegant low-calorie cuisine, plenty of personal attention, and expert beauty care. Add a total lack of worldly pressures, hours of peaceful repose, and you have a truly unbeatable vacation combination. You might even spot a few celebs working out next to you, but never fear: Homemaker or CEO, everyone looks the same in leotards and sweats!

Classic spa programs differ, of course; some emphasize fitness while others stress beauty—even to the point of providing their own lines of specially prepared cosmetics. Several spas offer highly individualized personal service. They range in size from an intimate 8 guests to more than 100. Some are for women only, offering special weeks for couples and men; others are strictly co-ed. To give you the best possible atmosphere in which to unwind and regroup, these spas are often off the beaten path, located in the mountains or by the seashore.

In addition to familiar services such as manicures and pedicures, the menu at a beauty spa may also include more esoteric treatments such as herbal wraps, salt-glo loofah massages, therapeutic baths, Thalassotherapy, and others you will find explained in the Beauty and Pampering Glossary.

SPAS WITHIN A HOTEL OR RESORT

What do you do if your idea of a vacation is to soak in a mud bath and hike three miles at daybreak, while your travel companion prefers only to laze in the sun and sip margaritas? Very simply, check out the offerings of a spa in a resort or hotel. A spa within a hotel or resort usually offers enough options to accommodate those who want to diet and exercise and those who want to eat, drink, and goof off. Depending on the size of the resort, you or your partner can play tennis, golf, shop, and party until the wee hours of the morning at the resort's nightclubs—options you won't find at a classic spa.

Today, hotels, motels, inns, and resorts of all sizes and descriptions offer services that only a few years ago would have seemed totally and unbelievably fantastic. Modern resorts, for example, have grown into minicities with their own recreation, entertainment, shopping, and conference centers.

In addition, what used to be just another amenity at many luxury resorts and hotels has become an integral part of their list of services. Many facilities have been renovated to offer state-of-the-art spa facilities that make it possible for one member of a couple to "spa" while the other enjoys more traditional vacation pleasures. For example, you or your companion can enjoy a massage and a facial while the other plays golf or tennis; then both of you can see a movie or go dancing after dinner, without ever leaving the grounds.

Of course, there are drawbacks for the spa vacationer at this kind of facility. For one thing, you might have to eat your low-calorie dinner while sitting next to someone devouring a meal of steak and fried potatoes topped with a huge helping of strawberry shortcake and a (gasp!) cigarette for dessert. For another, these big hotels and resorts often accommodate large groups of people, such as conventions, and you know how happy-go-lucky and noisy they can be. You'll have to put up with all sorts of temptations, as well as a majority who have no interest in changing their life styles. But, short of taking separate vacations, this may be your best travel plan.

THE LUXURY SPA

The finest luxury spas in the world share an almost tangible determination to offer their guests the very best of everything, down to the smallest detail. You can be assured of peaceful surroundings, privacy, superb services, ultramodern facilities, an impressive selection of programs and pampering treatments, gourmet cuisine, and cozy accommodations, plus many other amenities.

All of these spas give you a level of individual attention designed to make you feel like one of the most important people in the world. Some even limit the number of guests they can pamper at one time to as few as eight lucky people, each with his or her own personal counselor.

Food plays an important role at any spa, and luxury spas offer meals that rank high in flavor and low in calories. You'll enjoy dishes originated by some of the most famous chefs in the field, including Michel Stroot of Cal-a-Vie, whose name has become synonymous with nouvelle spa cuisine, and cookbook author Jeanne Jones of Canyon Ranch. Most spas will also teach you how to prepare these delicious low-cal meals at home. Of course, you pay for all this pampering and attention. A stay at a luxury spa can cost anywhere from $2,000 to $3,500 a week, or more.

NEW AGE RETREATS

The term "New Age" has come to describe everything from computer technology to alternative medical treatments to the search for spiritual enlightenment. Applied to spas, "New Age" suggests a program of health and wellness that takes into account a "whole-life" attitude. Such New Age retreats offer a wide variety of vacation experiences so you should have no difficulty finding one with a program of special interest that appeals to you.

You will exercise more than just your muscles at these retreats, because you will be challenged to expand your mental and spiritual concepts, as well. New Age retreats offer interesting alternatives to traditional spa vacations, with many different, often novel approaches to weight loss, stress reduction, smoking cessation, and various forms of homeopathy.

What can you do at a New Age retreat? Almost anything. Activities include yoga, massage, and bodywork techniques such as Shiatsu and accupressure, and even alternative beauty options such as aromatherapy. Some New Age retreats also offer saunas and hot tubs, hiking and horseback riding, and training in various forms of meditation.

New Age retreats offer nutritional programs ranging from juice fasting to strict vegetarianism, with great emphasis on whole grains, fresh fruits, and vegetables. Accommodations range from deluxe to economy, from the coziness of a private, peaceful cottage to the togetherness of a spartan dorm. At one retreat, you can sleep in a "yurt," a kind of geodesic dome resembling the portable tents used by Mongol nomads in Siberia. Most guests say they liked it.

A few New Age retreats espouse very specific philosophies such as Eastern religious disciplines, but most serve simply as health-conscious retreats for the spirit as well as the mind and body.

WEIGHT-LOSS SPAS

Once upon a time, people with serious weight problems signed themselves into so-called "fat farms," which often meant subjecting themselves to a prisonlike atmosphere and a strictly supervised program of deprivation. However, modern spas take a totally different, and far more pleasant, approach to weight loss.

Today, behavior modification and well-balanced, low-calorie nutrition are emphasized. These spas offer tasty-but-slimming meals, customized exercise programs, and instruction in weight-management, stress-relief, and relaxation techniques. You even have your choice of three types of weight-loss spas: medical, such as the Duke University Diet and Fitness Center; nonmedical, such as Bermuda Inn Fitness Resort (California); and fasting, such as the Deerfield Manor (Pennsylvania).

Whichever type you choose, you will find that weight-loss spas teach you to deal positively and effectively with the stress of obesity, how to build a favorable new self-image, and how to incorporate healthy eating habits into your daily life. Most spas also give you the opportunity to learn how the chef cuts calorie corners in the kitchen.

Weight loss often takes time as well as effort, so many weight-loss spas offer programs longer than the traditional six-night/seven-day spa week, an important consideration for those who want to check in for the duration and lose weight in a protected environment.

What do you eat at a weight-loss spa? Although nutritional programs differ among spas, you can expect to find some basic similarities in spa cuisines. Most serve a cuisine based on complex carbohydrates, built around pastas and whole grains, fresh fruits and vegetables, fish, and poultry. Doesn't sound like a starvation diet, does it? Eating light doesn't necessarily mean eating little, because spa menus include foods that make economical use of calories. First-time spa-goers are always amazed when they sit down to a huge salad, a generous portion of pasta primavera, whole wheat bread, and fresh fruit compote—high-fiber foods that keep portions low in calories.

Actually, spa menus served as the inspiration for the popular nouvelle cuisine of the eighties, while offering some of the most elegant eating you can find anywhere. Whatever your problem, and whatever your price range, there are a great variety of weight-loss spas to choose from.

MINERAL SPRING SPAS

In one often-quoted scene from the classic movie *Casablanca*, Claude Rains asks Humphrey Bogart why he came to Morocco. "I came for the water," Bogart explains.

Told that Morocco has no mineral spring waters, Bogart merely shrugs his shoulders nonchalantly: "I was misinformed."

Civilization discovered the benefits of mineral waters thousands of years ago, and folks the world over have sought them. Indeed, some cultures have long cherished mineral springs as sacred ground and credit the waters with providing cures for, or at least relief from, a wide range of ailments. Thermal therapy has earned recognition as one of the oldest continuous health therapies.

What you do with mineral waters depends to some extent on where you do it. Some waters you drink; others, particularly those from hot springs, you soak in. Hot spring enthusiasts say nothing can match the soothing effects of a relaxing soak in their effervescent warmth or the delight of a skin-smoothing mud bath. In addition, most mineral spring spas offer a variety of massages, saunas, blanket wraps, and other forms of hydrotherapy such as the century-old Kneipp water treatment (see Glossary).

Most mineral spring spas charge moderate rates—under $500 per week—and many of the most famous spas in Europe offer exceptional values. In this book we've listed spas that offer an endless array of services and deluxe accommodations in historic inns and castles for less than the cost of an *a la carte* stay at a deluxe domestic spa. (Note that there is no separate section in this book for mineral spas, although some spas are cross-referenced as such. Look for the notation "MS" on the spas-at-a-glance charts.)

SPAS ABROAD

Shopping for a spa that offers you historic charm in authentic Old-World surroundings, the opportunity to socialize with an international group of people, enjoy exotic beauty and pampering treatments, and soak up the curative powers of the famed fed mineral waters? That's a tall order, but spas in other parts of the world do offer those things.

These fitness, beauty, and vacation bargains await you in Europe and elsewhere around the world. For sheer value and remarkable variety, these spas are unequaled. But keep this in mind: Outside North America, "spa" usually means something quite different from what it signifies here. Spas overseas, particularly in Europe, specialize in medically supervised treatments and cures. Depending on the mineral contents of the waters and special treatments available, physicians prescribe visits to certain spas for specific treatments in the same way that doctors here prescribe medications for what ails you. Also, for the most part, spas abroad do not offer the kind of diet and exercise programs that you will find at domestic spas. Spa-goers abroad use spa facilities for treatment or cure of specific ailments. And because many countries abroad have socialized medical plans, and many foreign physicians believe in the healing properties of waters from natural mineral springs, the medical plans often pay for therapeutic spa treatments.

In the past, many spas in the United States enjoyed great fame for the curative powers of their mineral waters, and the affluent visited them in great numbers. Unfortunately, in the late 1800s, the U.S. medical establishment negated the value of natural cures. Many spas lost their popularity and were forced to close their doors. However, if physicians in the United States ever take a second, more positive look at the benefits offered by natural mineral waters, it could lead to a new boom for mineral spring spas on both sides of the Atlantic.

Currently, European spas, especially those in Eastern Europe, offer particularly good buys for those seeking to combine medical treatments with vacation pleasure. Because cure programs take time, however, many Eastern European spas require a minimum stay of one week or longer. Your medical insurance just might cover some of your treatments, so go over your policy carefully and check with your insurance agent or carrier. If you are partially or fully covered, don't forget to get the proper claim forms to take with you.

International spa choices range from historic Grayshott Hall in England, once the country home of Alfred Lord Tennyson, to the medical facilities of the high-rise resort Hotel Incosol near the Mediterranean in Marbella, Costa del Sol in Spain; from Brenner's Park Spa in Baden-Baden, Germany, gateway to the Black Forest, to the famed Clinique La Prairie, specializing in "fresh-cell therapy," in Montreux, Switzerland, on the shores of Lake Geneva; and from the luxurious Royal Hotel in Evian, France, to the stylish Daniel Hotel and Spa overlooking the Mediterranean in Israel.

You'll find that European spas cater to many special interests. For example, if you enjoy visiting classical ruins and ancient historical sites, take your camera to Montecatini, in the heart of Tuscany in Italy. The Incosol Spa in Marbella, Spain, has an equestrian school for those of you who take horseback riding seriously. All of this, plus the regenerative powers of soothing, mineral-rich waters!

What to Pack

The key to preparing for a spa vacation is to pack light! In general, spas have an informal and relaxed atmosphere and dress is equally casual. Jeans or slacks, t-shirts, and sweats are actually "dress" at most spas, though you may enjoy having a lounging outfit or two to wear on special evenings—arrival and departure days are common "dress up" times at most spas, if it's necessary at all. Although some spas are dressier than others, particularly the luxury spas and those at resorts where people do dress for dinner, you'll know exactly what to bring when you receive a pre-arrival packet of vital information.

It is far more important that you bring the basics: socks (you can never bring too many pairs), leotards and tights, sweatpants and shirts, a couple of swimsuits (so that one is always clean and dry), a robe, and rubber-soled slippers, your working wardrobe for a week. Most spas have laundry facilities on the premises, but why spend precious time rinsing out leotards and tube socks every night when you can enjoy an informative lecture or curl up with a good book?

Pack that swimsuit in a few plastic bags and you'll have a neat and tidy way to transport soggy items back and forth during your stay. And don't forget your swimming cap, goggles, and sunglasses. Bring lots of sweatbands or bandanas for tying hair out of the way while you work up a healthy sweat, and bring at least one good-size towel as even spas seem to think that all of us are postage-stamp-size when we step out of the shower or pool. For extra support during your workouts, men should bring athletic supporters and women should wear support bras.

Obviously, footwear is important for a spa vacation, and your first day at a spa is not the time to break in a new pair of expensive athletic shoes. Bring your most comfortable pair of broken-in walking or athletic shoes. If you must buy a new pair, break them in before you begin intense exercise. Although shoes needn't cost a fortune, very cheap sneakers may not provide the support and traction you'll need to do aerobic dance on wooden or carpeted floors. Look for a moderately priced shoe made specifically for aerobic activity or racquet sports. Also, there are several brands of special athletic socks on the market designed to minimize blistering, and although they're more expensive, they can be a real lifesaver on a seven-mile hike. Most spas have a nurse on staff to deal with minor aches and injuries, but you may want to pack a blister treatment kit like Spenco's Second Skin and a supply of bandages.

While you're putting your travel kit together, make sure you include your personal care items, as well as sunscreen and any medicines or prescription drugs that you use regularly. Many spas are well off the beaten path, and you won't want to hike to the drug store because you've fotgotten something crucial. Some spas do sell over-the-counter personal-care items, but why chance it?

Obviously, you'll pack appropriately for the season, but a light raincoat and folding umbrella always come in handy. Spa exercise is addictive, and you'll find you won't want to miss the morning hike just because of a light drizzle. At all the California spas you will need a light jacket for the morning and evening activities, no matter the season, because it tends to get chilly at night. This is also true for those in mountains and valleys across the country.

Items that top the "I wish I'd thought to bring list" include a personal stereo, favorite tapes (particulary relaxation and inspirational tapes), and extra batteries; camera and extra film for capturing images of newfound friends and scenic vistas; and a travel alarm clock so that you won't have to depend on someone else to get you up for morning meditation. Although most spas have a library, you should bring a good, long book to read during your quiet times. You will also need a notebook to jot down information you're learning, to record your experiences and the addresses and phone numbers of new friends; a tote to carry changes of clothing for the day; and an extra bag for carrying home souvenir sweatshirts and boutique purchases.

Leave your jewelry, high heels, hair rollers, as well as your preconceptions, prejudices and worries about spas at home. Above all, bring an open mind and relaxed attitude. Drop off any lingering pretentiousness at the front desk.

Spa Etiquette

As relaxed as the spa atmosphere generally is, there are some unspoken rules of etiquette that help to make it an even more pleasant experience for everyone. For the first time in years, some of you will be sharing a room with a stranger. Good roommate manners mean compromise, but if you find that your night-owl biorhthyms are completely incompatible with your early-bird roommate's, talk to the front desk about a possible switch. Smoking is usually prohibited in all public areas at spas, and often, even in your room. By all means observe the spa's no-smoking policy. In fact, consider using this time to give up this unhealthy, ugly habit. Many spas offer some kind of cessation program and the support you need to become smoke free.

The exercise studio and weight room also have some rules of etiquette. Popular classes can get crowded. Your best bet is to get to class early. But if you have to squeeze in late, remember to give your workout neighbors room to fully extend their arms and legs. In the weight room, don't monopolize your favorite exercise machine or stationary bike. Let others have a turn; you can always get back on and continue your workout.

Pool and Jacuzzi etiquette means always showering first, especially if you've recently had a massage or other body treatment and are covered with oil. It also means wearing a bathing suit or something to cover your private areas, even in the sauna or steam room. For protection of your own health as well as that of others, always wear shower shoes when padding around these wet areas, even from the shower to the dressing room.

Tipping baffles many first-time spa-goers, and customs do vary. Sometimes tips are included in the package price, but if a gratuity hasn't been added to your bill, it's customary to leave about 15 percent of your total to be shared among the service staff. Most spas are happy to accept an envelope with cash or check left with the front desk management and will make sure that your thoughtfulness is gratefully received. Beauty and massage staff often aren't included in staff tip funds, so you may tip these professionals as you would those at your home salon. And always feel free to tip any member of the staff—except management, of course—who took extra pains to make your stay special.

Mealtimes are generally the center of social interaction and they are heartily anticipated. Most spas have informal seating so you'll have a chance to meet lots of new and interesting people. Don't be surprised to find that the major topic of conversation is food! Although spa food is delicious, beautifully prepared, and satisfying, for some reason everyone insists on describing the tallest sundae they ever ate, or the best barbecue in eastern Oklahoma. That's okay, but please don't tell your tablemates about the Twinkies in your overnight bag if you've been foolish enough to sneak in contraband. Spas are not simply a wonderfully affordable retreat; they are an investment of time as well as money. If you're going to go for it, go all the way. Give your tastebuds time to adjust to the natural, wholesome flavors of crisp salads and healthful entrees. Most likely, you'll get over your cravings for red meat, sugar, and junk food in a day or so. By the way, tummy-rumbling is a reality when you change your diet abruptly; if you can hear your own abdominal grumbling during a serious evening lecture, don't blush; others will be hearing their own. However, if digestive discomfort continues, do check with a staff member who is familiar with the "sudden roughage" syndrome.

Say Goodbye to Stress

Like any new adventure, visiting a spa for the first time may create nervous anticipation. Relax. Your spa visit can be a warm, nurturing, and supportive experience, with a minimum of stress, if you know what to expect and how to make the most of it before you go.

The spa experience can provide that much sought sense of direction. Here in the protected environment of a spa, away from the pressures of personal and professional conflicts, it's possible to get a brand new perspective on what's really important in your life. At a spa you have the time, space, and support to explore avenues of living that can enhance your life style. You can actually acquire skills that enable you to get more out of life—do more, feel better, and recapture the pure joy of living.

The key to happy spa-ing is to allow yourself the freedom to try new things and not to measure your success against others'. You succeed to whatever degree you are ready and able. There are no report cards at a spa, no final exam; the only person you have to compete with or please is yourself. Don't let anyone push you into attempting an advanced aerobics class if you're still trying to coordinate your jumping jacks, and don't drive yourself to distress. Relax, kick back, and have fun!

One of the first lessons you will learn during your spa experience is to find a balance between activity and rest. This is probably something you've taken for granted. However, one of the biggest causes of stress during a spa visit, particularly among first-timers, is running frantically from one class to another. The enthusiasm behind this behavior is understandable, even admirable, but if you don't take it all in stride, you will soon be too sore and exhausted to really reap the benefits of this special vacation. You may even end up bed-bound and depressed for precious days of your stay. Be kind to yourself. Pace yourself and schedule activities realistically. If you've been sedentary for years, don't try to beat your body into shape in a week or attempt Herculean feats of all-day exercise just to get your money's worth. It's false economics.

The spa staff will undoubtedly do their best to meet your needs, but you'll be on your own once you depart. Begin to explore assertively how you can incorporate more exercise, better nutrition, relaxation techniques, and a positive attitude into your everyday life. Above all, be honest and realistic about your intentions and expectations. Hidden agendas and fears often prevent your experiencing a program to its full advantage. If food is a big issue for you and your goal is to lose weight at the spa, don't sabotage your efforts by packing snack food in your suitcase. To the world you are making a statement of commitment with your spa visit; inwardly, too, commit fully by giving the spa nutrition plan and your own success a fair chance.

The primary point to remember about stress—over a spa visit or any other area of your life—is that situations do not create stress; it is your reaction that counts. And that's good news! If you can create your own stress, you can also alleviate it. You are in control. Within your own mind is the power to control and reduce the stress in your life. Begin by setting realistic, attainable goals for your spa vacation. Let go of old stress-producing phrases such as "I should" or "I must." Above all, have fun and enjoy the incongruities and crazy moments as well as the joys of spa-ing. Remember, those who laugh . . . last!

Dr. Betsy Morscher, one of the best-known experts on spa-style relaxation and coping with stress, offers some additional tips to make your stay great:

- ▶ Plan ahead. Emotionally set the stage for a good time. Pack your bags with plenty of enthusiasm, flexibility, and an adventuresome spirit; leave guilt and "shoulds" at home.

- ▶ Begin the spa experience in advance. Add more fresh fruits and vegetables to your diet, drink more water, get up 20 minutes earlier, and go for a walk before work.

- ▶ Start taking a daily minivacation. Close your eyes and take a few deep breaths; listen to soothing music and stretch leisurely like a cat.

- ▶ Anticipate any problems at work or home and have a plan of action so you won't be interrupted during your vacation.

- ▶ Leave a list of contacts and "what to do ifs" at the office and at home.

▶ Find out exactly what clothing and essentials are needed for your spa experience. Many a spa holiday has been hampered by bringing enough baggage to outfit a safari.

▶ If you are one for carrying excess baggage, consider also how much extra emotional baggage of unresolved fears, anger, conflict, and guilt you're schlepping, as well. Leave it behind with the extra luggage!

▶ If this is your first time at a spa and you're anxious or fearful, imagine the worst thing that could happen, and then the best. Write down any fears and confront them on paper. Then, tear them up and consider them faced.

▶ Congratulate yourself for making a wise choice in embarking on a spa adventure. It's your passport to a newer, happier, and healthier life style.

1

Spa Exercise

Fitness is one of the most important components of overall good health, and it is a big part of your total spa experience. Most of the spas featured in this book have fitness programs that are geared toward getting you motivated and committed to a regular exercise routine.

The typical day at a classic spa begins with at least one early-morning fitness option to get you revved up for the day. A pre-breakfast walk or hike, usually between one and seven miles, is popular. These walks, however, are not leisurely sightseeing tours. They are designed for aerobic effect—heel-to-toe with arms swinging at or above your waist. A beginner's walk may be a brisk two to four miles with some small hills or inclines along the way. Of course, if you feel faint before hitting the finish line, you are free to turn around and go back. There's usually a guide at the front of the pack and one bringing up the rear.

For early risers who prefer to exercise their minds along with their bodies, spas often offer meditation exercises, such as yoga or Tai Chi, to break in the day. Sometimes, too, it is possible to do both, beginning with meditation, then throwing on a warm-up suit for the hike. A piece of fruit or a glass of fruit juice is usually provided for those who need an energy boost before breakfast.

After the first well-balanced, nutritious meal of the day, the schedule of fitness classes goes into effect. For the benefit of those who choose to sleep "late," the day's activities usually begin with a morning stretch or other gentle warming up exercises. At larger spas where several classes are held concurrently, low-impact aerobics training or some other activity may also be scheduled. Sometimes there is a lecture or a workshop, or guests may have appointments with their trainer, counselor, or nutritionist. Midmorning classes often include aqua aerobics, aerobic or other kinds of dance classes, and weight training. Some spas feature fitness classes designed to work on specific "target" areas such as abdominal strengthening or upper-body toning. Gentle, deeply relaxing exercises or water exercises to cool down fatigued muscles usually wind up the morning fitness schedule.

Afternoons at many spas bring yet more intense aerobic activity, weight training, water exercises, meditation and relaxation exercises, and team sports. However, many guests use this time to schedule massages and beauty treatments. Others swim laps in the pool, sweat off some stress in the steam room or sauna, or ease themselves into the Jacuzzi before dinner.

The current trend is for spas to offer some kind of health-oriented, though usually passive, after-dinner activity. Many facilities schedule a guest speaker to lecture or lead a workshop. Subjects range from astrology readings to low-calorie cooking, from positive imagery to weight management. Sometimes, too, an evening walk is scheduled; if not, guests may get together for an informal evening stroll. A few spas even offer bedtime massages. If the one you choose doesn't, you can probably still relax in the sauna or whirlpool before settling down to a sound night's rest.

Generally, the larger the spa, the more extensive the facilities and the more choices you have. The key, though, is that the choice is always yours. Rather than trying to do it all, you may not need or want to do much at all.

Preparing Your Body

If you haven't been exercising regularly before your spa vacation, it's a great idea to begin an aerobic dance class to get into the swing and learn the moves. At the very least, try to begin a serious walking program about six weeks prior to your arrival at the spa. Begin with a brisk walk around the block, if that's all you can muster; you'll quickly build endurance and leg strength and find that you can walk four miles daily in a little over an hour—just the aerobic conditioning you need to lose weight and build a healthy cardiovascular system.

Aerobic Conditioning

In case you're still having trouble getting motivated, perhaps you're not fully aware of the benefits of aerobic exercise: It increases metabolic rate, which aids in weight loss and weight management, and improves muscle strength, stamina, and flexibility. Aerobic activity is a way to release stress, tension, and frustration and gives you a well-deserved good night's sleep.

Aerobic exercise is defined as an activity that raises your heart rate to within 60 to 85 percent of its capacity and keeps it there, at the "target heart rate," for a specified amount of time, usually 20 to 40 minutes. To get a ballpark figure of your maximum heart rate: Men should subtract their age from 205; women should subract their age from 220. Multiply this number by 60, 70, and 85 percent to get a target heart rate range. Knowing your resting heart rate is also helpful. This should be taken as soon as you wake up in the morning, before getting out of bed.

You'll have an opportunity to learn a lot about effective exercise at your spa. The expert exercise professionals will teach you to find your own target heart rate and show you how to maintain that rate for the required 20-minute minimum. If losing weight is your goal, you'll need to follow their lead. Only by exercising within this aerobic zone for 20 minutes or more approximately four times a week will you reap the weight-loss benefits of exercise.

We've become a nation of aerobics fanatics, but with all this new awareness and enthusiasm for exercise has come a new kind of problem: aerobic-dance-related injuries. The culprit? Early aerobics videos and classes taught high-impact routines that were big on jumping but low on safety. Since you're going to a spa to begin to get into the best shape of your life (or to enhance an existing program), it makes sense to take it slow and easy, and above all, to do it safely.

Most spas offer safe and carefully designed routines that take novice exercisers' needs into consideration. If you find yourself being inspired to "keep up" or exercise at a level you don't feel comfortable with, it's important to be assertive and stick to your own pace. You'll never be chastised for marching in place while others jog, so don't be embarrassed to tailor each routine to your own abilities.

Every exercise program should begin with a warm-up. This is a brief period—about five to ten minutes—of gentle movements such as walking or marching in place, but not stretching.

A stretching class is a wonderful option at most spas and teaches you to limber up safely; stretching classes are often combined with relaxation techniques and are held at the end of the exercising day, making them a great way to unwind before getting ready for dinner.

After the warm-up comes aerobic conditioning. For most of us, this means doing aerobic dance. A short time ago we were injuring ourselves in droves doing hard-on-the-body aerobics taught by early aerobics enthusiasts. Now, even aerobics queen Jane Fonda has softened her routines. These days, most spas emphasize the recommended low- or soft-impact aerobic dance which keeps one foot on the ground at all times. It also avoids jerking or bouncing moves. Increased use of arms and upper-body movements are just as effective for aerobic conditioning and are far safer than the old routines.

Never do your aerobic workouts without shoes. It's too dangerous! At most spas, if you show up with bare feet, you'll be politely, but firmly refused entry into an aerobic dance class. A good aerobic dance shoe can provide the support you need to protect your delicate foot bones while keeping you from slipping or falling during your workout.·

The main part of your workout is always followed by a cooldown period, which allows the heart rate to drop back into the normal zone. This is medically important for exercisers of all ages because failure to end with a cool-down phase can result in heartbeat irregularities and even more serious consequences. Even if everyone else plops down on the floor in exhaustion, take five minutes or so to walk or march in place, allowing your body to wind down and recover.

Walking

Walking is just now receiving the attention and praise it deserves as a safe, accessible, and enjoyable aerobic activity. Walking is a great calorie burner and back strengthener, and it also benefits the legs, hips, and that trouble spot—the lower abdomen. Aerobic walking also calls for you to pump your arms when you walk, exercising your arms, shoulders, and chest muscles. In addition, walking is easy on the bones and joints, and walkers are not likely to suffer from injuries common among runners, making this form of exercise accessible to almost everyone.

Fitness walking is generally considered to be somewhere between three-and-a-half and five miles per hour, which translates into between 120 and 175 steps per minute. Keep in mind, however, that as you get in shape, you'll have to walk faster, swing your arms more vigorously, and/or walk up more hills to get the same aerobic benefits. Walking up hill takes less time to burn the same amount of calories, but it is more taxing on the legs, buttocks, and lungs. Begin with a gradual incline and slowly work your way up to bigger hills.

Since walking has come of age, a wide selection of walking shoes are available. When buying a pair of walking shoes, keep in mind that you'll be wearing thick socks, your feet will swell (sometimes as much as a full size), and that you need to be able to flex your foot. The shoes should be light, but firm, and made with natural fibers and lots of cushioning.

Hiking

Hiking is another great aerobic workout that, like walking, accommodates all fitness levels. The key to reaping the benefits of a good hike is to do it properly. An easy-does-it start helps to ensure your safety. Once you get your blood warmed up and circulating, get into a steady pace. To maximize the workout benefits, never stop moving, no matter how slowly you may have to go. On the ascent of a hill, walk so that your heel, not your toes, hits the ground first; this will help to avoid the aches and pains of sore leg muscles. On the way down, keep your knees slightly bent and loose. And as with any aerobic activity, it is important to take time to cool your system down. Slow your pace and walk leisurely for the last half mile or so.

Dressing for a hike always raises questions. Should you dress for the warm temperatures to come or the cool morning air? Should you wear all your clothes or bring some for later? The rules are actually rather simple. Layer natural-fiber garments so that you can take them off as your body temperature rises on the ascent; then put them back on for the trip down when you'll be exerting less energy and your body temperature drops. It's also important to cover your head from the sun and the rain.

Obviously, what you wear on your feet is important. The general rule of thumb is to wear two pairs of socks: First slip on a thin pair made of nylon or some other synthetic fiber that "wicks" the sweat away from your foot, then pull on a thicker pair made of a natural fabric such as cotton or wool. The point is to keep friction to a minimum. Petroleum jelly can also help. A hiking myth is that you need hiking boots, but the reality is that a high-quality running shoe with lots of cushioning and extra room in the toe will do just fine. Later, if the demand is there, you can invest in a pair of hiking shoes or boots.

Working Out with Weights

Our attitudes toward women's bodies are changing dramatically. Now, models work out alongside competitive female body-builders in order to acquire the healthy, lean, and muscular shape that's replaced the spindly "Twiggy" look women suffered with for so long. You, too, should treat yourself to an introductory weight-training class. You'll quickly learn that weight training doesn't create bulging muscles, but rather tones and shapes as no other form of exercise can.

Put simply, training with weights makes you strong. Once the sole domain of he-men, women are now enjoying the benefits of a stronger, sleeker body and improved self-confidence that a strong body brings. Through weight lifting and training, you can improve your posture and actually shape and mold your body. No other kind of exercise can claim that feat—not even all the sit-ups, leg lifts, or aerobic classes in the world.

The two components of weight training are the amount of weight you lift, called the "overload," and the number of times you lift it, called "repetition." The heavier the weight, the fewer repetitions you will be able to do. To build muscle you must lift enough weight so that the muscle becomes fatigued after about eight to ten reps. That will change the shape of a muscle. When you are satisfied with the muscle development, begin a maintenance routine to build endurance in which you can comfortably do 12 to 15 reps.

When it comes to weight training, less is always best to begin. Form is what counts. Strive for smooth, controlled movements during lifting and letdown. Once that goal has been achieved and you can do 8 to 12 reps without fatigue, it's time to increase the weight and begin the routine again. As with other exercises, it is also important to warm up before lifting. Walking, rowing, skipping rope, or a few light repetitions of the exercise you are planning to do will be sufficient. And remember to breathe—exhale on exertion and inhale on release. Afterward, stretch your muscles out, holding each stretch static for about 30 seconds. Rest for 48 hours between weight-training workouts; you can use that period to do aerobics or some other enjoyable fitness activity.

The debate over whether to use free weights (dumbbells and barbells) or weight machines is endless. However, keep in mind that free weights help to improve your balance and coordination, as well as strengthen your body. Also, they're relatively inexpensive and mobile. On the down side, because you control movement and technique which both require concentrated effort, you are slightly more injury-prone than when you are working out with weight machines.

Weight machines are safe, efficient, and easy to use, particularly for beginners. Used properly, they are effective at developing strength and building muscle. The drawbacks to machines over free weights is that they are generally too large and expensive to keep at home.

Once you've decided to weight train, get a professional to assist you with using the equipment and developing proper form for lifting free weights. If you're more than 10 pounds overweight, you might want to get closer to your target weight before building muscle, because weight training sculpts your body, it does not help you to lose the extra weight. Remember, too, that you are in control of how far you progress, so don't worry about bulking up.

Common Exercise Mistakes and Myth-Busters

Tummies are a major area of concern for all of us, but you can't flatten a stomach by doing thousands of sit-ups; nor can you reduce any specific area of your body. Sit-ups and leg lifts build endurance, and aerobic exercise promotes overall weight loss.

Avoid locking or anchoring your feet when you do sit-ups; by keeping your joints stiff, you will put far too much stress on the lower back, and, in fact, decrease the effectiveness of sit-ups and abdominal work. To avoid back injury, let your feet move freely while you work the abdominal muscles.

Another exercise error is stretching before the warm-up. Remember, warming up means preparing muscles for the workout ahead; stretching and flexibility exercises are part of the workout. Toe touches or any stretch that keeps the knees locked are also too stressful to delicate joints and ligaments. Always keep your knees slightly bent, even if everyone around you is working with straight legs. Ballistic or bouncing movements are dangerous and should never be a part of any stretch routine.

Muscle pain is not necessarily an indication that you're getting a good workout. It's more likely that you are not doing the exercise properly. Don't strain your muscles beyond their capabilities at any time.

The only exercise you should not do on consecutive days is weight train. Otherwise, if it feels good, do it.

Bringing Your Exercise Program Home with You

It feels fine to flex your pectorals and work your glutus muscles while you're visiting a health spa, but how do you keep up the momentum? Here are some tips to keep you moving:

▶ The best time of day to exercise is whenever you want to and whenever you have the time.

▶ If you're trying to lose weight, set goals that are realistic and give yourself enough time to realize the results. Generally speaking, it takes more than five hours of aerobics to work off one pound of fat. Those who have been sedentary for a long time will see results faster than those who are more active. Also, when you first begin to exercise, the scale may go up because muscle weighs more than fat.

▶ Don't judge your progress by the scale, anyway; judge by the way you feel, the way your clothes fit, and the way you look to yourself in the mirror.

▶ Determine the activities that you enjoy doing and make them part of your daily routine.

▶ Don't allow yourself to fall into a slump with the same routine. You'll get bored. Find alternate routines and activities that will keep your body moving, preferably something you can easily take with you on the road.

▶ The key is to be consistent. Don't try to make up for 15 years of a sedentary life style with a few sessions of high-intensity activity. You'll only hurt yourself, get discouraged, and end up quitting altogether.

▶ Many professionals suggest keeping a daily exercise log of what you did and rating how difficult it was; make notes of any discomfort you may have experienced and any positive feelings, such as a "runner's high." If you want to, you can also keep track of your weight this way.

▶ Exercising isn't punishment; it's a commitment to your health and well-being. Do it regularly, whether you "ate the whole thing" or not.

▶ Find an exercise partner who you couldn't bear to disappoint by not showing up.

▶ With each goal reached—an inch here, another mile there— treat yourself to something nice such as a massage, facial, or new running shoes.

▶ Eat foods high in complex carbohydrates, such as a banana or rice cakes, about an hour-and-a-half to two hours before an intense workout. A snack afterward, as well as lots of water to cool and rehydrate your body, are also highly recommended.

The bottom line of exercise is to move, no matter what, and to do it on a consistent basis. The more you exercise, the stronger you will be. Exercise raises your metabolic rate and may play a part in suppressing appetite. It definitely increases your awareness of your body, often making it easier to control your eating. Now that you know it takes 20 minutes of running to "work off" one chocolate chip cookie, you're likely to think twice before "pigging out."

2

Spa Pampering for Men and Women

Hour-long massages, deep-cleansing facials, and fragrant body wraps are just a few of the frills fitness vacations offer. And after all the physical exertion, you'll want to give yourself at least one well-deserved pampering treatment. These indulgences don't just benefit the body, but the mind, too. They are supremely relaxing, often therapeutic, and often come as part of a spa package. For men and women who have hesitated to try these kinds of personal care services, a spa visit is your chance to experience some of life's true luxuries.

Women, who are used to having their hair styled or their nails manicured, usually have an understanding of how satisfying and refreshing personal services can be. On the other hand, the closest many men get to personal service is having their shoes shined. No matter your sex, you are in for something special. The skin-care professionals and massage therapists who administer these services will help you feel comfortable and relaxed with dim lights and soothing music.

Some treatments go back many centuries, while others incorporate the latest in modern science and technology. In fact, many treatments and therapies mentioned in this book may be unfamiliar to you, so we've included a glossary of commonly used fitness and beauty treatments; get to know them so that you can make informed decisions about which therapies are for you. Don't let ignorance deter you from experiencing something that could enhance your life and transform your thinking.

The Magic of Massage

Massage is taken quite seriously at most spas, and for good reason. More a therapy than a beauty service, massage is highly regarded as a method of relaxing knotted muscles, soothing exercise-stressed tissues, and increasing circulation. But the real joy of massage is melting beneath the touch of a talented massage therapist. "Gifted hands" are much sought after by spa afficionados, and after you spend time on the table, you'll know why.

When you make your first massage appointment, you may be able to choose whether you want a male or female therapist, although male masseurs are more common. Female massage therapists are called masseuses, if you want to know how to tell at a glance. Many people prefer a masseur, since a man's hands are often stronger and can knead muscles more deeply. However, a good massage is not based on how strong or gentle the touch is, but rather on how comfortable you feel with the therapist. You can always ask him or her for a gentler or stronger touch.

Women may feel uncomfortable with a male therapist at first, but the feeling fades with each stroke. If, however, you're really distressed by the notion, notify the staff and they'll usually be able to provide a masseuse for you. Men, on the other hand, have less to worry about since there is almost always a male massage therapist on staff. No matter who administers the service, your private areas are covered at all times. (Swedish massage is the only kind where oil is used and, therefore, is the only massage where you have to remove all of your clothing.) Women may also question whether or not to have a massage when they're menstruating. Yes, by all means, have a massage during your period, but wear a tampon. Massage therapy does wonders for menstrual cramps.

Some folks may feel uptight about having a stranger's hands on their naked bodies, but a session in the steam room or sauna will help loosen you up for the next stage of relaxation. Remember that you are in the hands of a professional and there is absolutely no reason to be shy.

First-timers are often baffled about what to wear to a massage, but it's really quite simple. At most spas you can comfortably travel from your room to the massage area in a robe and slippers, slipping out of the robe in the privacy of the massage room. Or if you prefer, you can wear a loose caftan or lounging outfit that's easy to remove. If you're too shy to remove all of your clothing, talk to the masseur or masseuse about it. He or she may suggest that you begin your session wearing a bathing suit, knowing that within a few minutes you'll relax completely and feel comfortable about a full-body massage without extraneous clothing.

Massages are often available in half-hour sessions, but few people feel that anything under an hour is enough. Your first time around you may want to go for part of an hour, but before you leave your spa vacation, treat yourself to the maximum. And don't laugh, but any difficulties with ticklishness should disappear after your second or third massage.

There are many different styles of massage, but the ones you're most likely to be offered are Swedish, Shiatsu, and sports massages.

SWEDISH MASSAGE
Swedish massage is the type you're probably most familiar with. It utilizes gentle stroking, gentle slapping, kneading, and deep circular motions to increase circulation and relax the body. All of the major muscle groups are covered, and a massage oil is usually used. All clothing should be removed.

SHIATSU MASSAGE
Shiatsu is the Japanese finger massage that mimics the Chinese therapy called acupuncture, except no needles are used in the massage therapy. Shiatsu is based on the principle that there are eight meridians or energy pathways in the body. Massaging these meridian points releases energy in the body, helping to relax and tone organs and increase circulation. This, too, is a popular form of massage, especially good for those in the clutches of lethargy.

SPORTS MASSAGE
Athletes have long benefited from massage therapy. Sports massage, like other types of massage, is therapeutic in nature, utilizing deep kneading and circular movements on specific muscle groups, or areas strained or injured during physical activity.

Other kinds of massage that are lesser known, but are becoming more commonly available are lymphatic drainage and polarity, reflexology, and Trager massage.

LYMPHATIC DRAINAGE (MANUAL)
As the name suggests, this is a light massage of the lymph glands to promote the movement of toxins out of the body, which is what the lymphatic system is supposed to do. This therapy increases activity of

the immune system, reduces pain caused by fluid retention, and is especially recommended to those who suffer from colds, sinus problems, headaches, and arthritis.

POLARITY MASSAGE

A combination of Eastern and Western massage therapies, polarity therapy was developed by an osteopath and is based on the same meridian principle as Shiatsu. It involves light to deep pressure combined with lots of gentle rocking, holding, and stretching of the muscles until the body is in correct alignment.

REFLEXOLOGY MASSAGE

This therapy usually focuses on the feet. Reflexologists believe that reflexes in the foot correspond to certain areas of the body. By massaging these specific points on the feet, the therapist can improve your circulation, promote relaxation, and relieve pain anywhere in the body. It doesn't tickle, and you don't have to undress except, of course, for your shoes and socks.

TRAGER MASSAGE

This gentle massage involves rocking, stretching, rotation, and compression of the body. It promotes flexibility and relieves tight muscles in the neck, shoulders, lower back, and chest.

Putting Your Best Face Forward

Massage may be the most popular therapy at a spa, but facials win hands down when it comes to pampering. Both men (after being coaxed into it) and women rave about the sensations of having their forehead, cheeks, chin, and temples gently stroked. You may not know it yet, but a facial can be as comforting as a full body massage, and, in fact, a talented facialist or aesthetician can actually put you right to sleep!

Besides being incredibly luxurious, facials are one of the best ways to deep-cleanse skin that is exposed to damaging environmental dirt and abused by the elements. Utilizing equipment that looks like it belongs in a dentist's office, the aestheticians unplug pores, remove blackheads with painstaking care, and rehydrate and smooth the skin on your face and neck. A good facial helps to make skin taut, softens lines and wrinkles, and leaves you with a natural, healthy glow that lasts for days.

Before going in for a facial, strip off any makeup you may be wearing, but don't scrub your face dry. Gently wash your face with soap and water, and, unless you must confront the cold outdoors, skip the moisturizer. Wear a loose-fitting top that leaves your neck exposed. Afterward, schedule time during your spa day when you will be able to relax for a while without reapplying makeup to your face. Enjoy your natural, healthy-looking glow.

Herbal and Body Wraps

Body wraps are often touted as weight-loss treatments, but don't be fooled. At best, a small amount of water weight is forced out of the body, but this perceived loss is only temporary. However, herbal treatments and body wraps are quite soothing to the mind as well as the body, making this a luxury well worth trying.

In an herbal wrap, you are enveloped in a cocoon of steaming linen sheets that have been brewed in fresh herbs, such as chamomile or peppermint. You are then left in a dimly lit room to relax and unwind while savoring the fragrant smells.

In a paraffin treatment (usually performed on the back), your body is slathered in a warm paraffin wax which will leave your skin silky smooth and glowing.

Mud, Water, and Mineral Treatments

There is an almost endless variety of mud, water, and mineral treatments. Some spas, such as Murrieta Hot Springs in California, specialize in mineral and mud baths and other forms of hydrotherapy, while others offer treatments utilizing elements from the sea. One such treatment for the skin is the salt-glo (or salt-glow) rub, where therapists combine handfuls of coarse sea salts with a fragrant oil, such as almond oil. The result is a wonderful sloughing solution that is rubbed all over the body, leaving your skin supple and clean.

Aromatherapy is an increasingly popular treatment in which delightfully fragrant herb essences are combined with steam for a relaxing, therapeutic result. Sometimes, too, the oils are rubbed on specific parts of the body to relieve discomfort. You leave feeling refreshed, relaxed, and soothed all over, and smelling like a garden.

Kneipp herbal treatments, which have been used in Germany to treat everything from cardiovascular disease and respiratory disorders to digestive and nervous disorders, use various oils and herbs dissolved in bath waters.

Men and women throughout the ages have known the healing properties of mineral springs, and to this day folks travel long distances to bathe in their warmth. Depending on their mineral content, these waters have been purported to cure everything from arthritis to rheumatic ailments. Some of the best mineral spring spas in the country are listed in this book. Many of the European spas specialize in mineral water treatments.

Mud baths, too, are a specialized treatment not offered at every spa. "Why would anyone want to be covered in mud, anyway?" you ask. Once you've experienced the therapeutic as well as soothing result, you'll know why. This treatment doesn't just use ordinary backyard mud, but mineral-rich earth from specific parts of the world which is slathered on a specific part of the body. As it hardens, it extracts impurities and toxins from the skin. After being washed down with a hose, your body is left feeling smooth, tingling, and refreshed. If you're lucky enough to be at a spa that offers this treatment, by all means go for it.

3

Spa Cuisine and Nutrition

"This can't really be only 900 calories, can it?" You'll hear these words at spa dining tables nationwide, usually followed by the hopeful query, "Can we actually lose weight eating all this food?" It's one of the happy paradoxes of spa life: healthful nutrition that is both ample and delicious. So if you're packing for your first foray into the wonderful world of spa vacations with a care package of Twinkies and Cheese Doodles, confess now and have no fear. It may take your body a couple of days to adjust to a regular meal schedule and the limited amount of fats and sugar, but you won't go hungry.

The majority of American spas follow a nutritional program that falls somewhere between the recommendations of the American Heart Association and the diet guidelines set by Nathan Pritikin, creator of the Pritikin diet. The spa style of nutrition is a complex-carbohydrate-based cuisine, created around pastas and whole grains, fresh fruits and vegetables, fish, and poultry. It is low in sodium, cholesterol, sugar, and fat, and provides plenty of energy for working out. Spa menus, after all, inspired the Nouvelle Cuisine of the eighties, and offer some of the most elegant and delicious eating to be found anywhere. Most international spas do not have a "diet" program and do not serve low-calorie-based meals.

Eating light doesn't necessarily mean eating little. It does mean designing menus consisting of foods that make economical use of calories. First-time spa-goers are always amazed when they sit down to a generous portion of pasta primavera, whole wheat bread, and fresh fruit compote. All of these high-fiber foods keep hearty portions low in calories.

Most first-time spa-goers want to lose weight, and an unfortunate but all-too-common mistake is skipping meals in the hopes of losing that extra pound. That's a "no-lose" proposition if losing weight is your objective, because eating too little can throw your metabolism out of whack and lead to the infamous yo-yo syndrome that all spa nutritionists like to lecture about. Skipping meals and participating in more exercise in a week than you'd normally do in a year is a first-class ticket to spa burnout and not a pound less of fat to show for it. Do yourself a favor: Trust the nutritionists and the chef— they've created a carefully balanced menu that provides all the nutrients and calories required for optimal health and energized workouts while promoting sane and permanent weight loss.

Although there are as many nutritional programs as there are spas, you can expect to find some basic similarities. Breakfast is taken seriously at spas; although too many of us skip breakfast in our daily lives to the detriment of our health and our waistlines, you'll soon learn that you need to charge your nutritional batteries for the active day ahead. Spa breakfasts can range from whole wheat waffles with apple butter to fresh fruit and omelets (usually made with egg whites and a single yolk for color), plus yummy fillings. Some spa aficionados secretly judge spas by the heft of their breakfast muffins.

Lunch can vary from elegant sit-down affairs to brown-bag buffets, from whole wheat pizza to enchiladas. At dinner, you may be surprised to be served such mouth-watering favorites as Cornish game hen a l'orange and shrimp scampi. Often, an all-you-can-eat salad bar accommodates both lunch and dinner. And yes, you can expect dessert with dinner, and sometimes lunch, too! Between meals, many spas put out herbal teas, fresh fruit and vegetable juices, and high-energy potassium broth for you to enjoy.

If you really feel hungry, light-headed, or dizzy, don't hesitate to ask for a piece of fruit or some veggies from the kitchen. Some spas have scheduled midmorning and midafternoon snack breaks, plus an after-dinner munchy, such as popcorn, a perennial snacking favorite at spas throughout the country. (Guests at the Palms at Palm Springs have been known to pout over who got the bigger bag of after-dinner popcorn). Veggies and low-cal dips are another popular treat. The idea is to teach you a new nutritional outlook and help you live with it once you return home.

Spas take special care to create satisfying, aesthetically pleasing menus that you'll want to re-create for family and friends. At most spas, you'll be given the opportunity to learn how to cut calorie corners in the kitchen, as well as the theories of sound nutrition and sensible weight loss or weight maintenance. You'll learn to prepare healthy, low-calorie menus for parties and holidays by substituting wholesome ingredients for those that simply put on pounds and shorten lives.

If spa directors could convince you of anything, it would probably be to "eat and enjoy" food, but to make good, healthful choices as you do it.

Spa Cuisine for the Home Kitchen

Before you pack your bags and leave for that well-deserved spa vacation, you may want to do some last-minute shopping: not for workout clothes, but for wholesome foods to eat when you get home. Laying in a stock of culinary essentials to re-create the splendid meals you'll enjoy during your retreat will ease your re-entry into home cooking and help you stick with your program.

To get you started, we asked one of the smartest nutrition experts around to share her tips for preparing spa-style cuisine at home. Leni Reed Riley, M.P.H., is a Dallas-based registered dietitian, author, and lecturer. She is also the originator of *Leni Reed's Supermarket Savvy Tour*, an aisle-by-aisle excursion that teaches you how to shop smart for better nutrition with fewer calories; an audiocassette entitled "Dining Out Without Doing Your Diet In" (Nightingale-Conant, 1987); and a collaborator on a cookbook/survival manual published by the American Heart Association. Here are Leni's tips on preparing spa cuisine at home:

Of all the ingredients found in a spa kitchen, herbs and spices, vinegars and oils are the flavorful flourishes that make meals sparkle. Your spa chef probably uses only the freshest herbs available, and you'll be amazed to smell and taste how fresh herbs can enhance your own cooking.

If you have a green thumb, check out your local farmer's market or nursery where, in spring and summer, you may be able to buy potted herbs. These decorative plants are easy to grow, make an attractive window display, and remain in easy reach for snipping when you're creating your kitchen masterpieces. For starters, you might select mint, dill, chives, and basil, or any assortment that tickles your palate. If you're not much of a gardener, try your neighborhood supermarket, gourmet shop, or health food store where you may find a wide assortment of fresh-cut herbs, or at the very least, fresh parsley and dill. If your grocer's selection isn't what you want, try asking neighborhood restaurateurs to order fresh herbs for you when they order their own.

Keep fresh herbs as you would cut flowers—in a glass jar with stems sitting in about half an inch of fresh water. Unlike your vase of roses, however, keep the jar of herbs in the refrigerator with a plastic bag loosely enclosing the leaves. If you change the water daily, most fresh herbs will keep for about a week. One exception to this rule is basil, which should be kept in water but left uncovered and placed in a sunny window.

While fresh herbs are certainly the chef's choice, sometimes you just have to use dried herbs instead. When doing so, you can still add a little life to the dish with a dash of at least one fresh herb among the dried ones. The humble parsley, easily acquired, will usually do the trick. To release the full flavor of dried herbs, crush them in the palms of your hands before adding them to your cooking pot. In general, it's better to add herbs toward the end of the cooking process, so that the flavor is locked in rather than cooked out.

Since dried herbs lose their potency over time, it's best to store them in a cool, dry place for a maximum of six months to one year. However, if you have some herbs that are older and don't want to toss them out, you can often compensate for the inevitable loss of flavor by exceeding the amount called for in the recipe. And don't overlook the wonderful variety of new tabletop herb and spice shakers. Mrs. Dash offers four varieties to try. The American Heart Association also has a line of flavorful herb shakers.

Some of the other herb/spice blends on the market may taste bitter to you. That's because they contain potassium chloride, a salt substitute with a bitter aftertaste, especially apparent when it is heated. It should be noted also that too much potassium can cause medical problems for some people, particularly those taking diuretics or those with kidney problems. It's best to check with your physician before buying one of these.

For an economical do-it-yourself mix, pop dried black, white, and green peppercorns into your peppermill. (Another salt-free sea-soning blend using dried herbs calls for equal parts crushed basil, thyme, and parsley. You can add to that any or all of the following: sesame seeds, ground pepper, ground mace, cayenne pepper, onion powder, red pepper flakes, and garlic powder.) Garlic, onion, and shallots, in particular, are a chef's best friend. Not only do they add their own unique flavors to your home spa dishes, but they accentu-ate the taste of whatever they're paired with. (I'm especially fond of baked garlic and like to spread it on bread or mash it into baked potatoes. It's surprisingly mild prepared this way and low in calories—far lower than butter, margarine, or sour cream.) With flavors such as these, you won't need to reach for the salt shaker.

Two other special spices to add to your shopping list are vanilla beans and nutmeg. Both enhance perceived sweetness—the reason they're so popular with spa chefs—and they do it with much fewer calories. Freshly grated or ground nutmeg or scraped vanilla bean is far superior to anything you can buy in a can or bottle. If your supermarket doesn't carry whole nutmeg, try a gourmet store. While you're there, pick up an inexpensive little grater that's made just for nutmeg.

Along with herbs and spices, smart cooks stock up on flavorful vinegars and oils—yes, oils. Although oils are high in fat and calories, just a few drops of a truly fine oil can transform your dish from ordinary to exquisite.

The idea here is to get the most flavor with the least amount of calories. Buy the best and you can use less. Most connoisseurs particularly prize the Italian olive oils from Lucca and Sicily, as well as those from the south of France. (Olive oil is actually high in healthy monounsaturated fats, the kind that help to lower blood cholesterol.) Always buy "extra virgin" olive oil; you'll be getting the very best from the first pressing, without traces of chemical solvents used in manufacturing lesser grades.

As with all oils, rancidity can be a problem. Try to buy from a store that has a good turnover, and use the oil within six months to a year, at the very most. Always store your oil in the refrigerator, as this helps preserve the natural vitamin E, which in turn keeps the oil fresh. Since olive oils harden when refrigerated, you might want to keep about a week's supply in a covered jar in the cupboard. This way, you'll always have a little pourable oil whenever you need it. Remember to clean the bottle each time you refill it to avoid contaminating the new batch.

Flavored vinegars can truly transform a dish, and they make elegant *bon voyage* gifts for spa-goers. One that I find indispensable is balsamic. It is dark brown in color, slightly sweet, and intensely aromatic. I use it on a tossed green salad and there's no need to add oil or other seasonings. Fresh, ripe strawberries or fruit salad sprinkled with a touch of balsamic vinegar are also delicious.

Other vinegars you might want to add to your collection include tarragon and rice wine. They are mild and you can get by with much less oil (which means fewer calories) when preparing homemade salad dressings. Tarragon or rice wine vinegar add a spa-cuisine twist to an otherwise ordinary tuna or chicken salad. Just whisk the vinegar into a little reduced-calorie mayonnaise and a dollop of nonfat yogurt; then mix it with the tuna or chicken.

The trick to spa-style cuisine is maximizing flavor without high-calorie/low-nutrition additions. Smart spa chefs trick tastebuds into enjoying natural flavors—the tang of lemon or the pungency of fresh herbs—making it a snap to create delightful meals that are low in fat, sugar, and sodium. By utilizing these tips at home, you'll be able to create your own spa cuisine and enjoy the healthy glow that comes from eating light and right.

Myths and Truths About Good, Low-Calorie Nutrition

▶ **Sugar substitutes are slimming.** Actually, artificial sweeteners sharpen your sweet tooth, causing you to crave foods loaded with real sugar. There's also evidence that artificial sugars can make hunger pains more intense. A smarter choice is to cut back on both imitation and real sugars.

▶ **If you limit your calorie intake, you'll lose weight.** Not necessarily. In fact, all calories are not created equal. Foods with high-fat calorie counts put on pounds more quickly because fat contains twice as many calories per gram as protein or carbohydrates, and fat calories are more readily stored as body fat than those from protein and carbohydrate calories.

▶ **Fat is a dieter's worst enemy and should be avoided at all costs.** Even if it were possible to eliminate all fat from your diet, it would not be desirable. Fats are fuel for the body. But there are "good fats" and "bad fats." Eliminate saturated fats—animal fats and coconut, palm, and palm kernel oil—completely. Polyunsaturated fats, such as safflower, sunflower, and corn oil, are healthier, but monounsaturated oils, such as olive oil and peanut oil, are your best choice.

▶ **Foods marked "light" or "lite" are lower in calories.** If you want fewer calories, look for labels that read "calorie-reduced." Mandated by the FDA, these products contain at least one-third fewer calories than the original. "Light" or "lite" may simply indicate a lighter flavor, texture, or color, but with the same caloric value.

▶ **When dieting, skip the starches—pasta, baked potato, rice, and bread.** Previously thought of as "fattening," these complex carbohydrates should be staples of a regular diet. They are stick-to-your-ribs foods and are the body's most readily used energy source. They are also essential for burning fat and losing weight.

A Gourmet's Guide to Spas with
Exceptional Cuisine

For a brief description of the meal plans at the spas mentioned below, check the individual listings.

CAL-A-VIE, CALIFORNIA
Thanks to master chef Michel Stroot, this spa has its own style of nutritious dishes, called "cuisine fraiche," which uses seasonal produce and herbs from the spa's garden. You'll get a fancy sampling of his creations with one of the 12-to-20-ingredient salads. The evening meal is served on Villeroy and Boch china in the French-provincial-style dining room. The culinary philosophy here dictates that meals are to be savored by your sense of sight, smell, and taste.

CANYON RANCH, ARIZONA
The "Granddaddy of spas" offers imaginative and varied dishes which helped to make this fitness resort famous. Such delightful entrees as broiled lobster and artichokes with dilled shrimp topped off with strawberries Romanoff serve to accentuate the positive.

DORAL SATURNIA, FLORIDA
This luxury resort spa offers a choice of two elegant restaurants featuring "nouvelle" selections such as Gulf red snapper grilled with herbs. At dinner, you even have a choice of wine or champagne. Menus list the calories and fat content of each item and calculators are on the table, leaving the calorie count completely in your hands.

THE KERR HOUSE, OHIO
It may be hard to believe, but you can actually lose weight dining on cheddar cheese soup and homemade granola at this intimate, for-women-only retreat. Fresh veggies, fish, and fowl served by candlelight make for elegant, calorie-conscious evening meals.

LA COSTA HOTEL & SPA, CALIFORNIA
There are at least seven restaurants to choose from at this mega-resort and spa, but you can easily stick to the selections of masterpieces created by executive chef Willy Hauser for the Spa Dining Room.

NEW LIFE SPA/LIFTLINE LODGE, VERMONT

From cold melon soup to moussaka, chef and spa director Jimmy LeSage has found a way to make such gourmet dishes as Veal Piccata fit his modified Pritikin diet program, pleasing the most discriminating palate.

SOUTHWIND, GEORGIA

This quaint southern retreat offers a creatively ethnic variety of dishes on its menus. Don't be surprised if you're served moo goo gai pan one day and Cajun-style blackened breast of chicken the next. Homemade (dietetic) ice cream is a pleasantly surprising specialty here.

4

Finding the Perfect Spa for You

When people come to Spa-Finders looking for the spa vacation of their dreams, one of the first things they are asked to do is to fill out a detailed questionnaire designed to give us the best possible idea of what they are looking for in a spa.

For example, single clients are often more interested in meeting people and shaping up than in pure relaxation. Couples often differ in their spa needs, and so the goal is to find a spa that will please both partners. Some people believe they want one service from a spa, and after completing the questionnaire, realize they actually want something else.

So to aid you in pinpointing the right spa for your needs, I have provided a questionnaire that examines your diet and exercise goals, your pampering needs, and various other life-style considerations.

After completing the questionnaire, you will have a much clearer idea of what you expect your vacation to accomplish, and will be able to narrow down your choices. In choosing your dream spa, the progression in which you narrow down those choices will depend on your priorities. However, no matter the order, you will be considering the following criteria:

▶ Geographical location
▶ Spa category
▶ Price range

▶ Accommodations

▶ Fitness facilities

▶ Diet regimen

▶ Overall spa cuisine

▶ Beauty and pampering services

▶ Holistic or other mind/body programs for personal growth

▶ Degree of personal attention offered

▶ Sheer variety of activities offered

▶ Co-ed versus same sex

▶ Average age of spa guests

▶ Stress-reduction program

▶ Stop-smoking program

▶ Other behavior modification programs

▶ The length of your stay

In addition to filling out this questionnaire, I encourage you to refer to the Spa Almanac on page 273, in which I have already broken down spas by a host of specific categories. You may want to consult the Almanac, even before you turn to the handy spas-at-a-glance-chart on page 52.

In answering the following questions, be as honest as possible, and have fun!

YOUR HEALTH PROFILE

Your Current Level of Health

___ Excellent ___ Good ___ Fair ___ Food allergies

Health Problems:

___ Tobacco/drug dependency   ___ Alcohol dependency

___ Cardiovascular difficulties   ___ Respiratory ailment

___ Sports injuries   ___ Difficulty walking

___ Wheelchair-bound   ___ Allergy to smoke

___ Diabetes   ___ Other health problems

Your Current Diet

___ Mostly meat and potatoes with no restriction of fat or calories

___ Some restriction on red meat, eating mostly fish and chicken

___ Semivegetarian (dairy and eggs but no meat)

___ Strict vegetarian (no animal products at all)

___ American Heart Association

___ Pritikin-style program

___ Weight Watchers Program

___ Eat-to-Win program

___ Fit-for-Life-type program

___ Eclectic/don't follow any pattern

Do You Suspect You Are:

___ Anorexic   ___ Bulimic   ___ A compulsive eater

If You Are Not Already Getting Help for Your Eating Disorder, Do You Wish to Do So Now?

____ Yes   ____ No

Do You Weigh:

____ The correct amount for your height and age

____ 5–10 lbs more than you should

____ 11–20 lbs more than you should

____ 21–30 lbs more than you should

____ 31–40 lbs more than you should

____ 41–50 lbs more than you should

____ Over 50 lbs more than you should

When You Diet on Your Own or with Medical Supervision, Which Method Works Best for You?

____ High-protein diet

____ High-carbohydrate diet

____ Balanced low-calorie diet

____ Pritikin diet

____ Weight Watchers Diet

____ Water fast

____ Juice fast

____ Opti-Fast or other protein powder diet

What Are Your Eating Habits?

____ I eat healthily most of the time

____ I eat pretty much what I want, but exercise it off

____ I skip meals to compensate for what I eat

____ I am *always* on a diet, but never seem to lose weight

____ I go from one binge to another

How Well Do You Maintain Your Weight?

_____ Not perfectly, but it's no problem

_____ Not well enough; I'd like to do better

_____ Not well at all; I need help

What Is Your Weight-Loss Goal?

_____ I don't need to lose weight   _____ To lose 30–40 pounds

_____ To lose 1–10 pounds   _____ To lose 40–50 pounds

_____ To lose 10–20 pounds   _____ To lose over 50 pounds

_____ To lose 20–30 pounds

What Kind of Spa Cuisine Are You Looking For?

_____ Primarily calorie restricted; the sparser, the better

_____ Low in calories, but exceptionally prepared

_____ Specially tailored to your exact requirements

_____ Not calorie restricted at all; just fabulous

_____ The cuisine is not important to me

▶ After Reviewing Your Diet Profile, It Is Clear to You That:

_____ Learning a new way of eating is an important requirement of your spa stay

_____ Although you already know how to eat sensibly, you are counting on your spa stay to provide a shot of motivation

_____ You would like to learn about good nutrition, although you don't really need to lose weight

_____ You intend to lose as much weight as you possibly can during your spa stay—even if you have to fast

_____ You just want to cleanse your system out

Your Current Fitness Exercise Program
(check as many as apply)

____ Low-impact aerobics at least three times weekly for 20 minutes
or more

____ A combination of high- and low-impact aerobics three times
weekly

____ Gentle stretching exercises

____ Calisthenics/circuit training regularly

____ Walk, swim, or do aerobic dance three times weekly

____ Weight training

____ Competitive sports

____ Sporadic activity, regardless of format

____ Other

____ No exercise at all

*What Have Been Your Previous Obstacles to Incorporating an Exercise
Routine into Your Overall Life Style?*
(check as many as apply)

____ Lack of motivation

____ I don't deem it necessary to good health

____ I don't like to work out alone/at home

____ I don't like to work out in a group

____ There is no health club convenient to my home or work

____ I haven't found an agreeable form of exercise

____ I get bored/discouraged after a short while

____ I have no time/energy for it

You Would Prefer to Exercise:

____ At your own pace with help available only if you request it

____ In a group with at least some personal attention if you need it

_____ With a great deal of attention by a fitness expert who tailors an exercise program to your specific needs

_____ Under the supervision of a medical doctor or nurse

_____ Only on state-of-the-art exercise equipment

_____ Through sport activities such as tennis, swimming, and bicycling rather than in a gym

_____ With women only

_____ With men only

The Exercise Facilities That Are Important to Me Are:

_____ Olympic pool

_____ Lap pool

_____ Tennis

_____ Racquetball

_____ Jogging track

_____ Indoor bikes

_____ Outdoor bikes

_____ Water sports

_____ Circuit training

_____ Hiking trails

_____ Separate facilities for men and women

_____ Aerobics

_____ Free weights

_____ Sailing/boating

_____ Horseback riding

_____ Downhill skiing

_____ Cross-country skiing

_____ Treadmills

_____ StairMasters

_____ Water aerobics

Your Exercise Goals Are To:

_____ Lose inches and promote weight loss

_____ Improve muscle tone, body strength, and coordination

_____ Find an exercise program you can live with for a long time

_____ Supplement an already healthy, active life style

▶ *After Reviewing My Fitness Profile It Is Clear to Me That:*

_____ I need to incorporate more exercise in my life and my spa visit is the time to learn how

_____ I'd like to try some of the equipment and exercise methods I've never tried before

_____ Although I'm primarily going to a spa for the relaxation and/or pampering, I will enjoy some exercise classes as well

Your Beauty and Pampering Needs

Which Pampering Services and Facilities Would You Like To Experience?
(Refer to the *Beauty and Pampering Glossary* at the end of the book for a more complete list and descriptions.)

Massage:
_____ Swedish   _____ Shiatsu   _____ Trager   _____ Sports
_____ Reflexology

_____ Herbal wrap   _____ Jacuzzi

_____ Loofah rub   _____ Sauna

_____ Salt-glo rub   _____ Whirlpool

_____ Aromatherapy   _____ Steamroom

_____ Seaweed treatment   _____ Body treatments for specific problems such as cellulite

_____ Hydrotherapy

What Beauty Salon Services Do You Require?

_____ Facial

_____ Hairstyling

_____ Hair coloring

_____ Hair perm

_____ Regular manicure/pedicure

_____ Paraffin manicure/pedicure

___ Waxing/depilatory

___ Facial hair coloring

___ Makeup consultation and application

___ Hand/foot massage

During Your Spa Stay You Intend to Take Advantage of:

___ At least one pampering service daily

___ Between three and five during the week

___ One or two in a week

___ None at all

▶ *After Reviewing My Beauty and Pampering Profile It Is Clear to Me that I Expect to Leave My Spa Vacation with:*

___ A whole new makeover

___ A refreshed appearance

___ A beauty program specifically tailored to me

___ A general feeling of renewal—feeling better about myself

Overall Vacation Preferences

I Will Be Traveling:

___ Alone

___ With someone of the opposite sex

___ With children

___ With friend of the same sex

___ With parent/older companion

Would You Prefer:
(check as many as are applicable)

_____ A nonsmoking spa

_____ That alcohol be available on request

_____ A spa for women only

_____ A spa for the entire family (with kids)

_____ A spa that caters primarily to people over 50

_____ A spa that caters primarily to people under 40

_____ A spa that caters to singles as well as couples

Are You Interested in Combining Your Spa Visit with Any of the Following?

_____ Buying real estate	_____ Hiking
_____ Quitting smoking	_____ Sightseeing
_____ Skiing	_____ Gambling

Your Environmental Preferences Are:

_____ A warm climate	_____ A moderate climate
_____ A cool climate	_____ Ocean/lakeside
_____ Wilderness	_____ A mountainside/top
_____ Urban	_____ Tropical

You Would Prefer a Spa Vacation in the Following Region(s):

_____ Hawaii	_____ Canada
_____ Southwest	_____ Caribbean/Bermuda/ Bahamas
_____ Texas	_____ Europe/Israel
_____ South	_____ Alaska/Pacific Northwest
_____ Northeast	_____ Rocky Mountain States

_____ Midwest   _____ Mexico

_____ Florida   _____ Central/South America

_____ New England   _____ Asia/Pacific

What Type of Accommodations Would You Prefer?

_____ Private room with bath

_____ Private room with shared bath

_____ Double occupancy with own roommate

_____ Double occupancy with assigned roomate, if possible

_____ Dormitory-style room with hall bath

_____ Cabin

_____ Villa

_____ Suite

_____ Condo/time share

What Level of Accommodations Do You Prefer?

_____ The most luxurious

_____ Deluxe

_____ Comfortable

_____ The most economical

_____ Spartan in an oriental/spiritual sense

_____ It makes no difference

How Long Will Your Spa Stay Be?

_____ A day

_____ A weekend

_____ Three or four days

_____ A week

_____ More than a week

Which Price Range Is Reasonable for Your Spa Vacation?
(excluding airfare)

_____ Less than $500 per week per person based on double
occupancy

_____ $500 to $999 per week

_____ $1,000 to $2,000 per week

_____ More than $2,000 per week

_____ Money is of no importance

▶ *After Reviewing Your Diet and Fitness Profile, Your Beauty and*
Pampering Profile, and Your Overall Vacation Preferences, It Is Clear
to You That What You Are Looking for Most in a Spa Is:
(number these choices in their order of importance, 1 being the most
important)

_____ To make significant life-style changes in diet and exercise and
to lose some weight in the process

_____ To lose an appreciable amount of weight in a structured
environment

_____ To combine health and fitness with vacation fun

_____ To relax and enjoy lots of pampering and beauty care

_____ To address specific behavioral problems:
      _____ stress   _____ overeating   _____ smoking

_____ A religious or spiritual/mental renewal in a peaceful, relaxing
atmosphere

_____ To be in a "self-improvement" atmosphere with others seeking
the same for general well-being

_____ To come away with a better understanding of your specific
health conditions and how to manage them

—— To meet new people

—— To meet both your *and* your traveling companion's very
different requirements

Now that you have pinpointed your exact needs, you can read the
individual spa listings with these needs in mind. Don't forget to flip to
the Spa Almanac on page 273 for a unique breakdown of spas by
special services and features.

SPAS-AT-A-GLANCE HANDY REFERENCE GUIDE

Index of North American Spas

Explanation of Symbols

FB-SC: Fitness/Beauty Spas—Self-Contained
FB-RH   Fitness/Beauty Spas—At a Resort or Hotel
 LUX: Luxury Spas
 WL: Weight-Loss Spas
 NA: New Age Retreats
 MS: Mineral Springs

   $ = Less than $699 per week
  $$ = $700–$1399 per week
 $$$ = $1400–$1999 per week
$$$$ = $2000 and over per week

Per Person Double Occupancy

	Page	Type	Price
Hawaii			
Dr. Deal's Hawaiian Fitness Holiday, HI	103	FB-RH, NA	$$
Hyatt Regency Waikoloa, HI	126	FB-RH	$$$
The Plantation Spa, HI	227	WL, FB-SC, NA	$$$
The West Coast			
The Ashram Healthort, CA	58	FB-SC, WL	$$$$
Bermuda Inn Fitness Reducing Resort, CA	209	WL, FB-SC	$
Cal-A-Vie, CA	183	LUX, FB-SC	$$$$
Carmel Country Spa, CA	61	FB-SC, WL	$
Claremont Resort, CA	102	FB-RH	$$
The Golden Door, CA	193	LUX, FB-SC	$$$$
La Costa Hotel & Spa, CA	190	LUX, FB-RH	$$$$
Lakeside Health Resort, CA	73	FB-SC	$$

	Page	*Type*	*Price*
The West Coast			
Jane Fonda's Laurel Springs Retreat, CA	67	FB-SC	$$$
Le Meridien Spa, CA	133	FB-RH	$$$
Marriott's Desert Springs Resort & Spa, CA	142	FB-RH	$$$$
Murrieta Hot Springs Resort & Health Spa, CA	144	FB-RH, MS, NA	$$
The Oaks at Ojai, CA	79	FB-SC	$$
The Palms at Palm Springs, CA	80	FB-SC	$$
Sonoma Mission Inn and Spa, CA	163	FB-RH	$$$$
Spa Hotel & Mineral Springs, CA	167	FB-RH, MS	$$
Two Bunch Palms, CA	95	FB-SC, MS	$$
Joe Weider's Shape, Muscle and Fitness, CA	176	FB-RH	$$
The Southwest			
Canyon Ranch, AZ	187	LUX, FB-SC	$$$
Loew's Ventana Canyon Resort, AZ	138	FB-RH	$$
Marriott's Camelback Inn Resort & Golf Club, AZ	140	FB-RH	$$$
Tucson National Resort & Spa, AZ	170	FB-RH	$$
Rocky Mountain Wellness Spa, CO	85	FB-SC, NA	$$
Westin Hotel Cascade Club, CO	177	FB-RH	$$
Aerobics Center Guest Lodge, TX	207	WL	$$$$
Four Seasons Hotel & Resort, TX	113	FB-RH	$$$
The Greenhouse, TX	195	LUX, FB-SC	$$$$
Lake Austin Resort, TX	70	FB-SC	$
The Phoenix, TX	203	LUX, FB-RH	$$$$
The Verandah Club, TX	174	FB-RH	$$
Green Valley Health Resort & Spa, UT	218	WL, FB-RH	$$

	Page	*Type*	*Price*
The Southwest			
National Institute of Fitness, UT	224	WL, FB-SC	$
World of Fitness, UT	182	FB-RH, WL	$
The Midwest			
The Heartland, IL	63	FB-SC	$$
The Spa at French Lick Springs, IN	115	FB-RH	$$
The Elms, MO	105	FB-RH, MS	$$
Aurora House, OH	59	FB-SC	$$$$
The Kerr House, OH	196	LUX, FB-SC	$$$$
Sans Souci Health Resort, OH	89	FB-SC	$$
Interlaken Resort & Country Spa, WI	128	FB-RH	$
The Fontana Spa at the Abbey on Lake Geneva, WI	110	FB-RH	$$
The Spa at Olympia Village, WI	149	FB-RH	$
The South			
Evergreen Manor, AR	215	WL, MS	$
The Spa at the Biltmore, FL	100	FB-RH	$$$
Doral Saturnia, FL	190	LUX, FB-SC	$$$$
Fontainebleau Hilton, FL	112	FB-RH	$$$
Hippocrates Health Institute, FL	238	NA, WL	$$
Lido Spa Hotel & Resort, FL	74	FB-SC	$
Palm-Aire Hotel & Spa, FL	200	LUX, FB-RH	$$$
Pier 66 Hotel & Marina, FL	151	FB-RH	$$
Ponte Vedra Inn & Club, FL	152	FB-RH	$$
Pritikin Longevity Center, FL	154	FB-RH, WL	$$$$
Regency Health Resort, FL	229	WL, FB-SC	$
Safety Harbor Spa & Fitness Center, FL	86	FB-SC	$$
Sheraton Bonaventure Hotel & Spa, FL	205	LUX, FB-RH	$$$

	Page	*Type*	*Price*
The South			
Sonesta Sanibel Harbour Resort, FL	162	FB-RH	$$
Turnberry Isle Yacht & Country Club, FL	172	FB-RH	$$$
Southwind Health Resort, GA	93	FB-SC	$$
Wildwood Lifestyle Center & Hospital, GA	232	WL	$$
Eurovita Spa at the Avenue Plaza Hotel, LA	107	FB-RH	$$
Duke University Diet & Fitness Center, NC	214	WL	$$$
Structure House, NC	230	WL	$$
The Charleston Retreat	211	WL	$$
Hilton Head Health Institute, SC	220	WL	$$
Coolfont Resort, WV	235	NA, FB-SC	$
The Greenbrier, WV	119	FB-RH, MS	$$$
The Woods Fitness Institute, WV	233	WL, FB-RH	$$
The Northeast			
Norwich Inn & Spa, CT	147	FB-RH	$$
Canyon Ranch in the Berkshires, MA	185	LUX, FB-SC	$$$
Le Pli Health Spa & Salon, MA	135	FB-RH	$$$
Maharishi Ayur-Veda Health Center, MA	241	NA	$$$$
Northern Pines Health Resort, ME	243	NA	$
The Spa at Bally's Park Place Casino Hotel, NJ	99	FB-RH	$$$
The Hilton at Short Hills, NJ	125	FB-RH	$$
The Spa at Great Gorge Resort, NJ	118	FB-RH	$$
The Shoreham Hotel & Spa, NJ	158	FB-RH	$$
Gurney's Inn Int'l Health & Beauty Spa, NY	121	FB-RH	$$$

	Page	Type	Price
The Northeast			
HRH, NY	65	FB-SC	$$$
Living Springs Retreat, NY	222	WL, NA	$
New Age Health Spa, NY	76	FB-SC, NA, WL	$
Pawling Health Manor, NY	226	WL	$
Deerfield Manor, PA	212	WL, FB-SC	$
The Evolution Spa at The Equinox Hotel, VT	108	FB-RH	$$$
Green Mountain at Fox Run, VT	216	WL, FB-SC	$$
New Life Spa/Liftline Lodge, VT	145	FB-RH	$$
Topnotch at Stowe, VT	169	FB-RH	$$$
The Woods at Killington, VT	181	FB-RH	$$
Canada			
The Hills Health & Guest Ranch, BC	123	FB-RH	$
King Ranch Health Spa & Fitness Resort, ONT	69	FB-SC, LUX	$
Schomberg Health Spa & Retreat, ONT	91	FB-SC	$
Wheels Country Spa, ONT	179	FB-RH	$$
Auberge Du Parc, PQ	97	FB-RH	$$
Spa Concept Bromont, PQ	166	FB-RH	$$
The Caribbean & Bermuda			
Lady Diane's Health & Fitness Resort, Jamaica	239	NA	$
Le Sport, St. Lucia	136	FB-RH	$$
Sans Souci Hotel, Club & Spa, Jamaica	156	FB-RH	$$
Sonesta Beach Hotel, Bermuda	159	FB-RH	$$
Mexico			
La Fiesta Americana Condesa Vallarta Spa & Club	131	FB-RH	$$$
Gran Spa El Tapatio	116	FB-RH	$$
Ixtapan Resort & Spa	129	FB-RH, MS	$
Rancho La Puerta	82	FB-SC	$$

Index of Spas Abroad

	Page	*Price*
Austria		
Grand Hotel Sauerhof Zu Rauhenstein	246	$
Hotel Schloss Lebenberg	247	$$$$
Aganthenhof	249	$
Josefinehof Hotel Im Park	250	$
France		
Royal Hotel	251	$
Germany		
Brenner's Park	254	$$$
Villa Christina Clinic	255	$$$$
Wiedemann International Health Centers		
Ambach, Germany	258	$$$$
Meersburg, Germany	258	$$$$
Meran, Italy	258	$$$$
Gran Canaria, Spain	258	$$$$
Great Britain		
Grayshott Hall	259	$$$
Hungary		
Thermal Hotel Margitsziget	261	$
Ramada Grand Hotel Margitsziget	261	$
Israel		
Daniel Hotel and Spa	262	$$
Italy		
Christina Newburgh's "Spa Deus"	266	$$$
Grand Hotel e La Pace	264	$$$
Grand Hotel Croce di Malta	264	$$
Hotel Des Iles Borromees	267	$$$$

	Page	*Price*
Spain		
Hotel Incosol, Marbella	269	$$$
Switzerland		
Clinique La Prairie	270	$$$$
Brazil		
Ligia Azevedo	271	$

FITNESS AND BEAUTY SPAS
(SELF-CONTAINED)

The Ashram Healthort $$$$ FB-SC, WL

P.O. Box 8009
Calabassas, California 91302
(818)888-0232

When you want to retreat from life's distractions, get in touch with nature by hiking up mountains and bathing in streams, check into the tranquil, secluded "healthort," The Ashram. A sensitive blend of spiritual fitness, vigorous physical activity, and self-imposed discipline, The Ashram provides the perfect setting and inspiration to get you in touch with your body and soul.

Dedicated to spiritual, mental, and physical well-being, The Ashram accepts only eight to ten men and women at a time and provides the optimum program for each individual. Upon arrival in the one-week program, guests are checked out by the doctor in residence who plans a personal program for each of them. Since a cardiovascular ergometer stress test is included, it is advised that guests avoid a big lunch and alcoholic beverages before arriving. Meals here consist mostly of raw foods—fresh fruits, vegetables, nuts, and juices, herbal teas, and various kinds of therapeutic fasting.

This spa is definitely not for the grossly overweight or those severely out of shape. A daily schedule begins with morning meditation and breakfast, followed by a two- to two-and-a-half hour hike and gym workout. After lunch, guests can have a soothing massage, jog, do aerobics, and go for an evening walk. Before dinner there's another yoga meditation session. By about 10 P.M. it's lights out.

Ashram's facilities, including accommodations, are located in one large building with spacious porches containing a gymnasium and exercise areas. Yoga and meditation classes are held under a geodesic dome perched on a hillside. Guest rooms are double occupancy and decorated with a Mexican flair. Single guests can expect to share a room, and all guests share one of the three bathrooms. There are no telephones in the rooms or televisions anywhere at the retreat. The spa provides sweatsuits, t-shirts, robes, kaftans, and most other accessories. Guests need only bring socks, a bathing suit, shorts, walking/hiking shoes, toiletries, a book or personal hobby materials, and an open mind. Street clothes and belongings are discouraged. The one-week, all-inclusive program runs from Sunday to the following Saturday with scheduled meals, yoga, meditation, gym workout, water exercise, and massage. The price includes accommodations and roundtrip transfers from Los Angeles Airport.

GUEST FEEDBACK

Perhaps the most spartan spa in the United States, The Ashram has no luxury suites or fancy meals. What it offers is the chance for you to "stop the world and get off" and renew body, mind, and spirit. The absence of luxury may, in fact, account for its attraction to many people and to such celebrities as Barbra Streisand and Raquel Welch. And this challenging and invigorating way of life keeps guests coming back for more: A whopping 70 percent of visitors who have visited The Ashram return to renew.

Rates

	Single	*Double*
6-Night Package SUN ARR/SAT DEP	Not Available	$1,800

Aurora House $$$$ FB-SC

35 East Garfield Road
Aurora, Ohio 44202
(216)562-9171

Affectionately known as the Victorian Palace of Pampering, the Aurora House has garnered a reputation for its innovative body treatments in luxurious surroundings, top-of-the-line hairstyling, and gourmet spa cuisine. Located southeast of Cleveland on its own secluded island, Aurora House underwent over a million dollars in renovations to transform the century-old Victorian manor into a cozy, full-service beauty and fitness facility that includes the Manan Island Inn & Spa.

Specializing in head-to-toe pampering, Aurora offers more than a half dozen facials, including a nonsurgical face lift, makeup lessons, and an extensive array of massage and body treatments, from aromatherapy to Massercise (a cellulite treatment) to Thalassotherapy. In addition, guests have a choice of four relaxing heat retreats, including the Environmental Habitat which transforms a glass enclosed niche into an hour-long simulation of changing environmental forces for a journey from the seashore (steam) to the desert (sunlamp tanning) to a tropical rainforest (a warm, massaging rain shower). Other services include a variety of manicures, reflexology, and paraffin softening treatments.

At the Hair Studio, run by local celebrity stylist and co-owner Mario Liuzzo, you can choose from a long list of hair-care services—from a basic wash and set and choice of three kinds of drying to Henna treatments and neon highlighting. Hair waxing and permanent hair removal are also available.

Aurora has no shortage of fitness options either, with sessions based on guests' personal physical fitness goals. Dynastics is the resort's own "artful blend of dance, aerobics, yoga, and stretching." Other fitness and sports activities include cross-country hiking, trailside biking, aquacise, swimming, weight training, tennis, golf, horseback riding, and skiing (in season). Shopping and antique hunting are nearby.

Accommodations at Aurora are Victorian in design with antique wicker, brass lamps, lace curtains, and wooden floors. There are nine rooms and suites in the manor house for a maximum of 12 overnight guests. The newest accommodations all have Jacuzzis in the room. Additional housing is located in the Treadway Inn across the street.

The majority of Aurora's visitors are from the local area, but overnight guests can take advantage of discounted rates for stays of a week or longer. The longest package deal is the five-night Complete Retreat which includes up to 16 face and body treatments. A two-night Shape Escape and a one-night retreat also are available. All-inclusive prices cover accommodations, three meals daily, a full spa program with daily heat treatments, personalized fitness sessions, and body treatments.

For special occasions, there is a Pampered Paradise package that includes champagne and private in-room whirlpool bath, a country breakfast, environmental room, steam bath, and a half-hour massage or a facial. Business travelers can take advantage of the spa Break Away which offers one night's accommodations, heat treatments, a choice of either a half-hour tonic massage or perk-up facial, champagne and dinner by candlelight, a country breakfast, private whirlpool bath, and cable and closed-circuit television. Day-trippers can choose from the Spa Preview sampler for $99 or the Day at the Spa for $150 that includes all spa services. Guests can also choose services *a la carte*, with prices ranging from $7.50 for eyebrow tinting to $175 for a series of four Massercise cellulite treatments.

Aurora House is undeniably the place for a total makeover, inside and out. Guests rave about its services, particularly the beauty treatments.

GUEST FEEDBACK

Most guests thought the spa offered good value for the money, would visit again, preferably for a shorter period of two or three days, and would recommend the spa to a friend. When booking your vacation, you might want to ask how many others are booked during that time. One woman was the only guest for a week, and while she undoubtedly received all the personal attention she could want, she was expecting to meet other guests.

Rates

	Single	*Double (per person)*
1-Night Retreat	$299–349	$284.50–334.50
2-Night Shape Escape	$839–889	$799.50–844.50
5-Night Complete Retreat	$1,739–1,789	$1,654.50–1,699.50

There is any-day arrival.

Carmel Country Spa $ FB-SC, WL

10 Country Club Way
Carmel Valley, California 93924
(408)659-3486

In the expanse of rolling hillsides, where the ambience is casual and the options are varied, Carmel Country Spa offers a low-budget escape to weight loss, relaxation, and education on nutrition and alternative healing.

The beauty and simplicity of the spa, as well as its low-calorie cuisine, are appealing to folks who want to concentrate their energies on reducing body fat and getting in touch with themselves. There are nature walks around the scenic Carmel Valley and Lover's Point Beach, aquathinics in the Olympic-size pool, beginning Hatha yoga, and low-impact aerobics. If all else fails, the therma-trim wrap—an infra-red heat treatment that promotes cellulite reduction and weight loss with slimming, trimming, and toning—is touted to take off up to five inches in just one treatment!

Carmel Country Spa accommodates up to 50 guests. With the spa's low cost per night, guests can also afford to pamper themselves with a full line of beauty services such as hair care, facial, massage, salt rub, manicure, and pedicure, which range in price from $1.50 for a color rinse to $55 for artificial nails. While getting beautified, guests can peer out beyond the rolling hills. There is also a boutique on the premises where you can pick up anything you may have forgotten, as well as a full line of herbal, hypoallergenic cosmetics.

Nutritionally, water and herbs are an important part of the spa's diet plan. Meals are prepared with ingredients that have specific nutritional purposes, combined to give guests maximum inch and weight loss. The low-calorie, low-carbohydrate diet consists of approximately 700 to 800 calories per day. For lunch, the main meal of the day, there is a choice of meat or fish. Guests also receive a multivitamin, licorice root, and LBS II (lower bowel stimulant). Licorice root gives a gentle energy boost, while LBS II, which is equivalent to one bowl of bran cereal minus the calories, keeps the digestive tract regular. There is a morning broth break and a happy hour with light vegetable *hors d'oeuvres* and diet soft drinks before dinner.

To help maintain weight loss, the spa has its own specially prepared mayonnaise (five calories per teaspoon), tartar sauce, three kinds of salad dressing (14 calories per teaspoon), Insta-Butter, salt-free sweetener, powdered broth seasoning, and special potassium broth.

Why not take an evening soak in the Jacuzzi while watching the sunset? Or, often there's entertainment after dinner. Sometimes there's a guest speaker, a presentation, or an excursion into Carmel or Monterey. If nothing has been scheduled, guests can simply watch the 50-inch-screen television with cable channels, or view a movie from the spa's library. There are assorted table games from which to choose. You may also want to bring something good to read.

Besides the standard spa attire—leotards, bathing suit, jogging suit, terry robe, and slippers—the spa recommends that guests bring a warm sweater or jacket for cool evenings and a pair of well-broken-in walking shoes.

Picturesque pathways lead to single-, double-, and triple-occupancy bungalow-style accommodations nestled in well-maintained gardens. Fresh flowers and vegetables are brought to rooms daily. Prices are per night with a two-night minimum and include accommodations, food, exercise instruction, and full use of spa facilities.

GUEST FEEDBACK
Most guests found their vacation at Carmel very rewarding, particularly if they were attempting to lose weight. Because there is only one fitness instructor, guests cannot expect a lot of personal attention when working out independently with weights or other gym equipment, or while a fitness class is in progress. However, because it is a small spa, there is a chance to pull the instructor aside and get the information you need.

Rates

	Single	*Double (per person)*
Per Night	$150	$95

There is a two-night minimum stay and any-day arrival.

The Heartland $$ FB-SC

18 East Chestnut
Chicago, Illinois 60611
(818)683-2182

Tucked between farms and corn fields, just 80 miles outside of Chicago, is The Heartland, "a California-style spa with heartland hospitality." This fully equipped retreat motivates its guests toward meaningful life-style changes with a generous fitness plan and sound education in nutrition and stress management.

This former country estate consists of a barn that was converted into a three-story complex and now houses exercise studios, whirlpools, sauna and steam rooms, an atrium pool, massage and facial facilities, and men's and women's locker rooms. The guesthouse, which overlooks Kam Lake, is also connected to the spa complex by an underground passageway that shields guests from the midwestern winter. There are 13 guest rooms accommodating a maximum of 28 people, a colonial dining room, and two sitting rooms, both with a fireplace. One sitting room has a library and the other has a television, VCR, and videotaped movies.

After weighing in and having their blood pressures checked, guests at The Heartland can utilize the hi-tech equipment; pneumatic resistance weight machines (CAM II, which uses air pressure for resistance), exercycles, rowing machines, a StairMaster, and free weights all give the best possible cardiovascular workout. In season, guests can also take advantage of the outdoor tennis courts, quarter-mile jogging track parcours, cross-country ski trails, and ice skating on Kam Lake.

A typical day begins with an early morning wake-up call over the in-room intercom, followed by stretching or yoga, breakfast, hiking, calisthenics or aerobics, pool exercises, or free-weight training. After the main meal of the day is served shortly after noon, there is a rest period and/or lectures, race-walking or cross-country skiing, and pool volleyball. Before, after, in between, or instead of any of the fitness training, guests can treat themselves to any of the pampering services available, including full back treatment, deep pore cleansing and conditioning, massage, facial hair and makeup consultation, manicure, and pedicure.

For nutritional fitness, guests of The Heartland eat about every two-and-a-half hours. The menu is gourmet vegetarian supplemented with fish, whole grains, and low-calorie dairy products. In addition, meals are high in complex carbohydrates from fresh fruits and vegetables and grains and legumes and low in sodium and fat. Women are allowed about 1,200 calories per day, while men are allotted about 1,500. There are three meals daily with midmorning and midafternoon snacks. Delicious desserts—fresh fruit sorbets and frozen yogurts—are served around 9:00 P.M. to help combat late-night snack attacks and to inspire sweet dreams.

After dinner there is always a lecture. Common topics include nutrition basics, food preparation, and behavior modification techniques for weight control. Acupuncture, creative problem-solving, and personal achievements are others. In addition, guests are instructed on how tensions accumulate in the body and are introduced to various attitudinal approaches to defusing stress—strategies such as positive thinking and calming mental imagery.

Accommodations in the guesthouse are designed to make you feel at home. Each room has a private bath stocked with The Heartland's private-label shampoo, conditioner, and lotion, plus most of the clothing you will need during your stay. There's no need to pack sweatsuits, shorts, t-shirts, robes, socks, wool hats, gloves, hair dryers, slippers, rainwear, or evening loungewear. And as soon as any of these get soiled, it will be replaced. All you need to bring are pajamas, toiletries, street clothes, and most important, an open mind.

This co-ed resort offers weekend, five-, and seven-day packages that include room, meals, classes, use of all facilities, exercise and evening clothing, roundtrip transportation from O'Hare Airport and downtown Chicago, and all taxes and gratuities. The two-day package includes a massage, while the five- and seven-night programs include four massages and a facial. From July through September, The Heartland gives a 10 percent discount off regular rates and 14 percent off during the first week of those months. Roommates are provided for single guests requesting double occupancy.

GUEST FEEDBACK
Rated as "one of the Ten Best Spas in the U.S.A." by *Shape* magazine in 1986, The Heartland has been host to many satisfied guests. The warm and friendly staff is particularly inviting, and because of the small number of guests, you are able to take advantage of the staff's personal attention and knowledge. Although the resort claims to include stress management as part of its services, many of our otherwise satisfied clients wanted more information on ways to combat stress. All, however, would return to The Heartland and would recommend it to a friend.

Rates

	Single	*Double (per person)*
2-Night Weekend FRI ARR/SUN DEP	$660	$440
5-Night Program SUN ARR/FRI DEP	$1,650	$1,100
7-Night Program FRI OR SUN ARR/FRI OR SUN DEP	$2,175	$1,450

There is a two-night minimum stay.

HRH $$$ FB-SC

Rural Route 3, Box 19-C
Pound Ridge, New York 10576
(914)764-4033

This Japanese-style beauty and fasting spa is an idyllic place for a beauty makeover from the inside out. Open only on weekends, it offers women a unique two nights and two days in a private suburban mansion just outside of New York City. Here, group sessions for eight to ten women and private one-on-one programs are designed for the woman who wants to rejuvenate herself, shed a few pounds, get a grip on stress, or recover from a physical or emotional crisis. HRH offers exercise classes interspersed with body treatments to coddle and to energize.

Its fitness program consists of controlled body/mind movements performed to jazz fusion and classical music. Tranquil nature walks, yoga, and stretch classes are also available, but the true beauty of HRH is the opportunity for you to indulge in head-to-toe pampering. There are private steam rooms and herbal saunas, a Jacuzzi with sliding shoji screen for privacy, Swedish and Shiatsu massages or a combination therapeutic massage, a motor table for concentrated back muscle massage and alignment, and an organic mud body treatment that will soothe and soften.

HRH's beauty and pampering program features Chanel skin- and nail-care products for such treatments as a hot paraffin facial and makeup application and a hot oil manicure. Chanel consultants also offer lessons in how to apply theatrical and corrective makeup. In addition, the salon offers full-service hair care, braiding, weaving, and trichology (scientific hair analysis). There are also special services for wedding hair designs as well as makeup and hair grooming for portfolio shoots. Head-to-toe waxing and hair tinting are also available. All of these services can be bought *a la carte*, even without a spa stay. They range in price from $10 for chin waxing to $90 for a one-and-a-half hour therapeutic massage.

The ages of guests at this elegant spa range from 20 to 50. Guest rooms, which are single or double occupancy, have piped-in mood music, and are designed in Japanese style with futons—Japanese mattresses—that take the place of traditional beds. Baths are shared. Meals here are vegetarian and Oriental, and water fasting is available for those who want a more thorough internal cleansing.

For overnight guests, the spa offers two weekend retreat options. The Health and Beauty Weekend begins on Friday evening with a stretch/yoga class, private steam/sauna or Jacuzzi, and a Shiatsu massage. Saturday morning begins early with a brisk hike or stretch/yoga class, a breakfast of grain and fruit, followed by another exercise class. Around noon, lunch is served, after which guests are treated with a massage and Chanel facial, pedicure, and manicure. Evening begins with an Oriental dinner, and then after a meditative twilight walk, there is a lecture or workshop on body awareness or nutrition. Sunday begins the same way and ends after a gourmet Oriental lunch, herbal body wrap, nutritional lecture and workshop, Chanel makeup lesson, and hair design consultation.

Day-trippers can choose a Makeover Day for $200 that includes beverages, Jacuzzi, whirlpool, steam room, sauna, body massage, European facial, pedicure with foot whirlpool, hot oil manicure, makeup lesson, designer hair cut and conditioning treatment, and a gourmet lunch. The Day of Total Beauty is devoted to a facial, pedicure, hot oil manicure, hairsetting or blow dry, and a gourmet lunch. Beverages, herbal steam room, sauna, body massage, and whirlpool are also included for a total cost of $160. The Marvelous Morning costs $120 and includes relaxation in an herbal steam room, sauna, shower, body massage, facial, manicure, and beverages.

GUEST FEEDBACK
A few of the guests were surprised by the sparseness of the guest rooms and the relaxed, informal schedule. All, however, were pleased with the meals. For those of you who wish to pamper yourselves without "paying the price," a day trip may be just the thing.

Rates

	Single	Double (per person)
2-Night Weekend FRI ARR/SUN DEP	$650	$600

Jane Fonda's Laurel Springs Retreat $$$ FB-SC

Star Route
Santa Barbara, California 93105
(805)964-9646

Situated in a lush oak grove on Jane Fonda's own ranch, Laurel Springs offers very personal and very intense fitness activity and behavior modification. The three-bedroom redwood chalet is perched 3,500 feet high in the Santa Ynez Mountains and offers spectacular views of the Pacific Ocean and the Channel Islands.

Upon checking in, guests, limited to nine, get a fitness evaluation by the staff physiologist. Then, a personal trainer guides each guest through daily activities including biking, hiking, stretching, low-impact aerobics, circuit and strength training, body sculpting, aerobic machines, and pool exercises. You can burn fat and improve cardiovascular fitness while gazing out at an oak grove and meadow where peacocks and guinea hens strut their stuff. There are also evening presentations on nutrition, stress management, and food preparation. Facilities at the resort include a gym, hot tub, Jacuzzi, outdoor swimming pool (there's also swimming in mountain pools), rowing machines, sauna, treadmills, and weight-training machines. In addition, each guest is scheduled for a daily massage.

The cook develops delicious, nutritionally balanced, low-calorie menus in accordance with guests' requirements. Barbeques, fresh vegetables, homemade breads, and natural sorbets are part of the weight-control program. Emphasis is on a low-fat, low-cholesterol, high-fiber diet. Cooking lessons will help you incorporate this dietary approach into your everyday life.

Much of the lodge life revolves around the 17-foot stone fireplace. The folk art, Adirondack, and craftsman antiques add a warm and personal ambience. There is also a well-stocked library, a game room with the latest audio-visual equipment and tapes (including, of course, Jane Fonda's own popular workout videos), and private sunbathing decks. All three guest rooms are done in varying decor, but all are comfortable and homey.

The one-week package runs from Sunday afternoon to Saturday afternoon and includes cardiovascular, strength, flexibility, and body composition tests and exercise prescription, accommodations; meals; daily massage; nutritional counseling; cooking classes, a personal trainer; and evening programs. Net proceeds from Laurel Springs Retreat go to The Temescal Foundation, a nonprofit corporation that supports research in health and fitness and in child development and education.

GUEST FEEDBACK

The lucky guests of Laurel Springs are pampered with personal attention and are encouraged to make life changes. Many have been so pleased with their stay that they've returned and/or recommended it to a friend. Guests particularly liked the structured environment within the comfort and beauty of this retreat. They also enjoyed working with a personal trainer.

Rates

	Single	Double (per person)
6-Night Package	$2,500	$1,500

SUN ARR/SAT DEP

There is a six-night minimum stay.

King Ranch Health Spa & Fitness Resort $$ FB-SC, LUX

PR #2
King City, Ontario
LO6IKO, Canada
(416)833-8332

The brand new King Ranch Health Spa & Fitness Resort is expected to hit the spa scene with much fanfare. The C$38 million project, which will open in June 1990, is owned by Murray B. Koffler, founder of Shoppers Drug Mart and a director and co-founder of the four-star hotel chain Four Seasons Hotels Limited; Adam H. Koffler; and Tiana Koffler Boyman. The staff and management of the well-known and popular spa retreat Canyon Ranch Vacation and Fitness Resort of Tucson, Arizona, are the development consultants.

Conveniently located 20 miles from Toronto's International Airport and a half-hour drive from downtown, the resort hopes to attract guests from Canada, the United States, and Europe. In addition, King Ranch "will offer a productive business environment combined with a spa program designed to meet the needs of executives and their accompanying spouses." The ranch will accommodate up to 150 guests and invites executive groups to use their facilities as a meeting site.

Part of King Ranch's appeal will be its setting. Just beyond the cosmopolitan excitement of Toronto, guests come upon the gently rolling hills, winding streams, charming villages, and country estates of King Township. The Township is steeped in history and dotted with antique and collectibles shops, general stores, arts and crafts galleries, historic landmarks, and Canadian vistas. The resort is set on 177 acres of lush meadows and verdant countryside that provide seasonally changing vistas and diverse opportunities for summer/winter, indoor/outdoor sports. The majority of the grounds will be used for walking and hiking trails and cross-country skiing.

Touted as Canada's first international health spa and fitness resort, the co-ed spa will provide integrated programs of vigorous exercise, proper nutrition, advanced relaxation techniques, body and beauty treatments, and comprehensive preventive-health consultations. The resort features health-risk appraisal, stress testing, cholesterol screening, fitness consultations, biofeedback therapy, and hypnotherapy. The King Ranch also will offer special programs such as smoking cessation and tennis weeks. Fitness choices include aerobic and strength training, weight training, swimming, aqua aerobics, hiking, racquetball and squash, biking, jogging, tennis, horseback riding, and skiing, snowshoeing, and ice skating in season.

The actual spa facility houses exercise studios; weight room; racquetball, squash, and tennis courts; an elevated indoor/outdoor running track; lounges; showers; massage and steam rooms; sauna, and whirlpools; and body/beauty treatment rooms. Fitness-testing and stress-management facilities are offered in the preventive medical center. The spa's vaulting glass windows allow guests to maintain contact with the exterior surroundings, keeping the great outdoors in plain view.

Special ultramodern features of the new resort are its private screening theater, which will present current-release films, and an international waters bar which will serve imported spring and mineral water. The Club House will be the gathering place for guests to relax, dine on low-cal cuisine such as poached salmon and pasta with veggies, and socialize. It houses a dining room, living room, demonstration kitchen, den/music room, boutique, and the theater.

The guest accommodations consist of 120 rooms with either a balcony or ground-floor terrace. The decor includes earth tones, tactile textures covering the furnishings, and Canadian native art in guest rooms and throughout the resort. All rooms are interconnected with the spa and Club House for easy access. The resort offers four-, seven-, and ten-night packages that include accommodations, three low-cal meals daily, fitness classes, use of resort facilities, choice of sports, and health, beauty and body treatments.

Rates

		Double
Nov. 1–Mar. 31	*Single*	*(per person)*
4-Night Package	C$1,010	C$830
7-Night Package	C$1,850	C$1,530

There is a four-night minimum stay. Any-day arrival. U.S. dollar prices are approximately 15 percent lower.

Lake Austin Resort $ FB-SC

1705 Quinlan Park Road
Austin, Texas 78732
1 (800)847-5637 (Nationwide)
1 (800)252-9324 (in Texas)

At Lake Austin Resort in the rolling Texas Hill Country, you've got lots of options. On the shores of peaceful Lake Austin, guests have a total experience in renewed vitality and well-being, with emphasis on wellness as a working lifetime philosophy. The program provides a week of rest and relaxation, as well as vigorous activity and education. Under the direction of a staff that includes health educators, motivation specialists, an exercise physiologist, a nutritionist, and a registered nurse, the program is tailored to meet the guests' needs.

To get the body in shape, over 16 fitness classes are taught daily, ranging from gentle stretching and water aerobics to circuit weight training and early-morning Hill Country walks. Facilities include a lakeview gym, indoor/outdoor pools (including one for swimming laps), Jacuzzi, hiking and jogging trails, and stationary bikes.

After an invigorating day of workouts, guests can enjoy a European-style massage, body polishing, herbal clay treatments, a facial, manicure, pedicure, and hair-care services. Clarins skin-care products are used. Evenings are spent visiting the resort's boutique or at a lecture or film on health, fitness, exercise, nutrition, or psychological well-being. There's also varied evening entertainment in the lakeview lounge.

Nutrition, being an important part of the spa experience, consists of balanced eating based on wholesome, calorie-controlled cuisine, featuring low-sodium, low-fat, low-sugar versions of Southwestern dishes. The resort will teach you how to prepare some of the meals at home. Weekly low-fat cooking and nutrition classes in the demonstration kitchen are part of the crucial take-home program. Guests with special dietary needs, such as those with diabetes, food allergies, or who are vegetarians, should notify the reservations clerk in advance. A $50 weekly food preparation charge will be added to the bill.

This year-round resort houses a maximum of 70 adult men and women. Teenagers, 14 to 17 years old, are allowed only if accompanied by a parent. Although the resort will not assign a single person a roommate, it will provide telephone numbers of other single guests requesting roommates. Otherwise, a single guest pays the single room rate. Both deluxe and standard rooms have views of Lake Austin and the Hill Country, telephones, and color televisions. Newer deluxe rooms have ceiling fans, exceptionally large dressing rooms, and double sinks in the vanity area.

Included in the package price are accommodations, three meals daily, fitness classes, all programs and lectures and transfers to and from the airport in Austin. There are over a dozen fitness classes to choose from daily, as well as special evening programs such as fashion shows in which guests can be models and receive a discount toward boutique purchases. Plus, Lake Austin has its own excursion boat for daily trips on the lake.

Here are some tips to make your trip just as rewarding. Massages and facials are done by appointment and they tend to book early, but you can book up to three massages when you make your reservation. Since the spa provides ground transportation to and from the airport at specific times, let the reservations clerk know your flight schedule so that he or she can arrange for you to be picked up.

GUEST FEEDBACK

The "best kept secret in Texas" isn't quite a secret anymore. Guests have come from as far away as Ontario, Canada, and New York City to "the great escape to health and fitness." And almost all said they would do it again. Many of the guests were particularly pleased with the exercise staff and thought the programs were well structured. Meals were consistently rated very good and excellent, and guests thought the package was a good value.

Rates

Jan. 1–Jun. 2	*Single*	*Double (per person)*
4-Night Program WED ARR/SUN DEP	$591–636	$441–481
7-Night Program SUN ARR/SUN DEP	$990–1,060	$738–808
10-Night Program SUN ARR/WED DEP	$1,353–1,448	$1,011–1,105
14-Night Program SUN ARR/SUN DEP	$1,841–1,970	$1,377–1,506
Jun. 2–Nov. 19		
4-Night Program WED ARR/SUN DEP	$486–520	$366–401
7-Night Program SUN ARR/SUN DEP	$815–871	$613–669
10-Night Program SUN ARR/WED DEP	$1,115–1,191	$840–915
14-Night Program SUN ARR/SUN DEP	$1,519–1,623	$1,147–1,251
Nov. 19–Dec. 24		
7-Night Program (only)	$745–795	$563–614

There is a four-night minimum stay.

Lakeside Health Resort $$ FB-SC

32281 Riverside Drive
Lake Elsinore, California 92330
(714)674-1501

This co-ed retreat in Lake Elsinore Valley is about 75 miles from Los Angeles and attracts a slightly older crowd, whose average age is between 40 and 60, all of whom are on diets. Situated on five acres in the foothills of the Ortega Mountains, Lakeside promises all the fitness and some of the pampering that other, more posh spas offer, only less expensively—and to many people, this spa delivers.

As a guest here, your daily activities might include a three-mile or one-and-a-half mile morning walk, stretching classes, pool exercise, low-impact aerobics, afternoon yoga or relaxation classes, and a sit 'n' fit class that features full-body movements while sitting in a chair. This is particularly appreciated by some of the more sedentary guests. The Better Backs and Bellies class exercises the abdominal and lower back muscles, while Legs, Legs, Legs tones and strengthens the legs, hips, thighs, and buttocks.

To further help "balance the scales of your life," guest speakers offer advice and workshops on behavior modification, assertiveness training, self-hypnosis, stress management, and other life-enchancing strategies. A registered nurse is on the staff to help monitor your progress.

Exercise facilities at Lakeside include an indoor exercise pool, heated outdoor pool, sauna, herbal bath, dance exercise room, and gym. Treadmills, stationary bikes, rowing machines, circuit training, and free weights are available to tone and firm your figure.

For those of you who expect a very regimented exercise class schedule, you should know that a few of the guests commented on the resort's fairly relaxed program, with some classes starting a little late.

In the full-service beauty salon you can enjoy a massage, facial, body wrap, manicure, and pedicure. Also available are hair-care and hair-removal treatments that range in price from $3 for a hair conditioning to $40 for a frosting. European tanning beds help give you that healthy, well-cared-for glow.

In addition to activities at Lakeside, Lake Elsinore Valley offers boating, water skiing, horseback riding, fishing, hiking, bowling, tennis, and golf. There is even a casino there.

Lakeside serves its guests down-home meals that have a total count of between 700 and 900 calories per day. Fish, poultry, fresh fruit, and fresh vegetables are the mainstay of the low-salt, low-sugar, and low-fat, high-in-complex-carbohydrates menu. Cooking demonstrations help you maintain your progress once you get home—an important feature of any spa.

Resort rates are per night, but 7- and 30-night packages are available. Rates include accommodations, three meals and three snacks daily, exercise classes, and unlimited use of facilities, as well as evening programs, lectures, and entertainment. Lakeside also offers a free massage and body composition analysis with a seven-night stay, one night free after ten days, and a 10 percent reduction on all personal services and merchandise for return guests. There is no minimum stay and you can begin your vacation on any day of the week.

The guest rooms at Lakeside are not exactly luxurious, but they are clean and comfortable, and you can drive up to your own private entrance. Accommodations are available in single, double, or triple occupancy, and each room has air conditioning, a telephone, and color television. The resort will make an effort to match single guests with a roommate, upon request.

GUEST FEEDBACK
Guests who were looking for an affordable resort at modest prices and who took advantage of the exercise facilities more than the beauty services were the happiest here. Most of the guests were very pleased with the fitness program. If you are hoping to meet people your own age, be aware that Lakeside has a younger clientele on weekends.

Rates

	Single	*Double (per person)*
Per Night	$129	$99
7-Night Package	$903	$693
30-Night Package	$3,483	$2,673

There is no minimum stay and any-day arrival.

Lido Spa Hotel and Resort $ FB-SC

40 Island Avenue, Venetian Causeway
Miami, Florida 33139
(800)327-8363 (Nationwide)
(305)538-4621 (in Florida)

On Miami's "Gold Coast" sits Lido Spa, a resort, hotel, and health spa rolled into one reasonably priced vacation package. Guests, most of whom are in their middle years (although families are welcome), can lose weight with the help of fitness classes and special dietary plans. This resort offers the opportunity to incorporate life-style changes while enjoying resort recreation and the beauty and charm of the "Sunshine State." Located on a private island just 20 minutes from Miami International Airport, Lido is close to all of Miami Beach's shopping, culture, and sporting.

The fitness program features mild aerobics, water exercises, yoga, and dance classes. There are two complete gymnasiums for men and women, a whirlpool, mineral baths, and a diagnostic laboratory and examination facilities where guests are examined upon arrival, two saunas, two heated swimming pools (one with salt water), massage rooms, hot tub, wet and dry steam room and individual steam cabinets, exercise equipment, an outdoor solarium, and a beauty salon on the premises. Diet instruction and lectures are also available.

Other non-health-related activities include nightly entertainment in the Lido Spa Theater featuring top names in television and nightclub acts, music for dancing, movies, bingo, bridge, backgammon, and horse racing. There is also a card room, shuffleboard, table tennis, and croquet. Golf and tennis are just five minutes away and complimentary transportation is provided. Daytime activities include handicrafts, bingo, dancing lessons, discussion groups, and art lessons.

Meals here are special. Each is prepared according to a guest's diet, and all are high in protein, carbohydrates, and fiber and low in fat, sugar, and salt. For those on a diet, meals are between 600 and 1,200 calories a day; nondieters can dine on regular meals as well. The wide range of meal options guests have to choose from includes kosher dishes, and there is a staff dietician to help. Two snacks are served daily.

In resort style, guest rooms are air conditioned and have color televisions, telephones, and private baths. There are three types of rooms to choose from, each moderately priced and with pleasant views of the gardens, pool, or Biscayne Bay. Rates are as low as $42 per person per night in a double garden-view room, and no minimum stay is required. Daily rates include accommodations, three meals daily, use of all facilities, medical examination, daily massage, individual diet supervision with guaranteed weight loss, special diets, daily entertainment, free in-room HBO, and limo service to and from the airport. The co-ed spa, which accepts about 100 people at a time, is closed from May through October.

GUEST FEEDBACK
Guests who went to the Lido were generally pleased with their vacation and thought it offered a lot for the money. Some guests have been
returning since it opened 25 years ago. Although true fitness buffs
may find the lax exercise schedule and mild classes slightly beneath
their fitness levels, those who are just beginning to work muscles
previously unused for a decade or more will find this program is just
what they need to begin a life style that includes physical fitness.
Guests were particularly pleased with the daily massages and the
staff. This resort is also a great place for grandparents to vacation
with their grandchildren because it offers something for every age
group.

Rates

Per Night	*Single*	*Double (per person)*
Mar. 20–Apr. 5	$70–86	$51–67
Apr. 6–18 and Apr. 27–May 7	$50–66	$43–60
Apr. 19–Apr. 26	$55–71	$48–65
Spa closed May 8–Oct. 28		
Oct. 29–Dec. 19	$50–66	$43–60
Dec. 20–Jan. 19	$70–86	$51–67

There is no minimum stay and any-day arrival.

New Age Health Spa $ FB-SC,NA,WL

Route 55
Neversink, New York 12765
(800)682-4348 (Nationwide)
(914)985-7601 (in New York)

In the spirit of healing, the New Age Health Spa is a holistic health
retreat on 155 wooded acres of enchanted forest in the heart of the
Catskills. Beautiful surroundings, an outstanding physical fitness program, nutritional counseling, pampering services, behavior modification, group support, soothing physical therapies, and education are
all integral parts of the program, which you partake in as desired.
    Now under new management (former Wall Street executive Wer-
ner Mendel and wife Stephanie Paradise, a social worker, former para-
medic, and all-around athlete), New Age offers one of the widest array

of untraditional health options available. This spa literally offers an A to Z choice in holistic health and healing—from astrological consultations to Zen meditation and wonderful surprises in between. And, modeled after the old European spas, this resort makes it all affordable.

The fitness lineup usually begins with a guided nature walk on local roads and country trails around the Catskills. After breakfast, the class schedule includes a gentle warm-up stretch to prepare the body for the day's activities. Next is a calisthenics class that focuses on arms, abdominals, legs, hips, and thighs. Low-impact aerobics, aquatics, and weight training are also offered.

It would be hard to find a bigger selection of pampering and treatments for the body at a spa of this size. New Age offers such rare treatments as the Dead Sea mud treatment using imported mud from the Dead Sea to detoxify, cleanse pores, relax muscles, and relieve the discomfort of arthritis and rheumatism, plus a therapeutic treatment that includes an invigorating loofa scrub. During the two-hour paraffin body treatment, the body is lathered with warm, penetrating cream and covered in a thick layer of paraffin wax to seal in moisture and assist in cleansing pores of impurities. If more drastic measures are called for, try the Thermo Trim cellulite treatment for the entire body or specific target areas. Mineral and herbal Jacuzzi baths, reflexology, Swedish and Shiatsu massage, loofa scrub, and aromatherapy are also available. There's also a sauna and steam bath.

The full-service beauty salon offers all hair-care services and house facials using New Age skin-care products or the world-famous Jurlique facials featuring products made from herbal and flower essences. And, you can choose to have these treatments for 45-, 60-, or 90-minute sessions.

There's no shortage of sports activities at New Age. Each season brings something new. Swimming is available year round in an indoor pool. Summertime warms the outdoor spring-fed pool. In winter, the setting is perfect for cross-country skiing and horse-drawn sleigh rides.

For mental workouts, New Age provides an hour-long exercise consultation during which your needs and past stumbling blocks are discussed and a personalized fitness plan is designed. Nutritional consultations help you understand your current nutritional condition and offer direction on how to modify your eating habits to achieve better health. And the astrological consultations provide a tool for growth and a framework in which to view yourself in the present and future. Psychological and behavioral dynamics are explored as well as the timing of predictable cycles based on your astrological chart. The astrologer will also give you a birth chart to help you understand all this information, and a cassette tape to refer to later. For this two-hour session, be sure to know your time and place of birth. These services cost between $50 and $100.

Nutritionally, New Age also offers a variety of meal plans, including supervised water and juice fasting. Daily enemas and colon hydrotherapy are also available. To break a fast, they recommend the Breaker Diet which is approximately 350 calories per day and consists of fruit, salad, and steamed vegetables. Their Spartan Diet is only slightly higher in calories (450) and contains no dairy products; grains are served at one meal per day. The Lite Diet is 650 calories, and the Pro-Lite Diet, which adds chicken or fish to the dinner, comes to 850 calories. Nondieters can have the Pro-Lite Plus Diet which is prepared with all natural foods and has an unlimited calorie count. There's an additional $10 daily fee for this plan.

In the rustic charm of this homey no-frills spa, accommodations are simple. There are no phones or televisions in the rooms. All are clean and comfortable and have a private bath and scenic views. Guests can choose single, double, or triple accommodations. There is a large variety of packages to choose from, depending on the services and diet plan you choose. The most basic plan priced below includes accommodations, meals and snacks daily, use of spa facilities, exercise classes, and evening lectures.

GUEST FEEDBACK

Spa-Finders considers New Age a genuine "find," having sent more guests here than to any other spa in the country. Guests are often repeaters due to the spa's extraordinary value for the money. Those who are looking to incorporate a truly holistic approach to health and fitness find New Age to be just what they need and keep coming back for refresher courses and just to renew.

Rates

Jan. 1–May 14	Single	Double (per person)
2-Night Weekend Package FRI ARR/SUN DEP	$279–535	$186–363
5-Night Package SUN ARR/FRI DEP	$662–1,290	$441–879
7-Night Package ANY-DAY ARRIVAL	$875–1,724	$583–1,180
28-Night Package ANY-DAY ARRIVAL	$3,293–5,085	$2,195–3,114

May 15–Dec. 31

2-Night Weekend Package FRI ARR/SUN DEP	$353–535	$224–363
5-Night Package SUN ARR/FRI DEP	$837–1,290	$531–879
7-Night Package ANY-DAY ARRIVAL	$1,107–1,724	$702–1,180
28-Night Package ANY-DAY ARRIVAL	$4,166–5,084	$2,643–3,114

There is a two-night minimum stay.

The Oaks at Ojai $$ FB-SC

122 East Ojai Avenue
Ojai, California 93023
(805)646-5573

This is one of two spas run by Sheila Cluff, a well-known personality in the fitness field, whose spa programs are designed for folks who want to slim down and shape up. To prove she means business, The Oaks features ultra-low-cal meals totaling about 750 calories per day, and provides more than a dozen fitness and exercise classes to choose from. Evening lectures further enhance your health and fitness mindset, while games and arts and crafts sessions offer diversions right on the premises.

After an active day of mountain hiking and weight training in the mirrored gymnasium, exercising in the pool, and body dynamics classes, guests can soothe muscles in the sauna and whirlpool, or have a massage. For a little pampering, the salon offers facials, nail care, makeup design, and a full line of hair-care services for men and women. The Winner's Circle is the gathering room where diet snacks and low-calorie drinks are served before dinner. Meal plans range from 750 to 1,000 calories per day, and calories are printed on the menu. Food is prepared with no salt, sugar, or dietetic products.

In the mountains near Santa Barbara and Ojai is a lively art colony famous for the Ojai Music Festival, Folk Dance Festival, and tennis tournament which take place in the park directly across the street. The city itself offers interesting gift shops, boutiques, arts and crafts supply stores, a movie theater, and more. The lull of the pacific Ocean is just minutes away, and there's boating and fishing in nearby Lake Casitas, as well as golf, tennis, and horseback riding.

The Oaks offers a variety of lodgings and can accommodate up to

86 men and women. There are guest rooms with balconies in the main lodge and oak-shaded bungalows clustered around the pool. All rooms have air conditioning and color television. However, not all rooms have full baths; some come with only a shower, but the double and triple cottages have both a tub and a dressing room. The spa will try to match up single guests who want a roommate, but they do not guarantee it.

Each month the spa runs special programs and packages. A five-day Stop Smoking program, Spa Cuisine Cooking Week, Mother/Daughter Days, and Aerobic Activities Week have been featured in the past. But guests to The Oaks are welcome to come on any day and to stay for any length of time. Rates here are per night and include accommodations, three meals and snacks daily, fitness classes, and use of all resort facilities.

GUEST FEEDBACK
Guests were pleased with their vacations at The Oaks and found the program well structured and worth the money. Accommodations rated adequate to good, and the exercise programs rated high. Meals were generally satisfying, but guests emphasized that they thought the spa was particularly for people who wanted to lose pounds and inches. It's worth noting that there is a certain amount of street-noise level due to the spa's location on a main street and across from a park.

Rates

	Single	Double (per person)
Per Night	$155–165	$105–135

There is no minimum stay and any-day arrival.

The Palms at Palm Springs $$ FB-SC

572 North Indian Avenue
Palm Springs, California 92262
(619)325-1111

This desert resort, run by Sheila Cluff, offers much the same program as her other spa, The Oaks at Ojai. Here, too, guests escape the ignorance of poor eating habits, lethargy, and stress of everyday life. The Palms offers the opportunity to unwind, slim down, and tone up while basking in a sun-drenched, informal setting. The resort's activities are designed to increase flexibility, decrease body fat levels, condition the heart and lungs, and develop strength and muscle tone.

A typical day's choice of fitness options begins with a vigorous three-mile walk or a shorter, more leisurely nature walk before breakfast. Afterward, guests can choose from a body awareness stretching class, the more challenging body dynamics aerobics (recommended for the very fit), a creative low-impact aerobics class, or an aqua-toning session where specific muscle groups are toned by using water resistance. At noon, lunch is served and then an afternoon agenda of body shaping and strength training with weights, aqua-aerobics, aerobic body conditioning (low-impact movement with light wrist weights), and yoga begins. Happy Hour, when guests get together over a juice cocktail, begins an hour before dinner, after which guests can return to the Winner's Circle Lounge for card and board games or a movie. Or, guests can unwind in the sauna, with a massage, browse the boutique, have a manicure or pedicure in the full-service hair salon, or get a facial.

The menu here, as at The Oaks, consists of approximately 750 slimming calories per day and is supplemented with the spa's own vitamin-mineral pack. Emphasis is on natural, whole foods that include fresh vegetables and fruits, low-fat proteins, and whole grains. No salt, sugar, or artificial sweeteners are used in preparation. Alternative high-protein or high-fiber salads are available for lunch and dinner. Guests who plan a particularly strenuous day or who are not dieting can request cereal at breakfast or a baked potato or brown rice at lunch or dinner to increase their intake to about 1,000 calories for the day.

The Palms offers a choice of accommodations from poolside rooms to bungalows with private patios. Package rates are per night and there's no set day of arrival or minimum length of stay. For a limited time, first-timers at The Palms who book their vacation through Spa-Finders will receive a complimentary, comprehensive cardiovascular evaluation test. The $45 offer includes a cholesterol test, blood pressure check, body composition analysis, and cardiovascular risk factors all printed on a computer report.

In addition, The Palms frequently offers discount packages such as Mother/Daughter Days, Bonus Time at the Palms, and Friendship Days. They also periodically feature a 21-Day Stop Smoking program. The regular all-inclusive cost covers accommodations; three meals, snacks, and beverages daily; fitness classes and walks; use of the swimming pool, sauna, and spa; and evening lectures and entertainment. Beauty treatments and services are extra.

Near the spa, guests can use facilities around Palm Springs, such as public tennis courts and municipal and semiprivate golf courses. Bike rentals, horseback riding, the Palm Springs aerial Tramway, and movie theaters are all within walking distance.

GUEST FEEDBACK
Almost all of the guests surveyed found The Palms vacation rewarding, having met their expectations. The caring and knowledgeable staff further enhanced their spa experience. By resort standards, The Palms does not offer luxury accommodations and amenities, but it is a good value for your vacation dollar and just the place to shed pounds and firm up flab.

Rates

	Single	*Double (per person)*
Per Night	$160–$185	$105–135

There is no minimum stay and any-day arrival.

Rancho La Puerta $$ FB-SC
P.O. Box 2548
Escondido, California 92025
(800)443-7565
(619)295-3144

La Puerta lies at the foot of sacred Mount Cuchuma, known for its legendary healing powers. It is the home of hawks, quail, and hummingbirds, of coyotes, and countless cottontail bunnies. When it opened 50 years ago on the outskirts of the Baja Peninsula, an hour and fifteen minutes drive southeast of San Diego in Tecate, Mexico, Rancho La Puerta was the first fitness vacation where guests took up residence. Today, it still offers a pioneering approach to physical and spiritual fitness, attracting socialites, celebrities, professionals, and housewives from all over North America.

In fact, the facility has grown to such an extent that guests are given a map to find their way around the property. There are six aerobic gyms that offer 30 classes a day, six lighted tennis courts, an ultramodern weight-training gym, five swimming pools, four whirlpools, three saunas, and miles and miles of mountain and meadow hiking trails. Cardiovascular workouts; strengthening and toning classes such as Absolutely Abdominals, Bottom Line, and Kinetic Toning; and stretch and flexibility and coordination and balance activities are also offered. The co-ed resort, which can accommodate up to 150 guests, has separate facilities for men and women and takes the special needs of both sexes into account. For men, there are aerobic circuit training, body awareness, and flexibility training classes, as well as stress and blood pressure control classes. La Puerta also offers classes for women only. The ratio of staff to guests is an impressive two to one.

Morning routines include a choice of hikes, walks, and yoga sessions. For relaxation during the day, the resort offers yoga, meditation, hot tubs, and saunas. To reward themselves, guests can get a facial, herbal wrap, massage, hairstyling and scalp treatment, manicure, and pedicure. Beauty and body treatments are very affordable, with massages at $17.50 and an herbal wrap just $10. There is a four-treatment package for $57.50 and a seven-treatment package for $105 that include two or five massages (respectively), one facial and one herbal wrap, or a scalp treatment. Skin-care consultation and makeup application are complimentary. The new state-of-the-art Men's Center offers scalp and facial treatments and its own private hot tub, steam room, and sauna. There is also an equally well-equipped center for women. In the evening, there are guest lectures, craft classes, films, games, and billiards in the recreation center.

The menu here is low-calorie spa and modified vegetarian cuisine, with fish served twice a week. A buffet breakfast consists of fresh fruits from the ranch's organic garden, fruit juices, a variety of hot and cold cereals, hard-boiled eggs, the ranch's own stone bread and muffins, and several kinds of tea, as well as regular and decaffeinated coffee. The calorie count for each is clearly indicated, but you choose how much to eat. Menus change daily, but a typical midday meal is within the suggested 250- to 300-calorie range and consists of chilled fruit soup, garden salad with ranch dressing, and rice and vegetable casserole with Gouda cheese. Dinner, the only time guests dress a bit more formally, has a calorie count of between 450 and 500. A typical sampling might be a garden salad with cucumber-lemon dressing, broccoli and onion soup, enchiladas with vegetables and jack cheese, refried black beans, and brown rice with tomato sauce; Mexican flan is a favorite dessert.

Guest accommodations are nestled amid the oaks and sycamores that dot the 150-acre resort and are filled with one-of-a-kind Mexican furnishings. Options range from luxurious villa suites for three or four people to single rancheras, all with private baths, and some with private patios. Suites have a living room and dining area, two baths, two bedrooms, and a fireplace. Villa suites have a living room alcove and fireplace. Haciendas have a living room, one or two bedrooms, one bath, and a fireplace, and rancheras have a studio bedroom and bath.

The week-long package includes your choice of accommodations, three meals daily, use of all facilities, classes, hikes, evening program, entertainment, and roundtrip transportation from San Diego International Airport. Arriving guests should ask for the Rancho La Puerta hostess at the Traveler's Aid Desk in the luggage claim area at San Diego International Airport before picking up their luggage. If you miss the shuttle bus, which has four pickups for Saturday arrivals, Orange Cab will take you to the resort. A passport or other proof of citizenship, as well as a Mexican tourist card, are required. The resort will match up single guests and offers specially priced weeks for couples.

Children under six years old get to tag along for free, while youngsters aged 7 to 14 are charged $375 per week. No childcare services are available. People who have serious health problems and those who are more than 35 percent overweight are not accepted. Much of La Puerta's clientele are in their midlife years, although there are some in their twenties and thirties.

GUEST FEEDBACK

Guests have come from as far away as New Hampshire to take part in the relaxing, rejuvenating activities La Puerta offers, and many return again and again. Guests were particularly appreciative of the staff's concern and knowledge and the other guests who they called "friendly and unpretentious." This resort has maintained its place as one of the world's great spas and it is often necessary to make reservations months in advance. Also, because it is often filled to capacity, it is wise to get the daily schedules from the spa before you arrive and try to plan when you'd like to schedule appointments for massages, facials, and other treatments. The pressure will be on to make these appointments when you first arrive. To maximize your visit, begin an exercise routine before you visit. Also, a couple of guests warned of missing items. So don't bring anything you can't bear to part with. Use traveler's checks whenever possible. Credit cards are not accepted.

Rates

	Single	*Double (per person)*
7-Night Program	$1,250–1,650	$1,000–1,500
SAT ARR/SAT DEP		

There is a seven-night minimum stay.

Rocky Mountain Wellness Spa $$ FB-SC, NA

Box 777
Steamboat Springs, Colorado 80477
(800)345-7770 (Nationwide)
(800)345-7771 (in Colorado)

The Rocky Mountain Wellness Spa is an inviting pathway to a more healthy, relaxed life style. Situated in the majestic Colorado Rockies on the edge of 150,000 acres of national forest, Rocky Mountain offers a scenic opportunity to renew, recharge, and educate yourself in the fundamentals of holistic living.

Just a few minutes walk from the world-famous Steamboat Ski Area, the spa offers panoramic views, luxury accommodations, balanced low-cal cuisine designed by professional nutritionists, varied levels of exercise activities, and an array of scientific analyses and evaluations. Emphasis here is on learning to get healthy and maintaining a new way of life.

Upon arriving, each guest receives a vitamin and mineral analysis, and cardiovascular, metabolism, allergy, body-fat percentage, and toxic-level evaluations by a staff of registered nurses. These evaluations are analyzed for clues to body system trends and for comparison testing when you leave. Based on the findings, the staff designs programs for diet and life style, exercise, and stress-release techniques to follow during the stay and upon your return home. You also get a 26-page personal wellness analysis. Guests are assured loads of personal attention due to the high staff-to-guest ratio.

Fitness activities include aerobics, water sports, mountain walking and hiking, ice skating, rafting, sailing, windsurfing, swimming, tennis, and volleyball. During the winter, a special cross-country ski program is extended to guests of all experience levels. Instruction and ski rentals are included in the package price. When it's time to relax, Rocky Mountain has a full line of options. If a massage doesn't get the kinks out, you can try an herbal sauna, a dip in the natural hot mineral springs, or a dry-brush and cold-plunge bath. At the beauty salon, guests can have a color analysis, facial, manicure, or pedicure.

At mealtimes, the spa offers nutritional allergy-free food high in complex carbohydrates, protein balanced, and low in fat. Two fresh juices are prepared daily and calorie counts are individualized. For nicotine addicts, there is also a smoking cessation program.

Lodging at the wellness spa consists of comfortable, European-style rooms with queen-size beds and private baths. The spa accepts a total of 15 guests at a time; two to six guests have access to a living room suite with a fireplace and balcony which offers spectacular vistas of the Rockies. Standard and deluxe rooms are available. Before retiring, guests can browse in the library or attend a health-related seminar in the lecture/film room.

Available package lengths range from five days (the minimum) to three weeks and longer. Guests who stay two weeks or more get up to a 15 percent discount. The five-day package costs $900 and includes lodging; three meals and two juice breaks daily; seminars on stress, nutrition, life-style modification, goal-setting, time management, and other related topics; personal instruction in stress-release techniques; use of all spa and resort facilities; fitness and exercise classes and individual wellness evaluations and counseling; three full-body massages; a spa cookbook; and roundtrip transfers from Steamboat Springs Airport.

GUEST FEEDBACK
Rocky Mountain Wellness Spa is highly recommended for those who want to change the way they live, who appreciate the great outdoors, and who want individualized attention and order to their day. As one guest put it, "When I arrived, my life was a mess along with my body. I was completely stressed out. Not only did I lose pounds and inches, I found an important and lasting formula for keeping my stress under control and for being happier and healthier than I can ever remember. I can honestly say I didn't want to leave."

Rates

	Single	Double (per person)
4-Night Program	$860	$760
7-Night Program	$1,495	$1,330
13-Night Program	$3,990	$3,590

There is a four-night minimum stay and any-day arrival.

Safety Harbor Spa and Fitness Center $$ FB-SC

105 Bayshore Drive
Safety Harbor, Florida 33572
(800)237-0155 (Nationwide)
(813)726-1161 (in Florida)

Tampa is famous for its colorful harbor, brisk salt air, Disney's Epcot Center, and the Safety Harbor Spa and Fitness Center. Located on the beautiful shores of Tampa Bay, Safety Harbor is an elegant full-service spa within an equally comprehensive resort hotel. The variety of activities—from boxing to water volleyball—make this an especially good choice for couples. Even world-champion athletes have found the facilities up to their mark, including Olympic Gold Medal boxer Mark Breland, who trained at the spa.

Upon arrival, guests receive a complete physical. Afterward, a fitness program is designed to suit their needs and goals. The list of fitness facilities and options at Safety Harbor seems endless. To begin with, there is a choice of custom-designed or regular fitness programs for striking the right balance between fitness and fun. There are 35 daily classes (separate for men and women and co-ed) to choose from in three aerobics gyms, and there are two equipment rooms. Low-impact aerobics (only), stretching, aquatics, calisthenics, rhythmics, body definition, and circuit training, plus free weights and cardiovascular circuit training, a four-mile race-walk, and two-mile walk are but some of the daily choices. In addition, the resort has indoor and outdoor solariums, 21 massage rooms for women and 15 for men, a lap pool, a regular pool, a therapy pool with natural mineral water, and a relaxation pool for women.

To pamper yourself during the day, try the Lancome Skin Care Institute, located on the premises, where guests can find massage therapy, herbal wraps, loofah scrub, mineral water bath, hair analysis, makeup consultations, steam baths, sauna, sundecks, showers, and solariums. Men and women have separate but identical pampering facilities.

Nouvelle spa-style cuisine is colorful, well presented, and filling. It is also low in fat, salt, and sugar and high in complex carbohydrates and fiber. Fresh fruits, vegetables, grains, chicken, and veal are served daily. The calorie count runs between 900 and 1,200 a day. The spa also gives guests recipes to prepare at home.

All of the guest rooms have spacious closets, private baths, and remote control televisions. Deluxe rooms have sitting areas and balconies or patios that overlook the pool or the green of the driving range with Old Tampa Bay glistening beyond. Some deluxe rooms have telephones and televisions in the bath area. Room service is available to all guest accommodations.

Safety Harbor boasts a wide choice of spa vacations. The four- and seven-day fitness plans include lodging, three meals daily, unlimited fitness classes, unlimited use of equipment rooms, a full medical screening, daytime tennis, on-site golf and greens fees, and a daily massage.

The three-day Fitness Weekend includes lodging, meals, classes, and all spa facilities such as whirlpools, saunas, steam baths, tennis, golf, two massages, and use of the equipment rooms. The eight-day total fitness plan includes not only a medical screening, but a blood chemistry analysis, unlimited exercise classes and daytime tennis, on-site golf and greens fees, personalized fitness profile, seven massages, one loofah scrub, two facials, two herbal wraps, a manicure, and a pedicure. In addition, women receive a Lancome makeup consultation and a shampoo and blow dry. Men receive a scalp treatment, haircut, and blow dry. The cost ranges from $1,365 per person in a deluxe room, based on double occupancy, to $1,645 for single occupancy in a deluxe room. There is also an abbreviated five-day total fitness plan that costs between $740 and $920 and includes everything except a pedicure, blood chemistry analysis, and fitness profile.

For tennis buffs, a Tennis Plan offers one class a day with the resident pro, all spa and recreational facilities, unlimited use of tennis courts, and a massage for every two days of your stay. And, if golf is your game, you should know that the on-site golf is strictly a driving range. However, the staff will arrange for you to play at any one of three courses in the area, charging only for the cart rental.

The newest option is a Medical Makeover Weight-Loss Plan for people who are at least 20 percent overweight. The plan averages weight loss of up to one pound a day. Designed by Dr. Robert Giller, the plan includes accommodations, three meals daily, a medical exam, fitness profile, stress test, electrocardiogram, blood chemistry, pulmonary function test, test for ketones, nutrition consultation, workout prescription, unlimited exercise and counseling, and continuous monitoring and supervision.

GUEST FEEDBACK
With so much to offer, this resort can be quite appealing. Since Safety Harbor's $12 million renovation, the spa has received very favorable reviews from the print media as well as from guests. Still, you should know that along with the resort-sized variety of activities come resort-sized crowds. Most, if not all of the guests surveyed, rated Safety Harbor quite high in the quality of its programs. However, more than a few commented on the rather lengthy process of scheduling classes and beauty treatments upon arrival. So, when planning your stay, be sure to ask if you can book some appointments ahead of time. If not, come prepared to do a little waiting.

Rates

Apr. 3–May 14	*Single*	*Double (per person)*
Tennis Plan NO MINIMUM STAY—NIGHTLY RATE	$215–230	$165–180
2-Night Fitness Weekend FRI ARR/SUN DEP	$360–390	$290–320
4-Night Fitness Plan ANY-DAY ARRIVAL	$820–880	$620–680
4-Night Total Fitness Package ANY-DAY ARRIVAL	$972–1,032	$796–856
7-Night Total Fitness Package ANY-DAY ARRIVAL	$1,631–1,736	$1,323–1,428
May 15–Dec. 31		
2-Night Fitness Weekend FRI ARR/SUN DEP	$260–370	$240–300
4-Night Packages ANY-DAY ARRIVAL	$580–980	$500–800
7-Night Packages ANY-DAY ARRIVAL	$1,236–1,645	$1,029–1,365

Sans Souci Health Resort $$ FB-SC

3745 Route 725
Bellbrook, Ohio 45305
(513)858-4851

Eighty acres of peaceful, wooded surroundings, riding stables, and the 600-acre Sugarcreek Reserve give credence to this spa's name, Sans Souci, French for "without worry." Run by owner-director-instructor Susanne Kircher, in what is essentially her home, Sans Souci offers a very personal and homelike ambience with a no-nonsense approach to weight loss and general fitness.

Upon arrival, you will be evaluated for fitness level, ideal body weight, and muscle-fat ratio; your body measurements, blood pressure, and pulse rate will be taken and your medical history outlined. Kircher, a registered nurse, nutrition counselor, and former nutrition and fitness consultant to Olympic and national sports teams, structures a plan to fit your needs and goals. With only seven live-in guests, you can be sure of very personalized attention.

The daily agenda begins at 8 A.M. with a positive, motivational reading and a glass of lemon mineral water. Activities include wake-up stretching and breathing exercises, morning walks on the parcours (a European-style fitness track), water exercises, dance classes, aerobics, slimnastics, and yoga. In addition, Kircher offers cooking classes, a weekly picnic lunch at nearby Spring Lake and Park, meditation walks to the Pine Forest, walks to the charming town of Bellbrook, and race-walking.

Sans Souci offers an exercise room, swimming pool, and Jacuzzi, miles of hiking trails through woods and meadows, and a peaceful, aromatic spot in the Pine Forest for meditation and horseback riding. There are also special classes for the disabled, those recovering from injuries, and pregnant women. Evenings are spent in group discussions, viewing films, and listening to lectures by experts. Therapeutic massages, facials, and a smoking cessation clinic are other options.

Meals are prepared to satisfy taste buds and to achieve nutritional balance and maximum weight loss. Enjoy tempting dishes such as French toast, pizza, quiche, or chicken and peapods with rice, topped off by some homey desserts. Guests' current eating habits, likes and dislikes, and food allergies are taken into consideration in food preparation. Calories average 600 to 800 per day and vary according to individual needs and goals. Vitamins, minerals, and mineral water are also part of the daily nutritional intake. A one-day juice fast is recommended for the first day. Weight loss averages six to eight pounds the first week. To help maintain your weight loss, Susie teaches cooking classes.

The resort's guest rooms are actually suites with dressing rooms, lake views, and whirlpools in the bath. Open from May through October, there are a variety of package options, including five-day, two-day, and one-day commuter packages. It also offers special rates for husband-wife or mother-daughter vacations, extended stays, and groups. Due to its size and popularity, it fills up quickly. Included in the price are all meals, massage, exercise, nutrition education, fitness testing, behavior modification, stress management, and assertiveness training.

GUEST FEEDBACK

All of the guests surveyed enjoyed their stay at Sans Souci. Those who wanted to shed fat reported weight loss and were grateful that the spa provided the tools they needed to maintain their new figures. Because of the highly individualized program, many guests would also recommend the spa to their friends, even if they weren't greatly overweight.

Rates

		Double
Open Only Apr. 29–Oct. 30	*Single*	*(per person)*
2-Night Weekend	$480	$350
FRI ARR/SUN DEP		
5-Night Program	$1,190	$880
SUN ARR/FRI DEP		

There is a two-night minimum stay.

Schomberg Health Spa & Retreat $ FB-SC

P.O. Box 189
Schomberg, Ontario LOG 1TO
(416)936-2328
(416)462-3855 (in Toronto)

In the quiet woodlands northwest of Toronto sits the quaint and rustic Schomberg Health Spa & Retreat. Accommodating no more than 13 women (no men), Schomberg has expanded its exercise area and added new massage and treatment rooms, an indoor swimming pool with bay windows, and a large deck. However, these additions don't detract from the homey, comfortable feeling of the original structure, a Norman stone manor.

This informal retreat offers a full range of European-style spa and beauty treatments, as well as some unconventional services. The spa's highly qualified staff is made up of registered therapists, natural health counselors, and estheticians who design individualized programs for guests. Besides the soothing sensations of reflexology and Shiatsu massage, guests can undergo iridology, a method of revealing aberrations in a person's health history and status by reading the iris of the eye. Another uncommon practice offered here is kinesiology, a method of discovering which food substances the body may have trouble tolerating.

Schomberg also offers more traditional body treatments such as algae wraps, aromatherapy, colonic irrigation, and body polishing, as well as specialized services such as treatments for acne, hydrorestoration, lymphatic drainage, and skin peelings. Makeup application, paraffin manicures and pedicures, and waxing are *a la carte*.

Fitness walks, low-impact aerobics, water exercises, yoga, and Tai Chi, the centuries-old Chinese exercise using slow, rhythmic movements, are all part of the workout regimen, but guests are not required to take part in any of them. Everything is optional here and there is loads of free time to pursue other stress-reducing options. Guests can go for a walk or bike along groomed trails in the surrounding countryside. When snow falls, there are cross-country ski trails. Of course, a soak in the whirlpool or a visit to the sauna in the glassed-in solarium will do just as well to alleviate worries. Then, guests are free to take in lectures and discussions on natural healing.

Shopping excursions for antiques and crafts in the nearby towns of Schomberg, Cookstown, and Kleinburg are open to folks looking for a diversion. Horseback riding at a nearby ranch and an educational visit to a health food store are sponsored by the spa. In the evening, many guests lounge on the pink chintz sofas in the living room to watch videotapes of their choice, or one from the in-house selection of health, diet, and exercise tapes. Some guests simply gaze at the fire crackling in the massive stone fireplace.

Low-calorie vegetarian cuisine, herbal teas, and juice fasting fill the spa menu. Many guests may not ordinarily order zucchini-oatmeal soup with soya, vegetable-stuffed peppers, millet, and salads of beans and grated carrots in a restaurant, but in the name of good health, why resist? A cozy dining room seats the 13 guests around a mahogany Queen Anne table.

The bedrooms are decorated in pastel colors and accented with fresh flowers. They are very comfortable, with plenty of space for clothing, but it isn't necessary to bring too much, particularly dressy outfits. The rule of thumb for packing is to wear what makes you comfortable.

The Schomberg has two-, four-, and six-night packages ranging from C$345 to C$775. The four-night package price includes accommodations, three meals daily (or juice fasting), one pedicure, one facial, a massage or body polishing, and a reflexology treatment, plus all classes and equipment. For the two-night package, exchange the pedicure for a manicure. During a week's stay, guests get two reflexology treatments, a body polishing, massage, facial, manicure, meals, classes, and equipment. There is a basic two-night package for C$250 that includes accommodations, meals, classes, and equipment. Additional services, ranging in cost from C$7 for a lip waxing to C$65 for aromatherapy and a jar of special oil to take home, can be purchased separately. And for an inclusive day trip, the rate is C$145 which covers lunch, a massage or body polishing, a facial, pedicure, manicure, and use of all facilities.

GUEST FEEDBACK
Guests have found this retreat to be a real buy and those who come here come specifically to take advantage of its New Age therapies. They are pleased with the range and efficiency of services, the quality of the staff, and the fact that the spa doesn't offend the pocketbook. Many would return and/or recommend it to their friends.

Rates

	Single	*Double (per person)*
2-Night Package	C$390–485	C$250–345
4-Night Package	C$845	C$565
7-Night Package	C$1,265	C$775

There is no minimum stay and any-day arrival. U.S. dollar prices approximately 15 percent lower.

Southwind Health Resort $$ FB-SC

Route 2, Sandtown Road
Cartersville, Georgia 30120
(800)832-2622 (Nationwide)
(404)975-0342 (in Georgia)

This 20-room country estate-turned-spa has attracted such notables as singer Gladys Knight and Coretta Scott King with its pampering and tranquil setting. Southwind is located on 16 wooded acres bordering Lake Allatoona, just 45 minutes north of downtown Atlanta. Catering to women only, it provides a refuge from everyday stress and a chance to improve self-image and to get weight under control.

The fitness regimens here combine nutrition with a common-sense approach to weight loss and exercise, although everyone decreases calories and increases exercise at her own pace. There are daily aerobics, water aerobics, and body sculpting classes; supervised fitness walks around the lake; and loads of free time to sit in the rocking chair and read on the two-story veranda or take a dip in the hot tub or custom-built swimming pool. Owner-director Doreen Mac Adams, a registered nurse, believes in teaching ways to improve your life, through information you can apply at home. Each day a seminar on nutrition, stress, and general well-being is scheduled. Fitness goal-setting, low-cal/high-energy cooking, and self-image and relaxation techniques are some of the other topics covered by health professionals.

In the remodeled third-floor attic, which offers a wonderful view of the lake, each guest can submit herself to the massage therapist and beauty consultant for a massage and makeover. Body and skin care treatments include 30- and 60-minute massages, reflexology, facial, makeup application lesson, and lash/brow dye. Depilatory waxing from head to toe and luxurious nail-care treatments, including a 60-minute European pedicure, are also available.

The dining room is the setting for three gourmet meals prepared by a professional chef who also gives cooking lessons in the large, modern kitchen. And there are menu choices for each meal. Breakfast options range from omelets to grits to fresh fruit and bran cereal. Lunch features appetizers such as Creme Senegale (a rich chicken stock thickened with puree of apples and flavored with curry), marinated mushrooms; a mexicorn (lettuce, onions, and corn) or french potato cucumber salad; chicken mozzarella, fish sandwich, stir-fried Chinese cabbage, or spicy cauliflower as the main entree; and a choice of fresh fruit or strawberry sundae for dessert. Dinner options are more extensive with a choice of three appetizers (chicken mushroom soup, asparagus with curry dip, or a fruit kabob); salads of spinach with mandarin oranges or tomatoes with basil dressing; Creole chicken, scallops Dijonnaise or shrimp scampi entrees with either snow peas or grated sauteed beets; and to finish the meal—banana with ginger, pistacchio mousse, or fresh fruit.

All accommodations at Southwind are shared in one of the eight comfortable guest rooms, each with its own bath. There is one basic package for either a week or a weekend stay that includes accommodations; three meals daily; all seminars and lectures; a beverage bar featuring herbal teas, mineral waters, decaf coffee, and popcorn nightly; use of all spa facilities (including the video library and extensive health library loaded with self-help books), nature hike, and transportation on spa outings, such as shopping at the local grocery store to stock up for home-spa cooking. All guests must present a signed medical release from their physician upon arrival at the spa.

In addition to the basic package, guests can purchase fitness/ beauty packages. For a week's stay, The Ultimate, featuring five body massages, two facials, a manicure, European pedicure, and unlimited fitness classes is available for $400. The Sleek and Chic week beauty bonus costs $325 and includes three massages, a facial, manicure, five cooking classes, and unlimited fitness classes; the Lite & Lovely package for $400 offers a fitness consultation, unlimited classes, three massages, and a facial. In addition to their lodging and meals, weekend guests can buy a beauty package for $150 that features unlimited fitness classes, a facial, two massages, a manicure, and a cooking class; or the $100 Revitalizer which buys unlimited fitness classes, a massage, and a facial. *A la carte* fitness and beauty services also include fitness consultations, nutritional profiles, cooking classes, psychologist sessions, and hypnotherapist sessions, as well as all the beauty treatments. These services range from $7 for a toenail polish to $100 for an hour with a psychologist. Southwind also invites groups of between 24 and 40 women to spend a custom-made day at the spa, which is priced according to their special needs.

GUEST FEEDBACK
Guests of Southwind rave about the informative lectures and motivating seminars led by professionals. Many of guests surveyed were also particularly pleased to learn methods of cooking that helped to reduce fat and calories. Southwind's staff were also commended for their expertise and general concern and care for the guests. As one guest put it, "Southwind was committed to creating a very healthful and relaxing atmosphere. It is very hard to leave. Thank you all for a very special weekend." Many also talked about returning to Southwind for a longer stay.

Rates

	Single	Double (per person)
3-Night Weekend Program THURS ARR/SUN DEP	not available	$395
6-Night Program SUN ARR/SAT DEP	not available	$795

Two Bunch Palms $$ FB-SC, MS

67-425 Two Bunch Palms Trail
Desert Hot Springs, California 92240
(619)329-8791

Surrounded by groves of giant palm trees on a gently rising hill, Two Bunch Palms is an oasis nourished by a natural force from deep beneath the earth that has created one of the richest mineral springs in the world. Legend has it that infamous gangster Al Capone built his fortress in this desert oasis during the early thirties. Al Capone's former hide-out is now a spa resort where every guest's privacy is closely guarded—both from the outside world and from other guests. It is a place where even Hollywood celebrities retreat for strict R&R&R—rest, relaxation, and romance!

There is *no* fitness program, no regimented schedule, and no calorically restricted diets. The plan here is no plan at all. Guests come for the natural hot springs that are fed into individual pools which look more like natural rock grottos than manmade structures, and offer you the choice of 95- and 105-degree temperatures 24 hours a day. Nude sunbathing bins are placed in secluded groves throughout the grounds. Of course, there is also the obligatory swimming pool and sun deck.

For those who want to mix a little exertion in with their relaxation, you can play tennis on the two tennis courts or go jogging down the four-mile jogging trail.

For pure contemplation, you'll find meditation and Jin Shin Do, a meditative acupressure technique designed to balance energy flow through the acupuncture meridians, a worthwhile experience.

In the body care and treatment rooms, both men and women can enjoy traditional or more exotic body luxuries. Swedish, Shiatsu, Esoteric or Trager, and reflexology massages relax muscles and replenish physical energy. Then choose from a clay, mineral water, or milk and honey facial, or treat your entire body to a salt-glo rub and herbal steam, a Roman Celtic Brush, or an aromatherapy bath. Two Bunch Palms has its own line of skin and hair products, made of its natural mineral spring water mixed with other natural ingredients, which you can pick up at the boutique.

Lodging here is an assortment of 40 beautifully restored bungalows and villa rooms in which Victorian furniture, Edwardian lighting, and Art Deco accessories are mixed together with charming results. There is also the Al Capone suite which accommodates up to four people. No matter which you choose, expect a telephone and television in your room.

The spa's cuisine features chicken and fish dishes prepared with natural herbs and spices. Vegetarian and kosher meals are also served upon request. Reservations in the restaurant are required. Or, if you prefer, you can sample the wide variety of gourmet restaurants in town.

The resort, which is closed during August due to the heat, serves a maximum of 94 guests at any one time, so be sure to book reservations well in advance. And while this may be a popular relaxation playground to the stars, don't expect to get autographs. Privacy is the pivotal point here. Attire is casual and comfortable, although guests may dress for dinner in the restored Casino, which is now a lounge and dining room, and at nearby restaurants. Prices per night at Two

Bunch Palms include accommodations, continental breakfast, and mineral showers. All other services and meals are *a la carte*. Beauty treatments start at about $28 for a scalp massage and go as high as $72 for an esoteric massage which uses sound, visualization, and color therapy.

GUEST FEEDBACK
Guests are usually very pleased with their stay at Two Bunch Palms. If you are looking for real support to shed pounds, change eating habits, work out a fitness plan, or just hobnob with celebrities, Two Bunch Palms is not for you. However, if you long for a private place to relax and be pampered, this spa is just what the doctor ordered.

Rates

	Single	*Double (per person)*
Per Night	$135–325	$67.50–162.50

FITNESS AND BEAUTY SPAS (AT A HOTEL OR RESORT)

Auberge du Parc Inn $$ FB-RH

C.P. 40, Paspebiac
Quebec, Canada 12, GOC 2KO
(800)463-0890 (in Quebec)
(418)752-3355

This former maritime company now houses a luxury spa specializing in passive seawater treatments and therapies, but also offers sports and recreation on land and sea. Located more than 500 miles north of Montreal on the Baie des Chaleurs, Auberge is bordered by a wooded park and overlooks the harbor and gardens. French is the main language spoken here, but don't worry about fishing out your notes from high school, the staff is bilingual.

   Now catering to the health conscious, Auberge accepts about 30 guests at a time. With Thalassotherapy as the main attraction, you are treated with mud, algae, and mineral-rich water pumped directly from the bay. Massage is part of the daily routine for guests on the one-week program. The staff consists of naturotherapists, nurses, masso-therapists, and estheticians. Each day you can enjoy a three-hour session of treatments. These include hydrotherapy in a heated sea water bath, which is used to reduce muscular pain, stress, and tension, to contribute to the gradual reduction of cellulitis, and to restore the psychic and physical tone; algae wrapping, a procedure of being wrapped in algae which assists in eliminating toxic waste from the body and revitalizes energy level; therapeutic massage, where three techniques are used: a jet stream shower, lymphatic drainage, and a complete massage; and pressotherapy, a process which activates blood circulation in the legs and exercises weak muscles.

In addition to this, estheticians can provide you with information on wrinkles, acne, skin revitalization, weight loss, cellulitis, and the care of hands, face, and legs. All of Auberge's treatments are administered with Algologie products which contain high concentrations of vitamins, minerals, and other organic substances.

In summer, you can stroll the landscaped grounds or enjoy a relaxing afternoon in the sauna and heated outdoor seawater pool. For those of you with sports in mind, challenge yourself to a game of tennis, shuffleboard, ping-pong, or the nine-hole mini golf course. If mountain cycling, trout or salmon fishing (in season), or just shopping is your thing, the staff here can point you in the right direction. During the winter, you have access to cross-country skiing, skating, or a nice brisk walk. There are some stretch and tone sessions and water exercises (weather permitting) in the outdoor pool. Most of your time, however, will be spent receiving treatments.

Lodging here consists of 30 modern bedrooms with private baths in a country manor house, a short distance from the Auberge, overlooking the Bay of Chaleur. The dining room offers some favorite seafood dishes, as well as tasty low-calorie meals prepared with fresh produce from local farms.

Auberge du Parc offers two-, three-, five-, and seven-night programs that include accommodations, meals, beauty treatments, and use of all facilities. For those looking for specialized body treatments and serious skin-care information, you needn't look any further.

GUEST FEEDBACK
Although the spa is a trek from the airport (most guests fly into Charlo Airport—two and a half hours away), guests return with very favorable reviews. There's something about seawater that soothes the soul and makes the sojourn worthwhile.

Rates

	Single	*Double* *(per person)*
2-Night Program	C$415	C$375
3-Night Program	C$615	C$555
5-Night Program	C$990	C$890
ANY-DAY ARRIVAL		
7-Night Program		
SUN ARR/SUN DEP		
Oct. 29–June 3	C$985	C$875
June 4–July 2 and Aug. 20–Oct. 29	C$1,170	C$1,025
Jul. 3–Aug. 19	C$1,295	C$1,155

There is a two-night minimum stay. U.S. dollar prices are approximately 15 percent lower.

The Spa at Bally's $$$ FB-RH

Park Place Casino Hotel
Atlantic City, New Jersey 08401
(800)225-5977 (Nationwide)
(609)340-4600 (in New Jersey)

Sitting on Atlantic City's famous boardwalk is Bally's Park Place. Straight out of a Hollywood fantasy, the place is complete with exotic plants, waterfalls, fountains, and magnificent luxury touches. It offers health, beauty, and fitness options by day and glamorous casino action by night.

The 40,000-square-foot facility is a world apart from the action of Atlantic City and the monotony and pressure of day-to-day living. There is state-of-the-art fitness equipment, including Nautilus and Lifecycles, plus stretch and tone classes for men only, co-ed classes in aerobics, body conditioning, jogging, and walking. Thirty-minute and hour-long private exercise sessions are also available. In addition, there are four courts for racquet sports.

For relaxing, try a Swedish or Shiatsu massage, herbal wrap, aromatherapy in the private MVP suite, or a 90-minute session consisting of relaxing in a private marbled whirlpool, steam shower, and 30-minute massage. In addition, men can have a loofah scrub, while women submit to a body cleansing loofa treatment. For personal hair care, do visit the renowned Bruno Le Salon of New York which offers both men and women the finest in microvision hair and scalp analysis, as well as styling, manicures, pedicures, and waxing. In addition, there are five tanning salons and swimming in the Coral Lagoon.

The Spa Cafe features spa cuisine for breakfast and lunch, along with your favorite beverages.

You have a choice of meals, including an appetizer, salad, entree, and dessert. The calorie count is written next to each item. For dinner, guests on the spa package dine at a gourmet restaurant, such as By the Sea or Prime Place, both of which have a special spa menu with food for the calorie-conscious. The Spa Cafe also has a regular full menu and daily luncheon specials for non-dieters.

The spa offers services *a la carte* with a $10 admission fee, day-long packages from as low as $99 which include a massage, unlimited use of the spa's basic facilities, a fitness class, herbal wrap, private whirlpool bath, loofah body cleaning treatment, free parking, and a 20 percent discount in the spa Pro Shop. The one- and two-night packages feature accommodations, meals, fitness classes, herbal wrap, loofah cleansing treatment, manicure, hairstyling, unlimited use of spa facilities, 20 percent discount in the spa Pro Shop, and $10 in coins.

GUEST FEEDBACK

Surveyed guests rated their experience at Bally's as excellent, including the location, facilities, and staff. All would return again and would recommend it to their friends.

Rates

	Single	Double (per person)
1-Night Beauty/Fitness Package	$360	$320
2-Night Beauty/Fitness Package	$575	$450

There is any-day arrival and the spa will custom design packages for longer stays.

The Spa at The Biltmore $$$ FB-RH

1200 Anastasia Avenue
Coral Gables, Florida 33134
(800)445-2586 (Nationwide)
(305)445-1926 (in Florida)

The Spa at the magnificently restored Biltmore Hotel in Coral Gables is now associated with Elizabeth Arden/Main Chance Salon and Spa and offers a revitalizing, weight-reducing program in an elegant setting. Located just minutes from Miami International Airport and downtown. The Biltmore's central location makes it a perfect hub for business or pleasure.

The Spa experience at The Biltmore includes all the luxury pampering treatments such as Swedish and Shiatsu massage, aromatherapy, seaweed and cellulite wraps, facials, manicures, and pedicures. Plus, there are luxurious hydrotherapies. Try a Vichy shower where hot and cold water, in showers of varying velocity, tone and invigorate while you recline on a special table. This full European spa also has a sauna and whirlpool.

For fitness, you can get one-on-one instruction and a comprehensive computerized fitness (cardiovascular endurance, strength, flexibility) evaluation leading to recommendations and exercise. In addition, there are aquatic exercise classes, aerobics classes, Keiser weight machines, and tennis and golf clinics. Children can enjoy arts and crafts, museum tours, cooking classes, and other organized activities.

At mealtime, choose from a number of restaurants and lounges, and enjoy a spa menu developed by the chefs of Le Cirque, a four-star French restaurant frequented by New York's elite. Some spa participants take the Spa Cooking Class where you receive a chef's apron and diploma at the conclusion. In addition, The Biltmore spa offers fashion shows and image enhancement sessions.

The Spa at the Biltmore offers two- and four-night packages that include accommodations, three meals in the Biltmore Club private dining room, individualized treatment program, a spa wardrobe, tax, and gratuities, plus some extras, such as facials, hydro- or Swedish massage, and herbal wraps.

GUEST FEEDBACK
If you plan to be in southern Florida and are looking for something special, former guests highly recommend the spa at The Biltmore for pampering and a change of pace.

Rates

	Single	Double (per person)
2-Night Package	$595	$435
4-Night Package	$1,450	$1,100

There is a two-night minimum stay and any-day arrival.

The Claremont Resort $$ FB-RH

P.O. Box 23363
Oakland, California 94623
(800)323-7500 (Nationwide)
(415)843-3000 (in California)

Long known for its elegance and personalized service, the imposing 70-year-old hotel in the hills overlooking San Francisco Bay is receiving rave reviews of its new health and beauty facilities. Incorporating the concept of famous spa therapy centers of Europe with an extensive line-up of fitness activities and body treatments, The Spa at The Claremont can compete with the best of them. Occupying a Victorian-style castle built in 1915, the hotel presides over 22 acres in the hills of Oakland and Berkeley.

Fitness is taken seriously here with classes running from 7:00 A.M. until 7:30 P.M. Three levels of aerobics, plus circuit aerobics and swimnastics, stretch and flex, yoga, and weight training are offered in the aerobic room and weight room. Lifecycles, rowing machines, and Nautilus weight machines are also available. In addition there is race-walking, swimming, and tennis. Personal instruction in both sports, children's clinics, and one-on-one workouts are also available.

Less strenuous activities also abound, with water therapies featured. There is a hydrotub where underwater jets massage, relax, and invigorate you. Or, have an aromabath in the Jacuzzi tub filled with aromatic essential oils to detox your body while reducing stress and tension. Then, too, there is the herbal bath that uses various herbal mixtures in the Jacuzzi to promote relaxation or stimulation or to soothe sore muscles.

The separate locker rooms for men and women feature whirlpools, steam room, and sauna. Besides submitting yourself for a soothing, energizing, deep-muscle massage, you can have an aromatherapy massage that works on the skin's connective tissue. A very gentle, relaxing massage technique is used with essential oils to stimulate the natural flow of the lymph system. Salon services include facials, body scrubs, manicure and pedicure, hair care, and makeup instruction and application.

When it comes to dining, the resort has a special Pavillion room that serves up calorie-controlled, low-sodium, low-cholesterol dishes such as mesquite-grilled swordfish with papaya chutney. There are regular resort dining options, as well. And you can expect all the lodging amenities of a world-class resort in the 239 guest rooms. Disabled spa-goers are accommodated with specially equipped rooms, ramps, and elevators. Located about 20 minutes from downtown San Francisco, area museums, beaches, wine country tours, and Oakland's Jack London Square with its entertainment, shopping, and arts, the hotel attracts locals and day-trippers. There are one- two-, and three-night packages, focus weeks, and local memberships. Packages include accommodations; exercise classes; facial; Swedish massage; herbal bath, loofah scrub, or hydrotherapy; manicure; and aroma or seaweed bath. Meals are not included in packages, but can be purchased for $50 per person per day for three spa meals.

GUEST FEEDBACK
Former guests of the Spa at The Claremont have all found it rewarding. They report having lots to do, but hardly enough time in which to do it. That means they all want to go back and take advantage of the things they didn't get to.

Rates

	Single	Double (per person)
Vitality Vacations		
1 Night	$297	$244.50
2 Nights	$444	$339
3 Nights	$640	$482.50

There is any-day arrival.

Dr. Deal's Hawaiian Fitness Holiday $$ FB-RH, NA

P.O. Box 1287
Koloa, Hawaii 96756
(808)332-9244

A holistic approach to good nutrition and weight loss is what this spa, on the beautiful island of Kauai, is all about. Dr. Grady Deal, a holistic, nutritional chiropractor with a Ph.D. in psychological counseling and a license in massage therapy, and his wife Roberleigh accept no more than 10 guests at a time so you are sure to receive all the personal attention you could ever want.

Most fitness classes are held outdoors, and you'll get a special lift from the tropical vistas of the Pacific Ocean. There are stretch exercises and yoga, designed specifically to promote a feeling of rejuvenation and to reduce stress, as well as to tone and tighten your body—after which you might want to take a dip in the ocean and sun yourself on the beach. Or if you prefer aerobics, you can choose soft-impact or a more vigorous kind. Also available are fitness machines and weight training, which you can follow up with some time in the Jacuzzi, steam room, and sauna to ease any sore muscles. This is a good place to remind you of the importance of being somewhat in shape *before* you go to any spa to reduce the chance of straining unused muscles. Fortunately, for those of you who overdo it, there are quite a few massages to choose from: Swedish, acupressure, reflexology, and deep massage, or you can ask for the best of each all in one massage!

You will learn a lot about the holistic approach to your health here, through fascinating lectures and slide shows on such subjects as detoxification, fasting, weight loss, and Hawaiian healing. Holistic approaches to conditions such as arthritis, heart disease, cancer, and allergies can also be addressed.

In addition, Dr. Deal offers chiropractic treatments that are a combination of massage, the application of hot packs, and specific chiropractic adjustments using nontraditional techniques such as kinesiology.

It will be no surprise that the cuisine here consists of natural whole grains, beans, seeds, nuts, vegetables, fruit, fish, and eggs. You will be indoctrinated in the philosophy that natural, wholesome foods improve health, clear thinking, uplift feelings, increase elimination, decrease toxicity, reduce weight, and generally make you feel more alive. How do German pancakes, tabouli, butternut squash, carob mousse, and pineapple upsidedown cake sound? By the time you leave, you'll be able to make these things at home. You'll also be given tapes of your personal nutritional counseling with Dr. Deal, along with his nutritional, weight-loss, and rejuvenation supplement program and an instructional workout audio tape designed for you by Roberleigh.

Guests of Dr. Deal's stay at the Lawai Beach Resort on Poipu Beach. Rooms have either an ocean or garden view. Dr. Deal offers packages from one to four weeks or longer. Bookings are heaviest from December 20 to around April 19, especially over the Christmas and New Year holidays. Whenever you want to go, you should make your reservation well in advance. The all-inclusive price covers accommodations, three meals daily, and use of all facilities. Also, exercise classes, six massages or chiropractic treatments per week, one nutritional counseling session per week, health lectures, cooking classes, a personalized detoxification and weight-loss program with a personal exercise and nutrition tape, plus transportation to and from Lihue Airport. A colonic therapy detoxification program is also avail-

able at an additional cost of $250. Other options include facials, mani-
cures, pedicures, and color consultations.

GUEST FEEDBACK

Guests usually rate their Hawaiian fitness vacation as rewarding in
every way, often remarking on what warm and friendly people Dr.
Deal and his wife Roberleigh are.

Dr. Deal's Hawaiian Fitness Holiday is idea for those of you who
take a natural, holistic approach to wellness and want highly personalized attention, while basking in the South Pacific sun. This is not
the place to go for fancy body treatments. Dr. Deal's is more concerned with helping to promote beauty from within.

Rates

Ocean View Deluxe Condominiums	*Single*	*Double (per person)*
7-Night Program	$2,195	$1,583.50
14-Night Program	$4,171	$3,009
Garden View Economy Accommodations		
7-Night Program	$1,050 & up	$945 & up
14-Night Program	$1,995 & up	$1,795.50 & up

The Elms (New Leaf Spa) $$ FB-RH, MS

Regent and Elms Boulevard
Excelsior Springs, Missouri 64024
(800)843-3567 (Nationwide)
(816)637-2141 (in Missouri)

This gracious getaway was opened more than a century ago to house
the throngs of folks who came to soak in the area's curative mineral
waters. The guests who've taken up residence include Franklin Roosevelt, Harry Truman, and the infamous Al Capone. Now completely
renovated, The Elms offers totally modern amenities, including the
three-level New Leaf Spa. Set on 23 lush acres, just a half an hour
from Kansas City, the New Leaf Spa features traditional mineral
baths, plus the latest in fitness, beauty, and relaxation programs.

The indoor fitness facilities include Nautilus equipment, a Liferower, Lifecycle, treadmill, and stationary bike. In addition, there is a one-lane lap pool with attached hot and cold tubs, surrounded by an indoor jogging track. The spa houses private lounge areas for both sexes, showers and locker rooms, a wet steam room and dry sauna, and two private mineral bath areas with sunlamps. The main attraction at The Elms is its ten Environmental Rooms, each with a different theme. All of the rooms contain double whirlpool hot tubs, AM/FM cassette stereo, and heat lamps. The Disco room has heat lamps, while jungle rain flavors the Egyptian room. In the Oriental room you'll be exposed to wet steam; and hot showers can be found in the African room. The Indian and Desert rooms feature a dry sauna, while the Polynesian and Roman rooms contain fountains.

Out of doors, the water is great. There's a pool and three kinds of hot tubs. The waterfall hot tub and the south Diamond hot tubs are a steaming 100 degrees, while the north Diamond tub is a hot 86 degrees. Swedish massage, herbal wraps, cosmetology, tanning beds, and hair and nail care soothe and refresh the body. For recreation, there is shuffleboard, horseshoes, volleyball, badminton, tennis, biking, and croquet. Evenings can be spent enjoying resort entertainment.

Meals are served in The Meadowlark Room where Continental, American, and New Leaf Spa entrees are served. There's the Front Page Lounge for dancing and a piano bar for those who want to end their day more serenely. The 106 guest rooms have been lovingly restored and are furnished with color televisions, ceiling fans, wooden dressers, and desks.

There are no packages for spa vacations at New Leaf, but the per-night cost includes admission to the spa and use of the facilities. *A la carte*, services range in price from $23 for an athletic massage to $19 for a reflexology session. Private mineral baths cost $7.50 and a stint on the tanning bed will cost $7.00.

GUEST FEEDBACK

Guests found that New Leaf met most of their needs. The facilities and location, massages, and staff concern ranked very good, while the beauty salon services were rated as excellent. Some guests liked the unstructured environment, while others needed a little more prodding to get moving.

Rates

	Single or Double
Per Night	$79–150

Nightly rates apply; there is no minimum stay and any-day arrival.

Eurovita Spa at The Avenue Plaza $$ FB-RH
Suite Hotel

2111 Charles Avenue
New Orleans, Louisiana 70130
(800)535-9575 (Nationwide)
(504)566-1212 (in Louisiana)

Travelers who like the Avenue Plaza for its location—just two minutes from the historic French Quarter, Dixieland jazz spots, and the downtown New Orleans business district—can also enjoy an excellent selection of fitness and beauty services at the Eurovita Spa.

Designed for maximum flexibility to work around busy career and personal schedules, the fitness program is unstructured but available when you want it. There are exercise classes in aerobics, stretching, yoga, strength conditioning, and body sculpting on an Exerflex aerobic floor. The fitness center houses Universal/Paramount Weight equipment, free weights, Lifecycles, Schwinn Air-Dyne bikes, Trotter treadmills, a computerized StairMaster, Ski Fitness Master, and a VersaClimber. Guests interested in more individual attention can get a state-of-the-art computerized nutrition, fitness, and wellness prescription.

There are separate locker room facilities for men and women, each with an array of international hydrotherapy units, such as a Scandinavian sauna, a Turkish steam bath, communal whirlpool, and Swiss shower, plus towels, robes, Eurovita's private-label toiletries, and a locker room lounge with VCR and cable channels. Water babies also have a heated courtyard swimming pool and a rooftop sundeck with hot tub.

When you want some personal services, an Acu-massage machine can give you a vigorous rub down, or you can opt for the human touch with a therapeutic massage by a therapist. If looking and feeling great for your next appointment is high priority, make time for a loofa salt-glo, herbal wrap, European facial, or a session on the tanning bed. Individual whirlpool baths and salon services—hair and nail care and makeup applications—will help make a great first impression.

Verdura is the spa's balcony restaurant, serving up fresh, light cuisine, healthy fruit and vegetable juices, beer, and wine. And don't worry about going overboard at the famous Cajun restaurants nearby. Eurovita's dietitians have created a calorie-conscious guide to the Crescent City's tantalizing eateries. Plus, Avenue Plaza's 240 suites come complete with kitchenettes and wet bars.

Eurovita offers two-, four-, and six-night spa getaways that include just about everything you'd expect out of a spa vacation. Guests on the spa package receive a health-risk appraisal, daily exercise classes, use of exercise and spa equipment, massage, loofa salt-glo, herbal wrap, manicure, pedicure, hairstyling, makeup application, and tanning sessions. Also included are accommodations in a one-bedroom suite and breakfast and lunch daily. You are on your own for dinner.

GUEST FEEDBACK
Former guests laud this popular spa for the good value it offers. They particularly liked the professional attention to detail of the exceptionally pleasant staff and the outstanding low-calorie cuisine.

Rates

	Single	Double
2-Night Package	$315	$256.50
4-Night Package	$705	$601.50
6-Night Package	$832	$711

There is a two-night minimum stay and any-day arrival.

The Evolution Spa At The Equinox Hotel $$$ FB-RH

Manchester Village, Vermont 05254
(800)362-4747 (Nationwide)
(802)362-4700 (in Vermont)

After 200 years, The Equinox Hotel and Resort has a new way to help guests get more out of their vacations—the Evolution Spa Optimum Health, Fitness, and Beauty Program. The grand old Colonial with a backdrop of the majestic Mount Equinox still has the same 7 front doors, 31 columns, 3 verandas, and countless green-shuttered windows so admired by former U.S. presidents.

Designed by Stuart I. Erner, M.D., one of New York's leading health, nutrition, and fitness experts, the Evolution Spa offers medically supervised, individually tailored plans that include a complete medical analysis, cardiopulmonary assessment, and nutritional profiles for a total of about 24 participants, mostly women—mothers and daughters. Tone up with aerobic and strengthening classes, Nautilus weight training, and free weights. Then, cool down with whirlpool, sauna, steamroom, indoor pool, massage, loofah, and cosmetology treatments. *A la carte* services run the gamut from an Aquamotion water exercise class for $10 to private exercise classes ($50), Thalassotherapy ($55), and tanning beds ($10).

The Equinox doesn't stop at improving your body; it also improves your mind with the Health Education Seminar series led by a panel of physicians, psychologists, nutritionists, and physical therapists. You'll explore the important medical and psychological factors that influence health and weight. You'll also get up-to-date advice on health maintenance, weight control, nutrition, stress management, and safe exercise.

This complete resort complex features an 18-hole golf course, outdoor tennis courts, and two indoor and outdoor heated swimming pools, hiking trails, bike rentals, and skiing. Horseback riding, canoeing, and romantic horse-drawn carriage rides are nearby.

There are 154 rooms and suites in this landmark hotel which has catered to the likes of Abraham Lincoln's family, Theodore Roosevelt, and Ulysses S. Grant. Accommodations are appointed in Victorian style and no two are the same, although they all have modern plumbing, heating, air conditioning, and lighting. Sunny views, Vermont pine furniture, armchairs, and pale walls with handstenciling give a sense of light and spaciousness throughout. For small groups, there are ten three-bedroom suites adjacent to the main building.

Dinner is served in the main dining room where a tuxedo-clad pianist accompanies dinner with classics and show tunes on a baby grand. Executive Chef Ken Paquin, whose loyalty is divided between the French culinary tradition and a passion for the calorie-controlled New American Cuisine, oversees the food preparation. And watch out for the Viennese bakery on the premises, because it promises a spectacular finale of deserts.

The spa offers three- and seven-night packages that come complete with daily massage, loofah scrub, herbal wrap, facial, exercise classes, salon services, computerized body composition analysis, tanning session, unlimited use of the pools, Turkish steam bath, Swedish sauna, whirlpools, gratuities, accommodations, and three meals daily.

GUEST FEEDBACK

Generally, guests found the hotel agreeable and would recommend it to a friend, although some wanted a more diverse schedule of exercise classes. Also, if you are easily distracted by the ring of a cash register and rationalize leg lifts as a way to get to the mall, note that there are more than 70 designer outlets and boutiques in the area to deter you from the primary purpose of a fitness vacation.

Rates

		Double
Jan. 1–Mar. 1 and Jun. 1–Oct. 31	*Single*	*(per person)*
Per Night	$274	$221
Apr. 1–May 31 and Nov. 1–Dec. 22		
Per Night	$252	$204

No spa packages available December 23–31. There is a three-night minimum stay and any-day arrival.

Fontana Spa at The Abbey on Lake Geneva $$ FB-RH

P.O. Box D
Fontana, Wisconsin 53125
(800)SPA-1000 (Nationwide)
(414)275-9751 (in Wisconsin)
(312)368-8515 (in Chicago)

This luxury resort facility received its first guests in July 1989. The new spa is a 27,500-square-foot All-Season Environmental Habitat Enclosure that provides an elegant, serene, and stress-free atmosphere with superb facilities for men and women. It offers a healthy balance of exercise, beauty, massage therapy, nutrition, and relaxation with nurturing, pampering, and caring for each guest.

For starters, guests can have a body composition analysis for $10, a submaximal test for $25, strength and flexibility test for $10, and a whole fitness evaluation for $40. To begin your workout, there's a weight and cardiovascular training room, plus a variety of daily exercise classes. Low Power Aerobics works major muscles and is paced for beginners and those who exercise on a whim rather than regularly. Accommodating all fitness levels is the Firm and Tone class which works the upper body with the use of light hand weights, resistance rubber bands, and floor work. It seems that almost everyone enjoys aquacize, which gives an excellent cardiovascular workout while strengthening and toning muscles with the resistance of the water. Regular exercisers aren't neglected; they can work up a sweat in the low-impact/high-energy aerobics class that burns calories and promotes cardiovascular fitness.

When it's time to relax, Fontana offers whirlpools, steam rooms, sauna, and pool, plus inhalation facilities. But a spa vacation here wouldn't be complete without personal pampering services. You can have a soothing massage, as well as thermotherapy and hydrotherapy sessions. Indulge yourself with a full-body or back fango pack, parafango, or herbal wrap. Or, those who prefer water-based therapies can have a Scotch hose/Swiss shower, private whirlpool, body polish, or loofa scrub. The full-service salon offers hair and nail care.

The menu here includes some low-calorie favorites, and there's always a choice of entrees. Breakfast can feature an omelette or zucchini and cheese frittata, cinnamon French toast with apples, or hot oatmeal. Lunch, served at noon, offers such choices as grilled tuna with pepper chutney, Cajun snapper, or barbecued chicken and rice. Midday desserts include sorbet, fruit brochette, and chocolate frozen cream. The evening meal offers such favorites as roast turkey, beef tenderloin with wild mushroom sauce, and game hens with rosemary.

You also have a choice of lodgings. There are lake-, garden-, park-, and poolside accommodations that start at $69 for midweek occupancy from October through April, and villa rentals that include two bedrooms, two baths, living room with fireplace, dining room, breakfast room, and patio or balcony. You will also receive an Abbey Welcome Basket, a complimentary carafe of wine with dinner, an herbal wrap, and a daily newspaper. Rates are $185 per day with a five-night minimum stay; $215 per night with a three-night minimum stay, and $266 per night in July and August.

The Fontana Unwinder Package includes a deluxe guest room with dinner in the Monaco dining room, breakfast or lunch, use of pool and health club facilities, a tanning session, two-hour bike rental, use of the Fit-Trail, and gratuities on food.

GUEST FEEDBACK
Some of the first visitors to the new fitness facility were rewarded by their stay and have vowed to return before the crowds discover this healthy resort.

Rates

Per Night	*Single or Double*
Jun. 1–Oct. 31	$120–170
Nov. 1–May 31	$100–140

There is no minimum stay and any-day arrival.

Fontainebleau Hilton Resort and Spa $$$ FB-RH

4441 Collins Avenue
Miami Beach, Florida 33140
(800)548-8886 (Nationwide)
(800)445-8667 (Hilton Reservations Worldwide)
(305)538-2000 (in Florida)

The dazzling Fontainebleau, one of Miami Beach's most famous land-mark resort and conference facilities, has added a delightful fitness and beauty center housed in an eight-story Spa Pavillion located on the beach. Medical services, provided by Mount Sinai Medical Center in Miami Beach, include pre-exercise exams and treatment of sports-related injuries.

The new spa at the Fontainebleau offers spa guests and members more than 70 exercise classes each week. Your spa vacation begins with a computerized evaluation with a fitness counselor to determine the proper exercise and maintenance program for you. Your program may consist of beach walks, reach and stretch classes, ballet stretch, total conditioning, aqua-aerobics, and level III aerobics. One-on-one workouts are also available. In addition, there is Nautilus weight training, steam room, sauna, and Jacuzzi. A real treat is having a massage alfresco. A spa wardrobe is provided during workouts.

The Spa is also home to the Christine Vlamy Salon where you can get spoiled with a full range of skin-care services and analyses. Choose from a variety of revitalizing facials such as ultra-live cell treatment or biogenic treatments, and fresh herbal or fruit masks. Manicures, pedicures, makeup lessons, and depilation and skin evaluations are also available. The Valmy Boutique carries a full range of homeopathic skin care products, which can be custom blended for special needs. Herbal wraps, loofah rubs, individual whirlpool mineral baths, solarium sessions, and massages are yours for the asking. Expert lecturers on nutrition, tennis clinics, and children's activities complete this fitness vacation package.

For recreation, the hotel features a wide variety of water and land sports, including tennis, wind-surfing, parasailing, aquacycles, volleyball, and a 2.5 mile boardwalk for walking and jogging. Golf and deep sea fishing charters are also available. Plus the half-acre free-form pool has cascading waterfalls and a natural food and juice bar beneath the rock grotto. An exercise pool and cabañas are located nearby.

Fontainebleau offers six dining options. All meals are *a la carte.* Spa guests have their own lunch encounter on the spa verandah,

Granny Feelgood's, which serves up nutrional, low-calorie salads, sandwiches, fresh juices, fruit smoothies, and natural desserts. Low-calorie dinner choices include broiled fish and chicken, but there are no specific diet items.

You can expect world-class accommodations here with a choice of room views (there are over a thousand rooms). Packages run from two nights to five nights and include accommodations, fitness classes, computerized fitness evaluation, nutritional consultation, exercise prescription, massage, hydrotherapy, salt-glo loofah rubs, facial make-over, and spa souvenirs. Meals are not included.

GUEST FEEDBACK
Surveyed guests found their vacations here very rewarding and would return. Next time they'll even tell a friend or two about it because a vacation here offers something for everyone.

Rates

	Single	Double (per person)
Jan. 30–Apr. 30		
2-Night Spa Adventure	$900	$600

Prices decrease from May to December. Call Spa-Finders for details. There is a two-night minimum stay and any-day arrival.

Four Seasons Hotel and Resort $$$ FB-RH

4150 North MacArthur Boulevard
Irving, Texas 75062
(800)332-3442 (Nationwide)
(214)717-0700 (in Texas)

When you want to combine business and pleasure, there's no better place to do it than at this comprehensive resort and conference center in the Las Colinas complex near the Dallas/Ft. Worth Airport. State-of-the-art communications, including computer modem links and other high-tech facilities, help you tend to business, while the superbly equipped fitness spa allows you to get away from it all. The spa even provides leotards, tights, and sneakers to do it in, so there's no excuse not to go for it.

The fitness program offers a variety of options. There are morning walks, low-impact aerobics in three different exercise areas, conditioning with hand weights, water exercises, weight training with Nautilus equipment, treadmills, stationary bikes, rowing machines, and alternative classes such as ballet, race-walking, basketball, and water volleyball. Even children can get into the action with ballet classes, tumbling exercises, and swimming. The extensive array of spa and resort facilities includes an indoor and outdoor pool, indoor and outdoor jogging tracks (you can even rent a portable radio to keep *you* on track), multipurpose gym, four indoor and eight outdoor tennis courts, racquetball and squash courts, pro golf course, dry sauna, steam room, cold-plunge pool, and full-service beauty salon.

Following the Four Seasons's tradition of service, the spa offers pampering and relaxation treatments such as a one-hour herbal wrap, loofa baths, massages, facials, and aromatherapy. Dry and wet saunas, whirlpools, cold-plunge pool, suntanning parlor, and outdoor sunbathing decks make guests feel well rested and cared for. Men and women have separate locker rooms with spacious dressing areas and salons.

For dining, the Four Seasons offers alternative selections of dishes low in calories, sodium, and cholesterol, without sacrificing taste. Alternatives is an American restaurant devoted exclusively to spa cuisine; however, you will find "alternative" spa cuisine selections at all of the resort's restaurants and eateries.

Whether your stay is for business or pleasure, or a combination of both, you'll be comfortable in the luxury guest rooms at the Four Seasons. Each of the 315 deluxe and superior rooms features balconies with views of the Dallas and Las Colinas skylines and the golf course, three telephones, radio, color television, a mini snack bar, and a bathroom, complete with bathrobe, hairdryer and personal-care items. Superior rooms also have a work area with a large desk, an overstuffed chair and ottoman, and computer hook-ups.

The spa offers services *a la carte,* by the day and in two-, three-, and six-night packages. Included are your accommodations, meals, unlimited access to fitness and spa facilities, classes and programs, personal fitness consultation, and beauty and body treatments. The six-night package also includes roundtrip transportation from the Dallas/Ft. Worth Airport.

GUEST FEEDBACK

The Four Seasons was well received by surveyed guests. One guest rated the spa excellent in every area, and thought the program was well structured and of good value. Business travelers should seriously consider tacking a few days onto their next trip to Dallas to enjoy the facilities and services offered here.

Rates

	Single	Double (per person)
2-Night Package	$580	$444
3-Night Package	$929	$725
6-Night Package	$1,745	$1,339

There is a two-night minimum stay and any-day arrival.

The Spa at French Lick Springs $$ FB-RH

French Lick, Indiana 47432
(800)457-4042 (Nationwide)
(800)742-4095 (in Indiana)

Set on 2,600 butternut-and-oak-covered acres, French Lick Springs Golf and Tennis Resort has symbolized beauty and grace for nearly a century. Today, you'll find the spa provides some of the most complete beauty and health-care services. You'll receive professional guidance through a personal program of proper diet; exercise classes; massage; Pluto Mineral Baths; European skin care; hand, foot, and hair care; and personal makeup classes.

Here guests work at their own pace, doing as much or as little as they please. Consultations with the spa director will set you in the right direction, but no formal program is offered. Daily exercise classes for total body fitness—stretching, aerobics, aquatics, and dance exercises—are offered, as well as Universal weight training, stationary bikes, a treadmill, and rowing machines. Recreational pursuits include swimming in the indoor and outdoor pools, golf, tennis, horseback riding, biking, bowling, skeet- and trapshooting, miniature golf, billiards, fishing, sailing at Patoka Lake, and skiing in winter at Pazoli Peaks; there is resort entertainment in the evenings.

European-type skin-care services, administered by aestheticians, clean, stimulate, and normalize your complexion with luxury facials. Special massage therapies, such as aromatherapy, lymphatic massage, and reflexology, plus whirlpool and sauna soaks help heal and soothe the rest of the body. Loofa scrubs, manicures, pedicures, and epibrasion treatments leave you feeling refreshed all over. The spa's real claim to fame is the Pluto Mineral Baths which you can bathe in or sip from a well beneath a gazebo. The beauty salon offers hair-care services and makeup classes.

Meals include low-calorie selections from the dining room menu and vegetarian meals are served upon request. Your accommodations in this 490-room hotel are either in deluxe suites or large double rooms furnished with king- or queen-size beds, antique furniture, a modern private bath, and color television.

The spa offers two-night midweek packages and five-night packages. Your accommodations, meals, use of spa facilities, massages, mineral baths, reflexology session, facial, fitness classes, and a stress-management workshop are all included.

GUEST FEEDBACK

Most guests cited the staff as one of the major highlights of their stay. After the recent renovation of the hotel and spa facilities, one client classified French Lick as "a great spa!" and can't wait to return.

Rates

	Single	Double (per person)
2-Night Package MIDWEEK ONLY	$379	$300
5-Night Package SUN ARR/FRI DEP	$905–1,250	$707–1,088

There is a two-night minimum stay.

Gran Spa El Tapatio $$ FB-RH

Boulevard Aeropuerto #4275
Apdo. Postal 2953
Guadalajara 4100
Jalisco, Mexico
(800)431-2822 (Nationwide)
(914)632-5102 (in New York State)
35-60-50 (in Mexico)

The newest spa south of the border, which opened in February 1990, is in sunny Guadalajara, now known for its wonderful shopping, great sightseeing, and exciting sports. It is also the home of one of the finest spas in Latin America. The new facility, associated with the luxurious Hotel Tapatio Resort, Golf and Racquet Club, features a completely computerized center employing the most modern wellness techniques and gym equipment. El Tapatio has one of Mexico's most renowned tennis facilities.

Gran Spa offers a host of specialized programs in stress management, weight management, cardiovascular training, hypertension, and general fitness. Guests of each of the programs begin their stay with a medically supervised battery of evaluations, including biofeedback, nutritional analysis, fitness evaluation, and when prescribed, a lean body mass evaluation.

Under the six-night stress-management program, for instance, your stay follows this routine. After the initial tests are performed, you can spend the rest of the day at the spa where you participate in the following activities: an hour-long class on nutrition, a half-hour in low-impact aerobics, a half-hour of aquatics, an hour-long facial and alpha sleep, 15 minutes in a whirlpool, and a half-hour herbal wrap. What's left of the day is spent at your leisure. The remaining days are also scheduled, beginning with breakfast, followed by a power walk. Activities are then timed: 15 minutes in the Swiss shower, half-hour aerobics class, half-hour aqua-calisthenics, half-hour cadiovascular conditioning, 10 minutes in hydrotherapy tub followed by a quick dip in the chiller pool, 5 minutes in the hydrotherapy pool, an hour-long massage, half-hour herbal wrap or fango pack, half-hour facial, hour-long evening class on stress management, and a half-hour biofeedback session. In addition, you will receive a loofa salt-glo, soap rub, Thalasso tub, sun bed, manicure, and pedicure. Guests on the weight-management program follow a similar regimen plus a 60-minute class each evening on weight control, nutrition, food preparation, and dining out.

The hotel itself offers deluxe accommodations and amenities. Each guestroom boasts a fully stocked bar, bedside music selector, oversized beds and dressing rooms, private terrace, and color satellite television. Meals are served at the enchanting El Meson de Chef restaurant.

All of Gran Spa's packages run for six nights and include your accommodations, meals, and program. Your choice of services includes massages, loofah treatments, soap rubs, salt-glo rubs, Swiss showers, Scotch douches, cosmetic facials, wrinkle-removing and toning facials, alpha sleep sessions, hydrotubs or Jacuzzis, Thalassotherapy, herbal wraps, exercise classes, medical evaluation and testing, diet analysis, and evening classes.

Rates

	Single	*Double* *(per person)*
6-Night Program	$1,243.75–$1,743.75	$995–1,395

There is no minimum stay and any-day arrival.

The Spa at Great Gorge Resort $$ FB-RH

P.O. Box 848
McAfee, New Jersey 07428
(201)827-2000

Physical fitness is the name of the game of this super-resort located in
the Vernon Valley, just 47 miles from New York City. From aerobics to
skiing, with some diversions besides, Great Gorge offers fun, fitness,
and relaxation for the entire family.

The Spa and Country Club at Great Gorge is a multidimensional
complex created from the marriage of a traditional country club with
a comprehensive health and fitness facility. Within are myriad ways
to achieve physical well-being. Fitness buffs have an evaluation center, three indoor tennis and three racquetball-squash courts, a 2,500-
square-foot Nautilus weight training gym, aerobic exercise room, indoor running/jogging track, and a full gymnasium that overlooks five
glass-enclosed swimming pools. Located poolside are saunas, steam
and eucalyptus rooms, a tanning patio, juice bar, and locker rooms.
The spa also has its own gourmet restaurant, banquet facilities, and
meeting rooms.

In winter, Great Gorge's three huge mountains transform this
wonderland into one of the Northeast's most impressive ski villages,
with 25 miles of interconnecting terrain skiable by novices and experts
alike. There are over 50 slopes and trails, 17 lifts and tows, and a rise of
more than 1,000 vertical feet. A specially designed chairlift and several
ski slopes serve the Great Gorge Village condominiums to provide
convenient slopeside access to the entire Vernon Valley/Great Gorge
ski area. In addition, snow conditions at Vernon Valley/Great Gorge are
guaranteed by the world's largest snow-making system. After a day on
the slopes, take a dip in the 90-degree outdoor swimming pool.

Other seasons offer 36 holes of golf on any of three Robert Trent
Jones and George Facio courses, wind-surfing in any of the numerous
lakes at the Mountaintop Recreation Center, or excursions to the
world-famous Action Park, just a quarter-mile down the road. Action
Park features over 75 rides, shows, and attractions, including the country's largest collection of original water rides and pools. There's also
horseback riding and hiking on dozens of green mountain trails, and
for the more adventuresome, hot air ballooning. Other diversions include the historical Village of Waterloo, the craft fair at Peter's Valley,
and the numerous outdoor festivals and concerts of Sussex County. In
autumn, you can even pick your own apples at local orchards, sample
freshly made cider straight from the press, or combine an afternoon of
antiquing with a search for the perfect pumpkin.

Besides the spa's gourmet restaurant, guests have a gourmet deli, other restaurants, and many convenience shops in the resort. Since accommodations are condominium-style with elegant interiors, cozy open lofts, and sunlit windows, you can fix your own meals.

Great Gorge offers a host of seasonal and spa packages. The per-night rate quoted includes your accommodations, admission to the spa, and use of all facilities. Meals and spa services are available *a la carte.*

GUEST FEEDBACK
Former guests felt that Great Gorge met their fitness needs and expectations. They called it a wonderful family vacation, and many of them vowed to do it again, perhaps next time in a different season than their first visit.

Rates

Mar. 15–June 15 and Nov. 1–Dec. 14	*Single*	*Double (per person)*
Per Night	$119–168	$83.00–132.50

June 16–Oct. 31 and Dec. 15–Mar. 15, 1990		
Per Night	$144–198	$100–152

There is a two-night minimum stay during peak periods, July 1–September 4 and December 15–March 15. There is any-day arrival.

The Greenbrier $$$ FB-RH, MS

Route 60
White Sulphur Springs, West Virginia 24986
(800)624-6070 (Nationwide)
(304)536-1110 (in West Virginia)

Guests have been coming here to "take the waters" for more than 200 years. The waters include White Sulphur Spring's sulphur water and Alvon Springs water, which is similar in mineral composition to the waters of Perrier, France. Superlative service, comprehensive facilities, and luxurious accommodations are a solid tradition at The Greenbrier. Beautifully housed in a newly constructed, multimillion dollar Spa Wing, the bath facilities include soak tubs, Thalasso tubs for underwater massage, specialized walk-in tubs for whirlpool baths, Swiss shower, and Scotch spray. There is also a steam room, sauna, and therapy rooms for massage, body wraps, European facials, and other treatments. The bath facilities for men and women were designed to afford each guest privacy while preparing for and receiving treatments.

To work up a sweat, the exercise studio offers a range of equipment such as treadmills, arm ergometer, hydra-resistance weight units, stationary bikes, and rowing machines. The adjoining exercise studio, complete with mirrors and ballet barres, has a specially designed impact-resistant floor for the variety of exercise classes held there. Aquatics classes are also held in the Olympic-size indoor pool; and there is a heated wet deck for lounging.

Outdoor enthusiasts can enjoy the parcours and miles of hiking, jogging, and biking trails in the foothills of the Allegheny Mountains. There's also horseback riding, skiing, and boating, plus 15 outdoor and 5 indoor tennis courts, ball machines, and professional instruction. For golfers, there are three 18-hole championship courses. Other recreational sports include bowling, platform tennis, fishing, carriage rides, and skeet shooting.

The European spa features a host of body treatments to tingle the skin. You can have an aromatherapy massage where classic techniques of Swedish massage are combined with the use of aromatics to deeply relax the body and soothe the spirit. The Sports Warm-Up treatment kicks off with a loofah body scrub, followed by a Swiss shower. Then, a special herbal aromatic oil and a talc rub leave you feeling fresh and ready to win. Other specialties include The Greenbrier, a sulphur soak followed by steam or sauna and Swiss shower and Scotch spray ending with a half-hour massage. The Greenbrier Bubbly is a refreshing herbal foam whirlpool of waters from the Alvon Springs combined with a Swiss shower and Scotch spray, followed by a half-hour massage. Body Purifier is a specialized European technique that combines a mineral soak with massage-like manipulation, followed by a nutrient-rich seaweed wrap, Scotch spray, and Swiss shower. For Perfect Relaxation, you begin with a sulphur soak and special underwater massage. Next, luxuriate in a soothing herbal body wrap, complemented by a half-hour of aromatherapy massage. Lymphatic massage, algae body wraps, cellulite treatment, paraffin treatments, facials, and body buffs are also available. The beauty salon offers a full line of hair- and nail-care services.

Besides juice and mineral water breaks during the day, and afternoon tea, traditional American fare and low-calorie alternatives at breakfast and dinner are served in the main dining room. There is a wide variety of accommodations, from guest rooms in the main building to deluxe cottages and guesthouses.

The Greenbrier offers a variety of packages, accommodating golfers, honeymooners, tennis buffs, and spa enthusiasts. The three- and five-night programs include your accommodations, breakfast and dinner daily, fitness classes, massage, use of exercise facilities and equipment, a variety of beauty treatments, and a collection of Greenbrier's own spa products and an exercise suit. Evening entertainment, open to everyone, includes chamber music concerts and ballroom dancing.

GUEST FEEDBACK

Guests have given favorable reviews of their Greenbrier vacations. Not only would they recommend it to their friends but many have returned themselves for a refresher.

Rates

Mar. 31–Oct. 31	*Single*	*Double (per person)*
3-Night Spa Getaway Package	$1,190	$820
THERE IS NO MINIMUM STAY AND ANY-DAY ARRIVAL		
Nov. 1–Mar. 31		
3-Night Weekend Getaway	$740	
THURS ARR/SUN DEP		
5-Night Programs	$1,180–$1,435	
SUN ARR/FRI DEP		

Gurney's Inn International Health & Beauty Spa $$$ FB-RH

Route 27, Sunrise Highway
Montauk, New York 11954
(516)668-2345
(516)668-3203

This marino-therapeutic spa uses the healing sea and marine environment for its therapies and services. Located on the easternmost tip of Long Island, frazzled executives and celebrities alike wind down and soothe away anxieties and tension with European-style seawater and beauty treatments.

Upon arriving at Gurney's, you'll visit with a physiotherapist who evaluates your medical history and current level of physical activity and then designs a detailed health/fitness profile and program for you. Supervised exercise sessions, stress-control minicourses, nutrition and beauty guidance, and massages of all types round out a well-designed program for the spa's 60 or so guests. For physical therapy, there are at least 16 varieties of activities, from beach-walk aerobics to yoga sessions overlooking the Atlantic. There are separate spa pavillions for men and women and each has indoor exercise rooms, massage rooms, steam rooms, saunas, hydrotherapy and treatment wrap rooms, and tanning lounges. The gym houses Nautilus and Universal equipment and an indoor saltwater pool. For outdoor fun there's a 15-station parcours, and tennis and golf are nearby. Evenings can be spent at lectures on such New Age treatments as reflexology and other health- and fitness-related topics.

For Thalassotherapy, aquamarine tubs are filled with body-temperature, filtered seawater while a therapist, employing an underwater hose, "massages" your body. To alleviate pain caused by stress, mud from the hot springs of Battaglia, Italy, is mixed with heated paraffin for an Italian fango pack and applied as a localized heat pack at points where muscular tension is most likely to strike. To soften the skin, draw out toxins, and promote elasticity, try a seaweed body wrap for head-to-toe nourishment. Other European-style treatments include herbal wraps, Roman baths, and Swiss showers in the Vichy rooms. There are also salt-glo rubs using salt from the Dead Sea. Plus, you have access to a full-service beauty salon.

Spa guests reside in the same accommodations as resort guests, and of the six guest lodgings, four have ocean views and two are directly on the beach. Most of the rooms are spacious and furnished in simple contemporary design with double beds.

During mealtimes, spa guests have their own dining room with bay windows overlooking the ocean. Of course, you can also dine in the main dining room, favored for its Italian dishes. Room service is also available.

Packages here come in two-, four-, and seven-night stays, although there is no minimum stay. The rate includes meals, fitness walks, exercise classes, massage, beauty treatments, and use of all facilities, but not accommodations, which vary in price.

GUEST FEEDBACK
Most guests were extremely pleased with their vacations at Gurney's. They thought the program was structured and presented well and was

a good value, although a few felt the room rate was on the high side. All would tell their friends about it.

Rates

	Single or Double (per person)	
May 5–Oct. 9		
4-Night Marine Renewal Plan	$399 plus accommodations (see below)	
SUN OR MON ARR/THURS OR FRI DEP		
4-Night Health and Beauty Plan	$495 plus accommodations (see below)	
SUN OR MON ARR/THURS OR FRI DEP		
7-Night Rejuvenation Plan	$775 plus accommodations (see below)	
ANY-DAY ARRIVAL THERE IS NO MINIMUM STAY.		

Accommodation rates for May 5–Oct. 9

May 5–May 26 Sept. 4–Oct. 9 Per Night	$200–290	$115–160
May 27–Sept. 4 Per Night	$230–320	$125–170

The Hills Health & Guest Ranch $ FB-RH

C-26, 108 Ranch, 100 Mile House
British Columbia, Canada 12, VOK 2EO
(604)791-5225

This year-round family vacation center features a full-service spa facility, but its claim to fame is its super cross-country ski program. Nestled in a wooded valley in the interior of British Columbia, The Hills also features horseback riding, hayrides, and western jamborees.

Each spa guest receives fitness testing upon arrival to determine his or her program content. The daily line-up includes three-and-a-half hours of aerobic classes such as no-bounce aerobics, jazz fit, aquatics, swimming, and circuit training. The gym is equipped with cardiovascular testing machines, a treadmill, exercise bikes, hydraulic and free weights, a midsection vibrator, and a rowing machine. There is also individual fitness counseling, and nutrition and wellness workshops. Facilities include a swimming pool, two whirlpools, Jacuzzi, and separate saunas for men and women. Besides horseback riding, golf and fishing are also available. Of course, there's also terrific hiking and skiing terrain. The ranch pampers its guests with massages, facials, manicures, pedicures, and a tanning salon.

Accommodations here are deluxe Swiss-style chalets with complete kitchens, living room, full bath, color television and two private balconies. Calorie-reduced, continental cuisine is the standard fare, but there is a regular meal plan for those who visit exclusively for the pampering and sporting. Families can take part in the jamborees, square dances, barbecues, hayrides, sleigh rides and Cowboy Breakfast rides that are regular events.

A variety of spa plans are available, from the Weekend Spoiler to the 11-day Weight-Loss Program. Packages include chalet accommodations, three meals daily, daily hike, exercise classes, fitness testing, daily massage, workshops, and use of all spa facilities and equipment. A manicure, pedicure, and facial are included in the Weight-Loss, Beauty Weekend, and Executive Renewal programs. Ski packages are also available.

GUEST FEEDBACK
At a "down-home" resort and spa such as this, where families can take part in activities together, The Hills has something for everyone. Guests consider The Hills a great value for the money, especially with the hearty ranch food, in addition to low-calorie selections, and the daily massage included in the package price. The range of activities makes this an inviting family destination. Plus, with most packages, guests get to choose their arrival day.

Rates

Jul. 1–Dec. 31	Single	Double (per person)
2-Night Weekend Spoiler FRI ARR/SUN DEP	C$274	C$194
2-Night Weekend Beauty Special FRI ARR/SUN DEP	C$366	C$286

6-Night Weight Loss Package	C$842	C$627
6-Night Executive Renewal	C$1,141	C$916
10-Night Weight-Loss Program	C$1,451	C$1,047

Prices are somewhat lower prior to July 1. U.S. dollar rate is approximately 15 percent less than the given Canadian dollar rate.

The Hilton at Short Hills $$ FB-RH

41 John F. Kennedy Parkway
Short Hills, New Jersey 07078
(800)HILTONS (Nationwide)
(201)379-0100 (in New Jersey)

The Garden State's "most luxurious hotel" also houses a full-service European spa facility where guests have the luxury of dining poolside on spa cuisine. Total fitness is the name of the game here, beginning with an individual fitness assessment and a one-on-one training orientation program by an exercise physiologist who goes through everything from warm-up to cool-down. A nutritional analysis and daily reviews of your program can also be arranged.

For working the body, the spa offers Keiser pneumatic weight machines, rowing machines, treadmills, StairMaster, free weights, and stationary bikes, plus a variety of exercise classes. Guests also have access to the raquetball and squash courts, a 50-foot swimming pool, an elevated Jacuzzi, lockers, private showers, and a sun deck.

When it's time to relax, you can have a Swedish or Shiatsu massage, herbal wrap, mud treatment, facial, body polish manicure, pedicure, or a makeup application and consultation. Spa services include personal trainers, personalized travel exercise programs, complimentary workout attire and laundering, robes and oversized towels, cooking demonstrations that showcase the latest trends in spa cuisine, plus shuttle service to The Mall at Short Hills.

The hotel itself is 15 minutes from Newark International Airport from which guests receive complimentary transportation. There are 300 deluxe rooms and suites. In all of the guest rooms, you can expect personal-care items, terry robes, and ample living space—all the amenities that have made Hilton a first-class hotel. In The Towers, there are two exclusive floors of guest rooms with their own concierge and private lounge, where a Continental breakfast, afternoon tea, and evening cocktails with *hors d'oeuvres* are served. Each of The Towers guest rooms also has bathroom scales, hampers, pants pressers, and extra toiletry items.

Enjoy spa cuisine poolside or in either of the hotel's restaurants.

Plus, spa guests can take advantage of the business center, lobby bar, and a club lounge.

Guests who want to take advantage of the spa can go for a day or for a week. Packages include your accommodations, three meals daily, admission to the spa and use of all facilities, taxes, and meal gratuities.

GUEST FEEDBACK
Visitors to The Spa at The Hilton at Short Hills have the benefit of both business and pleasure. Former guests were particularly pleased with the fitness facilities and the fact that the Hilton is close to New York City's many glamorous attractions. They would return to take advantage of both settings.

Rates

	Single	Double (per person)
Per Night	$145–185	$165–205
2-Night Package FRI ARR/SUN DEP	$365	$280
5-Night Package SUN ARR/FRI DEP	$995	$695

There is no minimum stay required

Hyatt Regency Waikoloa $$$ FB-RH

One Waikoloa Beach Resort
Big Island of Hawaii 96743
(808)885-1234

The fantasy never ends at this Hyatt resort located on 62 ocean-front acres of the Big Island's "Sun Coast." An ocean-fed lagoon where you can swim alongside dolphins, Venice-like waterways complete with canal boats, and a mile-long museum walkway with Pacific and Oriental art are just a few of its wonders. Not to be overlooked, however, is the resort's new spa, ANARA—A New Age Restorative Approach— which ranks as the largest and most extensive European-style facility of its kind in the Hawaiian Islands.

With approximately 20,000 square feet, the spa has separate facilities for men and women, both with Turkish steam and Finnish sauna rooms, private whirlpools, outdoor Jacuzzis, a locker room, and a relaxation lounge. A spa wardrobe, towels, and toiletries are provided for use during your stay. The weight room, with free weights and machines, and an aerobic gym featuring a range of fitness classes are co-ed. Personal training sessions, nutritional consultations, and computerized fitness evaluations are also available. No one under 18 years of age is allowed in the spa.

Of course, you could get a workout just walking around the lush gardens, thick forests of hau and bamboo, rolling lawns, and Japanese garden; or visit the wildlife collection of tropical birds, peacocks, penguins, flamingos, and ornamental fish. Then there's swimming in the free-form pool that's nearly an acre in size and features its own waterfalls, grotto bar, and twisting water slides. The $16-million championship golf course has a complete clubhouse with restaurant and pro shop, plus a golf academy run by the resort with practice holes, classrooms, and videotaping facilities. Those who prefer racquet sports have ten tennis courts and a spectator stadium, and two racquetball courts that can also be used for squash. Nearby are riding stables, deep-sea fishing charters, catamaran cruises, scuba diving, and helicopter tours.

There's no shortage of personal-care services, either. After a busy day, why not treat yourself to a Swedish, Shiatsu, or sports massage? Reflexology sessions, aromatherapy, and lomi-lomi, a Hawaiian-style massage, will also ease overworked muscles. If you require a little more luxury, you can choose among a variety of personal-care services. A loofah body buff, herbal wrap or herbal or aroma bath, body facial, or body masque are sure to leave even the most neglected body supple and fragrant. Facials and beauty salon services—manicures, pedicures, hair care, waxing, and makeup applications—will complete your new look. You may even muster up the urge to browse the 20,000-square-foot shopping arcade.

All this activity is bound to work up an appetite. Your only problem will be choosing where you want to eat. There are no fewer than 7 restaurants and 12 lounges to choose from: Continental, Northern Italian, Japanese sushi bar, Polynesian, southern Californian, seafood, or steak. The options will fit any whim, but the calorie count is up to you.

There are almost 1,300 guest rooms in three low-rise buildings—the Ocean Tower, the Palace Tower, and the Lagoon Tower. In addition, there is the Regency Club, which features 80 exclusive rooms offering VIP service such as concierge, private floors accessible only to club guests, complimentary breakfast and beverage service, afternoon *hors d'oeuvres*, and special room amenities.

The Hyatt offers spa services *a la carte* for guests. It costs $15 for daily use of spa facilities and $10 if you also have a treatment or use the spa after 4 P.M. Fitness classes cost $8 each, while individual training sessions or evaluations cost $35. Massages run from $65 for an hour-long Shiatsu massage to $25 for a half-hour reflexology session. Body treatments range from $15 for an herbal or aroma bath to $80 for a hour-and-a-half facial. A body masque costs $25, while a body scrub is $65. An herbal wrap costs $20 and a loofah buff is $35.

GUEST FEEDBACK

The guests surveyed have nothing but rave reviews of their vacations at this mega-resort. Although most were not out for a life overhaul, they were pleased to get away from their everyday stresses and indulge themselves with some pampering. The facilities, accommodations, and staff were rated excellent. All would return for an adventure in this wonderland.

Rates

	Single or Double
Per Night	$195–$360

There is no minimum stay and any-day arrival. Luxury suites and spa packages are also available.

Interlaken Resort and Country Spa $ FB-RH

Route 2, Box 80, Highway 50 West
Lake Geneva, Wisconsin 53147
(800)225-5558 (Nationwide)
(414)248-9121 (in Wisconsin)

Sitting on the shores of Lake Como, the Interlaken resort spa is a complete family getaway. The Country Spa is fully equipped with all the fitness and beauty amenities of a classic spa. The fitness staff here emphasizes weight loss, body sculpting, and cardiorespiratory development. Exercise classes are designed to improve self-image with routines that range from vigorous dance aerobics to special gentle routines for an older group of people. There are also aquacise classes. Weight-training equipment, free weights, and stationary bikes complete the fitness set-up.

  Relaxing and luxuriating at the Country Spa comes in many forms. For the 40 male and female guests, there are Swedish massages, facials, sauna, steam room, whirlpools, tanning salon, nail care, herbal wraps, and mineral baths. Many of these services are offered as part of a package deal.

As an alternative to the spa services, the resort offers a host of other activities the family can enjoy. There are indoor and outdoor swimming pools, tennis courts, fishing and boating, a game room, bicycles, and seasonal sports. In winter, you can ski, ice skate, and snowmobile. When the weather warms, golfers have the greens, water babies can water ski, and landlubbers can go horseback riding. All resort guests have a choice of dining areas and accommodations. There is the panoramic Lake Bluff Dining room and the elegant Newport Bar & Grill. There are selections for each meal with the calorie count next to each. Food is low fat and cooked with no salt. The daily calorie count totals 1,200. The choice of modern lodgings ranges from villas that sleep up to six adults, villa apartments (studio and one- and two-bedroom suites), and large, comfortable lodge rooms, all complete with standard amenities.

Interlaken also offers a choice of packages, beginning with the Getaway to the Romantic Interlude that's priced per couple. The two-night Spa Escape Program includes five meals, a massage, facial, makeup session, herbal wrap, mineral bath, tanning session, daily exercise program, and juice breaks—all at a very affordable price.

GUEST FEEDBACK

Interlaken guests almost unanimously found their vacation rewarding and would return. They liked the very informal, relaxed atmosphere and quiet evenings. Guests also praised the staff for their friendliness and concern.

Rates

	Single	Double (per person)
Per Night	$59–145	$186–305
2-Night Spa Escape Program	$246–430	

There is a two-night minimum stay and any-day arrival.

Ixtapan Resort Hotel & Spa $ FB-RH, MS

Paseo de la Reforma 132
Mexico City, Mexico 13
(905)566-2855

Take the waters in thermal mineral pools and Roman baths, lounge in the solarium, and enjoy the spring temperatures of this Mexican retreat located 70 miles from the capital city. Sitting 6,000 feet up in the Sierra Madre mountain range and on the site of thermal springs enjoyed by Montezuma in the 17th century, Ixtapan's waters have lured health-seekers for centuries. For the past two decades, this mountain resort has attracted guests who want a change from the beach scene and a place to relax. Also of note is the fact that there are completely separate facilities for men and women (50–60 spa guests in all), and of course, men can take pleasure in the pampering treatments.

Although the spa's main attraction is its thermal mineral baths, fitness fanatics aren't entirely out of luck. There are two exercise classes per day—a stretch-and-tone class and an aquatics class—and plenty of opportunities to enjoy recreational activities. A fresh-water swimming pool with a 500-foot water slide, shuffleboard, miniature golf, badminton, fitness walks, tennis courts, horseback riding, bowl-ing, billiards, a shooting range, Ping-Pong, volleyball, old-fashioned carriage rides, and a miniature train ride through the Park of the 13 Lakes can keep you busy. In addition, guests can take tours to markets in nearby towns or to Taxo, famous for its silver shops. But there are boutiques and shops right at the resort.

Accommodations for 500 hotel guests come in suites and private chalets with single or double occupancy. All are accented with Mexi-can touches. Three low-cal gourmet meals are served in the Diet Dining Room, but the calorie count—between 800 and 1,200 per day—is up to you. Enchanted evenings can be spent enjoying live entertainment, such as a Mariachi band, or dancing at the resort's nightclub.

Ixtapan's week-long spa package is chock full of extras. Even fitness fanatics may want to consider cutting back on their routines to have a daily facial, massage, and steambath. Three times during your seven-day stay you'll receive a mud wrap, reflexology session, loofah bath, hair treatment, manicure, and pedicure. Accommodations and meals are also included in the price. Roundtrip limousine service between the International Airport in Mexico City and the spa (about three hours) can be prearranged and costs $36 each way.

GUEST FEEDBACK

We've sent many satisfied guests to Ixtapan. Most found the resort a real bargain and said that it met most of their needs. Most would also return and recommend the place to a friend. The spa recommends that guests arrive in Mexico City on a Saturday and stay overnight at the five-star Hotel Emporio. A minibus picks guests up from the hotel Sunday morning and transfers them to the spa for a $15 fee.

Rates

	Single	Double (per person)
7-Night Program	$830	$650

SUN ARR/SUN DEP
There is no minimum stay.

La Fiesta Americana Condesa $$$ FB-RH
Vallarta Spa & Club

Carretera al Aeropuerto KM 2.5
Puerto Vallarta, Jalisco C.P. 48300
322-2-99-59 (in Mexico)
(800)345-5094 (Stateside)

Located in Puerto Vallarta, one of Mexico's west-coast resort areas, the Condesa Vallarta is a friendly, casual place to take a fitness vacation. Opened in June 1989, the spa program here features more than 30 exercise classes weekly; there's a fully equipped gym, computerized fitness and nutritional evaluation center to determine individual programs, a full line of body and beauty treatments, and a spa cuisine restaurant.

In the gym, which accommodates about 35 men and women, workout enthusiasts of all levels have 22 stations of Paramount variable-resistance weight equipment, five free-weight stations, and six computerized stationary bikes. In the aerobics room, guests have a choice of five different types of classes per day and two levels of aerobics. There's low-impact, stretch and tone, a water workout, and a total body workout, plus circuit training, jogging, and walking trails. To get you started on the right foot, first visit the fitness and diet evaluation center to determine your percentage of body fat, aerobic capacity, strength, flexibility, and overall fitness. A nutritional evaluation will measure vitamins and minerals, and percentage of fat, cholesterol, proteins, and carbohydrates needed in your diet. Horseback riding and a host of water sports—snorkeling, scuba diving, skiing, parasailing, wind-surfing—can be arranged at the hotel.

The spa has separate facilities for men and women. Each has a Jacuzzi, cold-plunge pool, sauna, eucalyptus inhalation room, steam room, and body-treatment rooms. Both sexes can treat their bodies to a massage, loofah scrub, or herbal wrap. Beauty salon services include facials, makeup applications (they have an exclusive line of natural face creams and makeup made with natural extracts and herbs), haircut and styling, and scalp treatments.

There's also a Natural Bistro serving juices, health shakes, yogurt, salad, whole-grain snacks, and fruits. The spa restaurant features low-calorie, low-cholesterol, and low-fat gourmet meals. Health and beauty lectures feed the mind. Although the spa provides light warm-up suits, tennis shoes, and bathrobes, there is a spa boutique on the premises, just in case you forgot to pack anything.

La Fiesta offers three- and seven-night programs. For a daily fee the program includes unlimited access to spa facilities and classes. Services, treatments, and spa cuisine are offered *a la carte*. The three-night vacation includes spa orientation, use of the spa facilities, spa wardrobe, massage facial, loofah scrub, herbal wrap, health and beauty lectures, and daily snacks. The week-long package includes all of this, as well as meals and computerized fitness and nutritional evaluations. Both packages include luxury, oceanfront accommodations.

GUEST FEEDBACK

Former guests have good memories of their stay at La Fiesta, and felt that it was a good value for the money, even though it is not inexpensive. They felt it was worth the money and would recommend the place to friends for a short stay. Most, however, did want more information on stress reduction, but commended the beauty staff, particularly the massage therapist, on their knowledge and concern.

Rates

June–Dec. 21	Single	Double (per person)
3-Night Deluxe Spa Program THURS ARR/SUN DEP	$499	$399
7-Night Deluxe Spa Program SUN ARR/SUN DEP	$1,590	$1,327
Dec. 22-Apr. 15		
3-Night Deluxe Spa program THURS ARR/SUN DEP	$699	$499
7-Night Deluxe Spa Program SUN ARR./SUN DEP	$1,999	$1,485

Le Meridien Spa $$$ FB-RH

2000 Second Street
Coronado, California 92118
(619)435-3000

Le Meridien Spa specializes in beauty treatments under the auspices of the Clarins Institut de Beauté that made Clarins of Paris world famous. Clarins skin-care products, established more than 30 years ago by Jacques Courtin-Clarins, have emerged as the premiere skin-care system of France and are very popular in this country, as well. Professionally trained beauty therapists utilize these products, developed and created from natural plant extracts such as chamomile, cucumber, mint, and myrrh, and combine them with specific massage techniques to provide a unique experience in facial and body treatments.

Clarins Institut de Beauté offers such luxurious specialties as a regenerating and firming facial that it claims will visibly minimize the appearance of lines and wrinkles; a desensitizing facial that meets the needs of sensitive skin, providing moisture and nourishment while working to "desensitize" skin; a facial for "instant" youthful radiance in 30 minutes; and the deep-cleansing facial, an ideal treatment to normalize skin, restore balance, and lift surface impurities. You can also treat your body to other goodies such as a firming body treatment designed to smooth, contour, and benefit stretch marks and slackened skin, promoting youthful resilience; a contouring body treatment that addresses the problems of spongy cellulite and offers slimming products that effectively help smooth and firm skin texture and tone; and an exfoliating treatment to give you super-soft skin.

Le Meridien has its own line of therapeutic treatments, including the Balneo bath (hydrotherapy), an underwater massage treatment administered by a therapist while you relax in a European-style hydrotherapy tub. The body is massaged with a special water pressure wand, for pure massage relaxation. There are also herbal wraps and Swedish, sports, and Shiatsu massages.

The spa offers fitness facilities and programs to physically sculpt your body. Exercise classes, water aerobics, a heated lap pool, and an exercise center with the latest in conditioning equipment give you a thorough and invigorating workout. In addition, you can enjoy a second heated swimming pool, sauna, whirlpool, and six tennis courts. You can also take advantage of individual fitness training with specific exercise prescriptions, cholesterol testing, body composition analysis, and a fitness profile. Then, indulge yourself with salon services such as a paraffin hand treatment and manicure, foot treatment (pedicure followed by a moisturizing massage and heat treatment), plus makeup application and instruction. All services and classes can be purchased *a la carte* and range in price from $6 for fitness class to $100 for a fitness profile.

The spa menu was designed by Le Meridien's consulting chef, Jacques Maniere, recognized as one of the world's leading authorities on cuisine that is low in calories and cholesterol. He's won many awards for his creative talents as a chef and restauranteur, and his book *Gourment Steam Cooking* won the Academie Culinaire de France prize as best cookbook of the year in 1985. His version of nouvelle cuisine is heavily influenced by French culinary traditions.

Accommodations at this posh pampering spa are spacious, and come with mini-bars, remote-control television, and terraces that allow for private samplings of the famous San Diego sunshine and sea air. You can take advantage of the spa and beauty institute during a day trip or for a full five-day program. Whatever you choose you'll be treated to accommodations; meals; massages; Clarins facial; body, hand, and foot treatments; makeup application; or scalp treatment (for men), herbal wrap; Balneo bath; and unlimited fitness classes.

GUEST FEEDBACK

Guests at Le Meridien Spa and Clarins Institut de Beauté report a wonderfully relaxing vacation. They rated the accommodations and beauty treatments, as well as the staff's knowledge, very high. All would return and would recommend it to their friends. This southern California spa offers the *creme de la creme* and you owe it to yourself to go for the most luxurious pampering around.

Rates

Jan. 1–Dec. 31	Single	Double (per person)
2-Night Spa Package ANY-DAY ARRIVAL	$690	$544
2-Night Spa-Finder Special Weekender Package FRI ARR/SUN DEP	$719	$553
3-Night Spa Package ANY-DAY ARRIVAL	$1,041	$822
5-Night Spa-Finder Special Package SUN ARR/FRI DEP	$1,530	$1,165

Le Pli Health Spa & Salon $$$ FB-RH

5 Bennett Street, Charles Square
Cambridge, Massachusetts 02138
(617)868-8087

Neighborhood residents and out-of-towners alike are welcome to the health and beauty facilities at this urban spa inside the deluxe Charles Hotel. Situated in the heart of Harvard Square, you'll find a state-of-the-art fitness facility plus European pampering in a luxurious setting.

Exercise enthusiasts will be at home at Le Pli, which has all the equipment necessary for a well-rounded workout. The club facilities include a glass-enclosed, four-lane swimming pool that overlooks the Charles River. Water exercise classes are performed in the pool to the rhythm of modern and classical music. Keiser CAM II and Nautilus weight-training center, StairMaster, free weights, rowing machines, treadmills, Lifecycles, stationary bikes, and a cross-country ski machine fill the Cardiovascular Conditioning and Weight Room.

If you want to further improve the shape you're in, have a complete fitness evaluation and an exercise routine designed just for you. For those who want undivided attention during their routine, personal trainers are available for $48 for nonmembers and $35 for members for a one-hour session. The exercise studio, with its sprung floor, is the setting for body-conditioning, stretch, dance, and yoga meditation classes. Workshops in weight and nutrition and stress management are also held here.

After working up a sweat, soak away aches and pains with eucalyptus in the steam room or try the huge hand-tiled whirlpool bath. A shower, locker room, and thick terry towels and robes are also at hand. Work the kinks out with Swedish, sports, or Shiatsu massage, or polarity therapy with a certified massage therapist. Other European techniques and therapies include hydrotherapy with underwater deep massage in an effervescent mineral water tub; Italian Fango mud treatments; and a variety of herbal steam and seaweed essence body wraps and brush treatments. The full line of salon services includes facials, waxing, makeup applications and lessons, and hair and nail care. There's also a suntan booth and a sun terrace.

Dining here, as in any first-class hotel, is a real treat. The Clubroom, with its view of the Charles and Memorial Drive, offers light food and full bar service in a relaxed setting. It features vintage wine by the glass and a cafe-style consisting of homemade soups and entrees, sandwiches, and salads. In addition, there is the hotel's four-star restaurant. When it's time to retire, guests can expect a room filled with all the amenities of a deluxe hotel, including terry robes and televisions in the bath, three telephones, and honor bars.

Guests can visit Le Pli for an hour, a day, or a weekend of intensive body and mind conditioning, massages, facials, body wraps, and fitness workouts. Two-, four-, and six-night packages include your accommodations, three meals daily, exercise classes, use of spa facilities, and beauty and body treatments.

GUEST FEEDBACK
Surveyed guests rated Le Pli very high for its facilities, accommodations, and location. The beauty and body services were also well received; mealtimes were very tempting since Le Pli has no spa dining room to serve up low-cal cuisine. The majority of the spa-goers here may very well be from the area.

Rates

	Single	Double
(per person)		
2-Night Package	$795	$695
4-Night Package	$1,221	$985
6-night Package	$1,742	$1,389

There is a two-night minimum stay and any-day arrival.

Le Sport $$ FB-RH

P.O. Box 437, Cariblue Beach
St. Lucia, West Indies
(809)452-8551
(800)221-1831 (Stateside)

A welcome addition to the tiny, lush tropical island of St. Lucia, Le Sport is a $15-million renovation and expansion of the Cariblue Hotel. Now owned and operated by the Barnard Group—which also owns Couples St. Lucia, another all-inclusive resort at Malabar Beach—Le Sport combines the best that a first-class Caribbean beach resort offers with the restorative body care of European Thalassotherapy, a system of body tonics based on the beneficial properties of heated sea water.

The Thalassotherapy Center is situated on a beautiful 18-acre estate and adorned with fountains, shimmer pools, courtyards, and a marble relaxation temple. For your Thalassotherapy treatments, water is drawn from the Caribbean and filtered to remove impurities. It is then heated before being used in sprays, showers, and baths and is never re-used. Before you undergo any treatments, a resident physician will give you a thorough check-up, to note stress-linked fatigue, muscle tension, circulation, and lymphatic drainage and to take your blood pressure, heart rate, and weight.

The treatment list is extensive. Hydromassage is rather like a Jacuzzi with sea water; the jet massage is a high-pressure jet that showers salt water to vigorously massage, stimulate circulation, and encourage the release of toxins; in the aqua gym—a salt water pool with sea water jets—you exercise under water while the jets help tone muscles, ease tension, and break down fatty deposits. Many people take special delight in the seaweed and sea mud wraps, which are particularly good for sufferers of arthritis and rheumatism. Le Sport also features Thai and Swedish massages, loofah rubs, saunas, facials, herbal wraps, Turkish baths, eucalyptus inhalation, hair and nail care, and relaxation therapy.

For those who'd rather just play in the sea, Le Sport offers a wide assortment of water sports such as snorkeling, scuba diving, waterskiing, wind-surfing, and sunfish sailing. Landlubbers can enjoy golf, tennis, squash, cycling, archery, fencing, weight lifting, horseback riding, and team sports such as volleyball and basketball. All equipment and instruction are included. There are also classes in calisthenics, dynamic swimming, and hydro-aerobics, as well as a Nautilus gym and free weights.

When the sun sets, Le Sport offers a nightly floor show, dancing to a live band, and a piano bar for those interested in a nightcap. And since the hotel is only 20 minutes from the capital city of Castries, you can easily check out local nightlife.

Cuisine at Le Sport's open-air restaurant features healthful gourmet dishes called Cuisine Legere, which are naturally low in calories.

Three meals and two snacks are served daily, and wine is offered with lunch and dinner. Breakfast may include a selection of fresh fruits and juices, brans, mueslies, two-egg omelets, smoked salmon, and a selection of homemade pastries. For lunch, you may have a fresh salad, stuffed chicken legs in a leek and cream sauce, and boiled wild rice garnished with julienne of carrots and zucchini. Dinner may consist of a brocolli souffle for starters, followed by escallope of veal with champagne saboyone, and fresh asparagus. To top off the meal, how do fresh pears poached in Grenadine syrup with homemade pear sherbet sound?

All accommodations in the 102-room hotel have undergone extensive renovations. You have your choice of deluxe, ocean-view, ocean-front, or beach-front rooms, which are connected to a lounge and dining room in this pavillion-style hotel. Rooms are decorated Caribbean-style with rattan furnishings, private balconies or patios, and modern baths. There are 200 guest rooms. Rates are uncompli-cated here.

At Le Sport, nightly rates apply. To make things even simpler, all single and double room rates include "everything you do, see, use, enjoy, eat, drink, feel, and participate in"—including the nightly entertainment and a shopping tour of the island. Tipping is not permitted.

GUEST FEEDBACK

The absence of cost considerations for treatments and activities en-hanced overall enjoyment and allowed guests to fully relax and par-ticipate in the resort's offerings. Many guests felt Le Sport offered a good value—even a bargain, would return here, and would recom-mend it to friends.

Rates

Per Night	Single	Double (per person)
Apr. 1–Apr. 21	$190–200	$170–200
Apr. 22–Oct. 13	$180–210	$160–190
Oct. 14–Dec. 22	$185–215	$165–195
Dec. 23–Jan. 6	$205–235	$185–215

There is no minimum stay and any-day arrival.

Loews Ventana Canyon Ranch $$ FB-RH

7000 North Resort Drive
Tucson, Arizona 85715
(602)299-2020

Nestled at the base of the Catalina Mountains and surrounded by the Coronado National Forest, this resort is situated on 93 exquisite acres of desert. It's a good choice for couples who may have different ideas about what a good time is all about. The resort offers recreational activities, plus a variety of fitness options and pampering services.

The fitness-minded can work out in the gym with Universal weight and exercise equipment, or in the mirrored aerobics studios. An 18-station parcours flanks the area with scenic views along a mile-and-a-quarter nature trail. There is a 50-foot lap pool and Jacuzzi, plus saunas, steam room, and showers. Tennis buffs can play on ten lighted courts, while golfers can glory in Tom Fazio's renowned 36-hole PGA golf course. Nearby there's biking, hiking, horseback riding, and skiing (in season). European-style massages, facials, and beauty salon services are also available.

Meals are not included in the spa package, but there are three restaurants and a poolside grill to chose from. Accommodations are luxurious; the 366 guest rooms and 24 suites offer all the amenities of a first-class hotel. Each has a fully stocked mini-bar and refrigerator, extra vanity area, three telephones, bathroom television, and a special double-sized bathtub. Bedroom views of the city skyline, mountains, or the natural 80-foot waterfall can be seen from private balconies. Rooms are furnished in a southwestern decor with pine and original works of art.

The resort offers three- and seven-night packages that include your accommodations, use of spa facilities, aerobic classes, massage, tax, and gratuities. (Meals are not included.)

GUEST FEEDBACK
Former guests consistently rated the physical location, accommodations, and facilities as excellent. Most were not upset by the very relaxed and unstructured program, but would have liked a diet menu. (They did note, however, that the hotel tried very hard to please.) Most had a rewarding experience and would recommend this retreat to their friends.

Rates

	Single	Double (per person)
May 1–25 and Sept. 6–Jan. 5		
3-Night Package	$535	$300
7-Night Package	$1,230	$690
May 26–Sept. 5		
3-Night Package	$300	$185
7-Night Package	$685	$417.50

There is no minimum stay and any-day arrival.

Marriott's Camelback Inn Resort, $$$ FB-RH
Golf Club, and Spa

5402 East Lincoln Drive
Scottsdale, Arizona 85253
(800)228-9290 (Nationwide)
(602)948-1700 (in Arizona)

You can unwind at the Camelback Inn Spa with an extraordinary array of recreational activities and services that follow the resort's tradition of award-winning excellence. Work out the kinks at the Fitness Center, receive body composition analysis and nutritional counseling at the Wellness Center, and luxuriate at the spa's full-service body and beauty salon amid centuries-old cacti and Paradise Valley's colorful desert wildflowers.

For total fitness, there are indoor/outdoor lap pools, a fitness center with weight stations and a full array of the latest equipment and computerized exercycles; aerobics and muscle-building classes; Jazzercise and water exercises; and an exercenter/playground complex complete with basketball and volleyball courts, table tennis, shuffleboard, and calisthenic stations.

The Wellness Center focuses on nutritional counseling, body composition, and relaxation. To ensure that's what you get, there are whirlpools, Turkish steam baths, Finnish saunas, natural sunbathing, and a relaxation lounge.

Personal services offered at the body and beauty salon include facials, herbal wraps, and loofah body buffs. The separate-but-equal spa facilities for men and women include Thalasso tubs, hot and cold plunges, an outdoor solarium, and 18 indoor and outdoor massage rooms.

Sports activities are a winner here. The Camelback Golf Club's two championship PGA-rated 18-hole courses offer some of America's best golf enhanced by splendid desert mountain views and lush palm-lined fairways. The pro shop features a full line of equipment for rent or purchase. There is also a nine-hole pitch 'n' putt course and putting green. Tennis buffs may be pleased by the ten all-weather courts, five of which are lit for night play. The professional staff conducts tournaments and clinics. There are also two swimming pools adjacent to the whirlpool baths, as well as paths suitable for walking, jogging, and cycling.

Dining here consists of a choice of gourmet specialities. The Chaparral Dining Room offers continental favorites with breathtaking views of Camelback Mountain. The Navajo Room offers a variety of daily specials for breakfast, lunch, and dinner in an authentic southwestern decor. The North Garden Buffet features outdoor buffets for breakfast and lunch amidst lush gardens. For a light meal or snack, try the Cactus Patch near the pool or the Oasis Lounge patio grill. Then, enjoy a drink and dance the night away at the Chapparal Lounge.

Each of the 423 adobe-style "casa" guest rooms and suites at Camelback are convenient to the restaurants and recreational activities. All rooms have private patios with picturesque views, kitchenettes, refrigerators and an array of five-star amenities. A variety of suites are available with luxurious living and dining areas, and many have large sun deck patios. Bilevel suites are highlighted by comfortable loft bedrooms. Deluxe suites feature private swimming pools.

Camelback spa packages include accommodations, breakfast and lunch daily, massage, haircut or style, nutritional consultation, exercise classes, use of all spa facilities, and your choice of beauty treatments. There is a two-night minimum stay; however, meals are not included in two-night packages.

GUEST FEEDBACK

Guests were very taken with the southwestern ambience and beauty of this resort spa. They were also delighted with the facilities, the fitness activities, and the pampering treatments. Some of the guests, however, thought it was rather pricey, especially since the evening meal is not included. Still others wanted a stricter diet plan. Most guests would recommend it to their friends.

Rates

	Single	Double (per person)
Feb. 1–May 20		
2-Night Package	$565	$375
4-Night Package	$1,330	$950
May 21–Sept. 9		
2-Night Package	$355	$270
4-Night Package	$910	$740
Sept. 10–Dec. 31		
2-Night Package	$525	$355
4-Night Package	$1,250	$910

Marriott's Desert Springs Resort & $$$$ FB-RH
Spa

74855 Country Club Drive
Palm Desert, California 92260
(800)255-0848 (Nationwide)
(619)341-2211 (in California)

Clean, dry air, sun-drenched days, and balmy, starlit nights will be
the backdrop to your stay at this spacious European-style spa within
the luxury Marriott resort. Light and airy and surrounded by gardens
and distant mountains, the spa caters to men and women of all ages
and conditions. It offers a complete range of personal fitness, beauty,
weight-control, and health services.

Indoors you can make use of the Turkish steam room, Finnish
saunas, hot- and cold-plunge pools, individual whirlpool baths, aerobics studio, and the multifitness gym stocked with Universal equipment. Outdoors you can enjoy the Olympic-size pool, exercise lawns,
and large whirlpool.

Fitness classes, which are held both inside and out, run the
gamut from waterworks and pumping rubber (rubberbands) classes
for beginners, to the white-water workout using hydrostatic resistance. The 2.5-mile Sunriser Walk, followed by a 20-minute Mountain
Vista Warm-up which combine Tai Chi with breathing exercises are a
great way to greet the day.

If it's pampering you pine for, this is the place to receive it. The
spa offers five kinds of massages, including a Swedish massage which
you can have in the privacy of your room, and an underwater massage, for women only, where water pressure is applied externally to
the body for "improved physical well-being." For facials, a system of
skin care known as the Beauty Point System (BPS), designed for skin
over 30 by Kerstin Forian, a Swedish skin-care expert, is utilized.
There are also herbal wraps, loofah body buffs, and aromatherapy
baths, as well as the services of the beauty salon for men and women
run by Beverly Hills hairstylist to the stars, Jose Eber.

Other options include the Super Space Relaxer where you can
"experience" relaxation videos, or Cybervision video and audio cas-
settes for weight control, tennis improvement, or whatever you want
to work on. You can also take advantage of the desert hiking program,
nutritional consultations, computerized body composition analysis
and fitness consultation, and the services of your own personal trainer.

The gourmet spa cuisine menu is restricted to 900 calories per
day and is served at the Lake View Restaurant. You'll be amazed what
they can do by substituting fresh herbs, fruits, and vegetables for your

usual high-calorie foods. At snack time you might head for the juice bar which serves fresh fruit and tropical drinks, herbal teas, decaffeinated coffee, and cold salad platters. In addition, there is a Japanese restaurant on its own island, a seafood specialty restaurant, a restaurant serving traditional cuisine, and the Golf Club Bar and Grill.

As a hotel guest, you can also take advantage of the 18-hole golf course, a practice range, and two putting greens. Tennis buffs will be pleased by the 16 tennis courts. And everyone gets to enjoy the over 200 acres of gardens and lakes. For swimming and sunbathing, you will want to use the unique 12,000-square-foot beach with white desert sand sloping to one of the fresh water lakes.

There are 900 rooms in the eight-story atrium resort, including 65 suites. Each is spacious and furnished with a refrigerator, minibar, large double-sink bathroom, and balcony.

For a spa vacation, you can arrive any day of the week and there is no minimum stay required. However, there are four- and seven-night deluxe packages, both of which include accommodations, three meals daily, arrival and departure fitness consultations, a medical screening upon arrival, individual program consultation, unlimited use of spa facilities and classes, and use of the spa wardrobe. The seven-night package includes such beauty and pampering treatments as four facials, six Swedish massages, four herbal wraps, a dry flotation session, loofah body buff, and a shampoo, blow dry, makeup application, manicure, and pedicure for women; or a shampoo, haircut, scalp treatment, manicure, and pedicure for men. The four-night plan includes three Swedish massages, two facials, three herbal wraps, a loofah buff, and a dry flotation session.

GUEST FEEDBACK

Guests usually rave about their visit to this luxurious resort spa. They give the staff high grades for their professionalism and kudos, as well, to the very tailored fitness program they each received. In fact, when asked if there was anything she wished she had known prior to arrival, one guest replied, "If I'd known it was this terrific, I would have stayed longer!" If you like large-resort hospitality and luxury, and you can afford the price, the Marriott's Desert Springs Resort & Spa is a place worth visiting.

Rates

Jan. 1–May 29	Single	Double (per person)
4-Night Deluxe Spa Program	$1,568	$1,178
7-Night Deluxe Spa Program	$2,744	$2,062

May 30–Aug. 31

4-Night Deluxe Spa Program	$1,446	$1,213
7-Night Deluxe Spa Program	$2,531	$2,123

Sept. 1–Dec. 23

4-Night Deluxe Spa Program	$1,594	$1,278
7-Night Deluxe Spa Program	$2,790	$2,234

There is no minimum stay and any-day arrival.

Murrieta Hot Springs Resort and Health Spa $$ FB-RH, MS,NA

28779 Via Las Flores
Murrieta, California 92362
(800)322-4542 (Nationwide)
(800)458-4393 (in California)
(714)677-7451 (in California)

This family-oriented health resort is located a little over two hours southeast of Los Angeles on 47 acres rich with mineral hot springs, some as hot as 140 degrees Fahrenheit. Specializing in polarity therapies, Murrieta Hot Springs offers a healthful blend of the physical and spiritual approaches to healing, fitness, and weight control, making it one of the largest and most unusual holistic spa resorts in the country.

The spa features exercise classes, polarity therapy training and certification, three natural mineral pools with varying temperatures, an Olympic-size pool, bubbling Roman Jacuzzi, 14 tennis courts, and an 18-hole golf course. The Nature Care Spa has 26 private mineral baths and areas for polarity body work, salt glow rubs, and body wraps.

Such bodywork treatments as mineral baths, energy-balancing sessions, and body wraps cost $35 for an hour. A natural mineral bath with bubbles, essential oils, or nature care wrap; popular Tule (pronounced "too-lee") Root Mud bath and European facials are also available. Fitness classes include polar-energetics exercises, aqua-exercise, and light aerobics. In addition, there are two daily seminars and workshops on diet and exercise, understanding emotions, food preparation, family stress patterns, and more.

Dining here is mostly vegetarian, although there is now a restaurant that serves fish and chicken and beer and wine. The Oasis Family Pub serves up such wholesome sweets as cheesecake, pies, juices, malts, and honey drinks. There is also a large television and a game room with pool tables. Healthland is a store specializing in vegetarian food products, skin and hair products, and therapeutic footwear. And the Natural Fibers Boutique carries a wide assortment of quality clothing for men and women.

The 240 guest rooms at Murrieta Springs are in private cottages or lodges with single or double occupancy. While they recently received a "face lift," our clients thought the rooms were adequate, but not special.

Murrieta offers a wide range of packages on physical fitness, weight loss, family relationships, and personal awareness. They range from the two-night Fit and Trim to the four-week Healing Yourself and Your Family to the six-week Holistic Training. Included in all package prices are accommodations, three meals daily, exercise classes, energy massage, mineral bath and wrap, Murrieta Mud Experience, (which includes the mud bath, the mineral bath, and body wrap), and use of all facilities.

GUEST FEEDBACK

Guests who went to Murietta Hot Springs for the wide selection of activities and not the deluxe accommodations, who didn't require a regimented schedule of classes and one-on-one instruction, were most pleased with their stay. The advantage of a resort spa is having the chance to substitute one activity for a more satisfying one.

Rates

		Double
Feb. 5–Dec. 31	*Single*	*(per person)*
2-Night "Fit 'n' Trim" Weekend Package	$375	$329
FRI ARR/SUN DEP		
7-Night "Fit 'n' Trim" Package	$1,395	$1,230
SUN ARR/SUN DEP		

Call for rates for four-week and six-week packages.

New Life Spa/Liftline Lodge $$ FB-RH

P.O. Box 144
Stratton Mountain, Vermont 05155
(802)297-2600
(802)297-2534

Owner Jimmy LeSage's personal touch is evident in every aspect of New Life Spa, from the tasty cuisine to the enthusiasm of the staff. This mountain fitness/ski resort, found amidst the invigorating beauty of southern Vermont's Green Mountain National Forest, takes a holistic approach to wellness, offering an innovative experience in fitness and diet for men and women of all ages and all physical capabilities.

The program consists of body awareness, aerobics, body contour, yoga, stretches and strolls, mini-lectures, and free time to pursue a host of recreational activities at the nearby Stratton Sports Center. Participants of the hiking program discover the beauty of the Vermont countryside—hidden waterfalls, spectacular vistas, sylvan valleys, and meadows of wildflowers. The hikes become more challenging during your stay, with the seven-day hiking program working toward treks up Bromley and Stratton Mountains.

During any season, each New Life Spa session (always limited to about 30 men and women) provides a wide range of activities, professionally structured and monitored to provide the level of aerobic effort that's best for you, including the opportunity to hike or ski amidst some of New England's loveliest mountain scenery. Brisk morning walks and small, personalized studio classes are especially appealing; in addition, there's swimming, tennis, and racquetball, and a bounty of bodily delights such as whirlpool baths, hot tub, sauna, steam room, massage, facials, and hand and nail care. All staff is trained in first aid and CPR, but other medical facilities are available at the Otis Clinic only five minutes away, and at the Mountain Valley Clinic in Londonderry just 15 or 20 minutes away by car.

Spa guests stay in the two-story chalet at the base of Stratton Mountain. Lodging is available in single or double occupancy, with private bath, color television (although reception is reportedly not very good), and a telephone. Bright and airy rooms are decorated with touches of wood, and there is a pine-paneled lobby and lounge with fireplaces and comfy chairs.

As well as being a fitness buff and certified yoga instructor, Jimmy is a professional chef who treats his guests to delicious low-calorie meals, consisting mainly of fresh fruits, vegetables, and lean meats. This high-in-complex-carbohydrate, moderate-protein, and low-fat diet is based on the findings of Pritikin and the American Heart Association. Vegetarian alternatives are offered at each meal. Don't expect to find caffeine or refined sugars at New Life. Diets begin at 800 calories per day, and you'll go home with Jimmy's *New Life Guide to Healthy Eating* cookbook to maintain your weight and health after your vacation is over.

New Life offers three-, five-, and six-night packages that come complete with accommodations, meals, exercise classes, massage, use of all facilities, and the New Life cookbook. The spa is closed in October but there are many spring and holiday specials. Also, down-hill and cross-country spa-ski packages that include lift tickets are available December through March. Year-round, the choice is yours. High-top walking shoes are required for the hiking program. Dress is casual for meals; in fact, you can wear sweats during your whole vacation, if you choose. Sports equipment is available, as well as film, writing materials, books, and sundries. You may want to bring your own towel or mat for the yoga classes.

GUEST FEEDBACK
New Life has been popular with many guests who were all pleased with their stay. There were no complaints, although one guest misin-terpreted the "vegetarian" diet to mean that dairy products would not be served. Others hinted that it might be a good idea to begin exercis-ing before visiting New Life so that you can take full advantage of the program.

Rates

		Double
Apr. 28–May 26 & Sept. 1 Only	*Single*	*(per person)*
3-Night Program FRI ARR/MON DEP	$525	$475
Mar. 26–Apr. 28		
5-Night Program SUN ARR/FRI DEP	$795	$725
Apr. 30–Jun. 24		
6-Night Program SUN ARR/SAT DEP	$995	$895
Jun. 25–Sep. 16		
6-Night Program SUN ARR/SAT DEP	$1,090	$990

There is a three-night minimum stay.

Norwich Inn & Spa $$ FB-RH

607 West Thames Street, Route 32
Norwich, Connecticut 06360

(800) 892-5692 (Nationwide)
(203)886-2401 (in Connecticut)

Escape to New England's cozy country resort where old-town charm
and classic elegance prevail. This private estate offers guided fitness
programs, luxurious body and beauty treatments, and good, old-
fashioned cuisine in very graceful and spacious surroundings.

The fitness program here includes classes in body awareness and
body parts, an isolation class concentrated on improving dynamic and
absolute strength, toning, sculpting, and tightening of the muscular
system; limber-and-tone stretching exercises with an emphasis on improving flexibility; power play, a monitored workout utilizing Keiser
CAM II weight equipment, free weights, and Lifecycles, Trotter Treadmill, StairMaster, Life-Rower, and Fit One Cross Country Ski machines; and waterworks, an invigorating pool workout utilizing the
natural resistance of water. Yoga is also available.

When it's time to relax, treat your body to aromatherapy, a body
scrub, deep-cleansing facial, foot massage, body massage, hydrotherapy, makeup consultation, mineral bath, neck and shoulder massage, nourishing facial, paraffin hand treatment, polarity therapy, or
Thalassotherapy. Of course, a relaxing session in the whirlpool, sauna,
or steam room always feels good, too. The spa can accommodate up to
30 men and women who work out together, but use separate sauna
facilities. Classes and appointments should be booked early.

New England ambience pervades the Norwich Inn. English country chintz, cozy quilts, four-poster beds, and bleached wood furniture
are hallmarks of this rustic, romantic inn. Spa meals are served in a
separate dining area. The food, based on New England-style recipes, is
limited to 1,200 to 1,500 calories daily for women and 1,800 to 2,000 for
men. You should know, too, that even if you are traveling solo, you are
expected to dress for meals, especially on the weekends.

Accommodations are standard, deluxe, or suite. All rooms have
private baths, color cable television, and ceiling fans. Some rooms
have raised four-poster beds with stepping stools. Villas are also available and come completely furnished, right down to the china.

Norwich offers two- and five-night packages, or nightly rates.
Your accommodations, meals, and a variety of beauty treatments and
fitness classes, as well as unlimited use of spa facilities are included
in the packages.

GUEST FEEDBACK
The exercise program consistently ranked excellent to very good, although one guest says that when she returns, she will "get a chic

outfit." Some guests noted that the spa dining room was secluded from everything else but guests were still expected to dress for meals. Still others felt dining alone was a bit awkward due to the formality. Almost all, however, would recommend the Norwich Inn and Spa to their friends.

Rates

Apr. 15–Dec. 31	*Single*	*Double (per person)*
Per Night	$115–185	$65–100
2-Night Norwich Revitalizer	$585–655	$470–505

MON OR WED ARR/WED OR FRI DEP
There is no minimum stay.

The Spa at Olympia Village $ FB-RH

1350 Royal Mile Road
Osonomowoc, Wisconsin 53066
(414)567-0311 (in Wisconsin)
(800)558-9573 (Nationwide)

Not all top spas are located on a coast. Midwesterners treasure this getaway at the Olympia Village. This spa is just one facet of a total resort complex. Families can share this vacation because there's literally something for everyone, including corporate and convention facilities. Located just two hours from Chicago and an hour-and-a-half from Milwaukee and Madison, the setting for Olympia Village is 400 acres of forest, hills, rivers, and lakes in southern Wisconsin's lake country.

Spa facilities include an indoor/outdoor pool, sauna, steamroom, and whirlpools, weight room, indoor and outdoor tennis courts and a resident tennis pro, four racquetball courts, a golf course, horseback riding, and bicycling. There are approximately ten fitness classes daily, including water exercises; gymnastics; low-impact aerobics, Rear Echilon for stomach, hips, thighs, buttocks, and arms; yoga; stretching and flexing; and walking. In season, there's downhill skiing for beginners and advanced athletes, an outdoor ice-skating rink, boating, sailing, and waterskiing; plus there's a beach, polo fields, and a lake that's stocked for fishing. Volleyball, badminton, softball, shuffleboard, and a social playground for children are also available. Indoors, there's a billiards room and the latest in video games. The classes and weight room are co-ed, but other spa facilities are separate for men and women.

The resort also offers shopping, lounges, a nightclub with live music and dancing, and a Twin Cinemas that features first-run movies.

Beauty services at the full-service salon feature Lancome products and include herbal wraps, Roman baths, facials, massage, loofa scrub, salt-glo, and scalp massage.

There are 400 rooms and suites. Guest rooms, which are intermingled with those of convention guests, feature double or king-size beds and all hotel amenities; suites have open fireplaces and private bars.

Spa cuisine is low-calorie, nutritionally balanced, high in carbohydrates and fiber, and low in fat, salt, and sugar. Caloric intake ranges from 600 to 1,000 daily. However, you can dine at any of four restaurants at an additional cost. (Note that all meals on the spa plans are calorie-controlled.)

A variety of packages are available, depending on your dieting needs. Olympia offers a week-long weight-loss program that includes accommodations, three low-cal meals daily plus a first-day juice cleansing, unlimited use of facilities, an hour of tennis or racquetball, unlimited bike use, individual nutritional and fitness consultation, and use of workout clothes.

An eight-day renewal program includes accommodations, three calorie-controlled meals daily, three massages, two facials, two herbal wraps, a Lancome loofah scrub, a deluxe manicure and pedicure, scalp massage and condition treatment, makeup lessons, shampoo and blow-dry, two individual whirlpool baths, and 21 exercise classes. Three- and five-day plans are also available. For each additional day you want to add to your original package, you get a massage and three exercise classes.

All of the spa plans include use of facilities, morning and afternoon refreshment break, meals, workout clothing, an hour of tennis and racquetball, bicycling in season, and use of the private beach on the lake. Additional use of spa facilities (whirlpool, steamroom, sauna, eucalyptus room, towels, and lockers) cost $5, as does robe and clothing rental. Other services purchased *a la carte* cost from $8 for an individual mineral bath or suntanning session to $46 for a special Lancome facial.

GUEST FEEDBACK
Guests were pleased with the beauty and fitness staff and services, but recommend bringing your own robes and towels since these were sometimes hard to come by.

Rates

		Double
Jan. 1–May 28 & Sept. 6–Dec. 31	*Single*	*(per person)*
Per Night	$129.95	$89.95
May 29–Sept. 5		
Per Night	$144.95	$97.45
7-Night Weight Loss Program	$700	$1,000
8-Day Renewal Program	$950	$1,200

There is a two-night minimum stay on some weekends and any-day arrival.

Pier 66 Hotel and Marina $$ FB-RH

2301 S.E. 17th Street Causeway
Ft. Lauderdale, Florida 33316
(800)327-3796 (Nationwide)
(800)432-1956 (in Florida)
(305)525-6666 (in Florida)

This 22-acre island resort is located in the heart of Ft. Lauderdale, on the famed Intracoastal Waterway. The property is just five minutes from the Ft. Lauderdale International Airport and close to the city's popular night life, restaurants, and beaches. Pier 66 also houses the Spa LXVI, a world of personal luxuries.

This facility is for pure indulgence. There are no exercise classes, weight machines, or spa programs, but you can leave there looking and feeling like a million dollars for a fraction of the cost. The spa services are purchased *a la carte* and priced very reasonably. They include a full-body Swedish- Esalen massage for $45; a deep-heat herbal wrap for $20; an invigorating massage with sea salts (loofa-glo) for just $25; and a rehydrating facial with a neck and face massage for $45. There's also a full-body massage with rare essences and oils derived from the petals, leaves, and bark of plants from all over the world. This aromatic massage technique and inhalation therapy was a favorite of the Egyptians. For a total makeover, you can get hair and scalp treatments and hairstyling, and a manicure and pedicure. There are also two professionally maintained regulation clay tennis courts overlooking the water.

The 145-slip marina has guest dockage and complete boat/yacht hook-ups, a marine store, fuel dock, boater's lounge area, and security force. There's the Club Nautico pleasure boat rentals, 24-hour room service, a newsstand, gift shop, concierge, babysitting, and laundry and valet services. The complimentary shuttle bus takes you to the nearby beach and shops. The resort also features elegant dining at Windows on the Green, featuring American Continental cuisine entrees such as mesquite-grilled chicken, fish, meats, and fresh pasta. Terrace Garden is the more casual alternative with a tropical atmosphere. The Pier Top Lounge is at the top of the landmark tower, revolving 17 stories above the sea and offering spectacular sunsets, ocean and city vistas, live entertainment, and dancing.

A $21-million expansion and redecorating program brought 132 new rooms and redecorated the property's existing 248 rooms and suites for a total of 380. In addition to standard features, all rooms and suites offer fully stocked bars and refrigerators.

A two-night spa spectacular at the island resort includes your accommodations, two 1-hour massages, herbal wrap, two facials, one loofah, use of facilities, tax, and gratuities. Meals are not included.

GUEST FEEDBACK
This is an excellent pick for yachtsmen and sailors, offering the best of beauty services, plus the amenities and convenience of a marina resort. Former guests were pleasantly surprised to find such treats at a marina and all would return and spread the word.

Rates

	Single or Double
Per Night	$220–260
2-Night, 3-Day Spa Spectacular	$580
There is no minimum stay and any-day arrival.	

Ponte Vedra Inn & Club $$ FB-RH

Ponte Vedra Beach, Florida 32082
(800)234-7842 (Nationwide)
(800)432-3498 (in Florida)
(904)285-1111 (in Florida)

One of Florida's premier oceanside resorts provides relaxing, well-appointed accommodations, superb food, and a spectrum of recreational activities in an unmatched locale.

The Ponte Vedra Spa is located directly on the beach and is housed in two quaint cottages, originally built in the thirties as beachfront accommodations for guests of the Ponte Vedra resort. For fitness, there's a complete Nautilus circuit, treadmills, stationary bikes, and free weights. Aerobics and exercise classes such as Splash Dance are scheduled during the morning hours, while body treatments and leisure time take up most of the afternoon. Evenings can be spent at seminars on stress, nutrition, and beauty. Throughout the day you are free to relax in the Jacuzzi, sauna, or steam rooms, or swim in any one of the four pools. (Two are heated.) A health profile, which costs $50, includes testing for heart rate, blood pressure, body composition, strength and endurance, flexibility, cardiovascular fitness, pulmonary function, height and weight, and health-risk appraisal; plus, you can have nutritional counseling by a nutritionist.

The co-ed spa is limited to about 20 people, many of whom may be accompanying their spouses on a convention or business trip. It offers massages, skin care and facials, herbal wraps, massotherapy, thermotherapy, hydrotherapy, and a full range of beauty salon services such as manicures, pedicures, complete beauty analyses, and consultations. With salon imaging services, you can see yourself on a computer screen with various hairstyles, hair colors, and makeup techniques before deciding on what works best for you.

Meals in the spa dining room are calorie-controlled for those on the spa program. Spa guests can also dine at one of the other Ponte Vedra restaurants while sticking to their diet since calorie-controlled selections are found on all menus. Casual clothing is acceptable in the spa dining room, but dresses and dinner jackets are required in the other restaurants for dinner.

Accommodations at this 175-room resort, which caters to the upper echelon of business travelers, come complete with all the amenities of a first-class resort. Many of the rooms are oceanside and have balconies; accommodations overlooking the Atlantic include the Ocean House, the Sand Dollar South, the Sand Dollar North, the Court, the Sand Dune, and the Sea Gull; ocean cottages are also available. Or try the Golf Cottage accommodations, which have wet bars and a panoramic view of the famed Island Ninth Hole.

Ponte Vedra Inn & Club offers half-day pampering packages, as well as four-night stays with the works. Included in the package are your deluxe accommodations, meals, fitness evaluation and exercise prescription, nutrition analysis, two massages, facial, seaweed wrap, manicure with paraffin, computerized makeup or hairstyle consultation, and makeup application, fitness classes, use of all facilities, and seminars. If you don't choose a package, all spa facilities are *a la carte*.

GUEST FEEDBACK
The surveyed guests thoroughly enjoyed the spa vacation at Ponte Vedra and would return, perhaps with a friend. One guest even extended his stay. Remember though, Ponte Vedra is in central Florida where temperatures can dip down into the thirties during winter months, so come prepared for outdoor activities such as brisk morning or evening walks.

Rates

	Single	*Double* *(per person)*
Per Night	$155	$155
½-Day Package (not overnight)	$165	
4-Night Spa Package	$900	$739

There is no minimum stay and any-day arrival.

Pritikin Longevity Center $$$$ FB-RH, WL

5875 Collins Avenue
Miami Beach, Florida 33140
(800)327-4914 (Nationwide)
(305)866-2237 (in Florida)

This newest Pritikin Center on the ocean in Miami Beach, offers the same world-renowned Pritikin program as the centers in California and Pennsylvania. The Centers claim not to be spas or fat farms, but educational facilities where you learn a new way of life to improve your health. Many participants have heart disease, weight-control problems, diabetes, and high blood pressure, but others are in normal health, interested in disease prevention.

The exercise program here is staffed by professionals with Master's or Bachelor's degrees in exercise physiology. Guests are assigned to an exercise class with classmates with the same exercise capabilities. Classes are conducted in the Center's gym, which contains motorized treadmills, exercise bicycles, rowing machines, and other resistance equipment. Instructors guide you through various kinds of aerobic exercise, check your heart rate, and chart your progress. You are also given a personal exercise prescription, which might mean two 20-minute walks along the beach, or for high-fitness individuals, running every day for an hour. Yoga, exercises for a healthy back, and cardiopulmonary resuscitation classes are also offered.

Education is a vital part of the program. Some of the material covered includes a lifetime eating plan, myths and realities of weight loss, coping with stress, exercise and your heart, and blood evaluation interpretation. In addition, there are group and individual counseling sessions on weight control, stress management, and life-style management, and a smoking cessation workshop.

Along with the seminars and exercise program are the services of a medical staff specializing in cardiology and internal medicine. Upon arrival you are assigned to a physician who gives you a complete blood chemistry test (each week you get a new one), plus a physical exam and a risk-factor analysis. Then, the two of you discuss your goals and program, and meet again at regular intervals throughout your stay.

The Pritikin Center contains a gym overlooking the ocean, lecture facilities, a dining room, medical offices, and an Olympic-size pool for aqua-aerobics classes.

Don't worry about going hungry here—you'll eat six times a day. Meals consist of potatoes, pasta, fresh fruit and vegetables, whole grain bread, and brown rice; lean animal protein, such as chicken, turkey, or fish, is served at least twice a week. The Pritikin Eating Plan is 75 to 80 percent complex carbohydrates, less than 10 percent fat and 10 to 15 percent protein. No salt, sugar, fat, or cholesterol is added to the food. All the daytime snacks and meals are buffet-style. Dinner is sit-down, served by waiters and waitresses. And, you'll learn to cook and live on the Pritikin Eating Plan under the guidance of registered dietitians at the Center. You'll also receive cooking classes and nutrition workshops on dining out, grocery shopping, entertaining, fast food, and traveling on the Pritikin Program.

The Center is in a six-story hotel that has 100 guest rooms, each with a color television, direct-dial phone, daily maid service, and individually controlled air conditioning.

The Center offers 7-, 13-, and 26-day programs at regularly scheduled dates. The 7-day program offers intensive training in the basic components of the Pritikin Program. It is geared to healthy people who want an accelerated course in starting and maintaining the Pritikin life style. A special Quit and Live seminar has been incorporated for those who want to quit smoking.

The longer programs are geared more to people on medication for hypertension, those with diabetes (on or off medication), and those with cardiovascular disease. The program fee covers your accommodations, health screening, tolerance test, two blood panels, all meals, exercise sessions, cooking workshops, stress-management workshops, and a comprehensive educational program focusing on nutrition, exercise, life-style change, and health.

GUEST FEEDBACK
The Pritikin Centers have gotten very favorable reviews from their guests. They've reported weight loss and attitude changes that have allowed them to implement a new, healthy way of life. For that they would share this place with a friend, and would return themselves for a refresher course.

Rates

	Single
7-Day Program	$2,967
SUN ARR/SUN DEP	

The Sans Souci Hotel, Club & Spa $$ FB-RH

P.O. Box 103, Ocho Rios
Jamaica, West Indies
(800)237-3237 (Nationwide)
(809)974-2353 (in Jamaica)

On Jamaica's sun-drenched north coast sits one of the island's most elegant and romantic resorts, which houses a fitness center and mineral spa. Charlie's Spa, which borrows its name from a giant green sea turtle that has lived there for almost 20 years, is situated in an intimate Mediterranean-style resort nestled in a tropical hillside garden with its own natural spring-fed mineral pool and private beach leading to the crystal waters of the Caribbean Sea.

Charlie's Spa, an affiliate of the Phoenix Fitness Resort in Houston, Texas, is a charming, tropical health retreat offering an action-packed fitness vacation for couples, singles, and families. The week-long program is a combination of exercise, body treatments, and low-calorie gourmet meals. Plus, spa guests have access to all the facilities and activities that this resort offers.

Your day at Charlie's begins with a wake-up call, followed by juice and a brisk morning walk, and a buffet breakfast of Jamaica's finest fresh fruit and juices, cereals, low-calorie muffins, and other tempting delights. At 9 A.M. you begin your first workout with gentle stretching and toning exercises, then a half-hour low-impact aerobics class. From there you can proceed to weight training and afternoon aquacise in the mineral pool, and an appointment for a massage or body treatment. The fitness and exercise pavilions, two facial rooms, sauna, and hot mineral water whirlpool are all at the edge of the Caribbean Sea. What better way to end a day than with a massage in a hilltop pavilion overlooking the sea, while watching the sunset? Body treatments are administered in specially designed rooms tucked away in the lush hillside grounds of the hotel where Jamaican and Caribbean music is always in the air. The hair salon offers both men and women a full range of hair design, conditioning, styling, coloring, perming, braiding, and other services.

Year-round water sports at the resort include wind-surfing, sailing, snorkeling, scuba diving, and—by special arrangement—deep-sea fishing. There are also four tennis courts and two croquet lawns.

Calorie-controlled cuisine is offered to spa guests, but for those of you not counting your calories, you may also take advantage of regular selections from the menu. Both breakfast and lunch are served buffet-style on Charlie's Terrace, a gazebo jutting out over the sea. Dinner is served under the stars on the Casanova Terrace and in the Casanova Restaurant. In the evenings, the resort offers dancing under the stars with the resident combo or performances by traditional Jamaican folk groups.

Guest rooms come in deluxe and one-bedroom suites, all with private bath and balcony, air conditioning or ceiling fan, color television, and telephone. The week-long program at Charlie's Spa includes deluxe accommodations; meals, unlimited fruit juices, bar drinks, cocktails, and French house wine daily; all hotel facilities; five massages or four massages and a body treatment; a facial, manicure, and pedicure; three daily exercise classes; and use of the sauna, mineral-water pool, and whirlpool. You may also avail yourself of a personal fitness counselor and a consultation with the spa director, should you desire.

Lastly, you are treated to a tour of Ocho Rios and Dunn's River Falls, a Charlie's Spa robe and tote bag, and roundtrip transfers from Montego Bay Airport. Tax and gratuities are included in the package price as well.

GUEST FEEDBACK

Guests have generally found the atmosphere and accommodations at Charlie's to be outstanding. The ultimate test is that most would recommend this spa within a resort to a friend—despite the spa's two-and-a-half hour distance from the airport. Charlie's Spa seems particularly appealing to those who want the amenities of a luxury resort and the health benefits of a mineral spa and fitness center and who want to mingle with both crowds. Guests particularly found the setting and location—on the water's edge—to be pleasing. As with most spas at resorts, Charlie's Spa is popular with casual spa-goers who do not want restrictions on their diets.

Rates

		Double
Dec. 14–Apr. 15	*Single*	*(per person)*
6-Night Charlie's Program	$2,297–2,560	$1,600–1,733
Apr. 16–Dec. 14		
6-Night Charlie's Program	$1,575–1,940	$1,225–1,315

There is no minimum stay. Sunday arrival/Saturday departure on Charlie's Program.

The Shoreham Hotel and Spa $$ FB-RH

Box 225, 115 Monmouth Avenue
Spring Lake, New Jersey 07762
(800)648-4175 (Nationwide)
(201)449-7100 (in New Jersey)

This Victorian hotel offers a quiet refuge in one of the loveliest communities on the New Jersey Shore. Shoreham is admittedly more of a hotel than a full-fledged fitness facility; however, when it comes to pampering and individually designed programs, the Shoreham delivers.

Emphasis here is on healthy living rather than on strenuous exercise. The physical fitness program consists mostly of walking or biking along the oceanside boardwalk or lake, although there are some aerobics and aquatic classes. There's swimming in the heated outdoor pool and at the beach, as well as a sauna and whirlpool; golf and tennis are nearby. To rejuvenate and beautify, have a massage, herbal wrap, facial, or makeover. Lectures on health and beauty supplement the program.

The co-ed spa program is limited to about 15 guests, most of whom are in their forties. In addition to the spa activities, the hotel offers an array of recreational activities such as fashion shows, live bands, luaus, bingo, ballroom dancing, and movies. The staff also conducts excursions for shopping, antiquing, and browsing through arts and crafts shops. Plus, Atlantic City and the Monmouth Race Track are nearby, as is the Garden State Arts Center which features famous entertainers.

Spa guests are served in the Victorian dining room where they choose meals from a special, set spa menu with a total calorie count of between 1,000 to 1,200 per day. Or, guests can dine *a la carte* at the Empress Room. There, pasta *du jour* is served either as an entree or as an appetizer. Dieters have a choice of two entree selections, such as a chicken and broccoli stir fry or a veal chop. Other regular menu selections range from a mixed grill of chicken breast, filet mignon, lamb chops, and andoullie sausage served with sauce bordelaise to pork stuffed with jarlsburg cheese, pears, walnuts and parsley and served with a roast walnut and orange sauce. The 108 guest rooms have ocean or lake views and private bath; some have a porch, and all have their own personality with unique furnishings.

The Shoreham offers two-, five-, and ten-night spa packages that include accommodations with private bath, three gourmet meals daily, your choice of treatments, massages, exercise classes, and use of all spa facilities.

GUEST FEEDBACK
Many guests thought Shoreham was a cute, quaint little inn, although some of our clients were disappointed with the accommodations. Most would not quite qualify it as a place for a full-fledged fitness vacation.

Rates

	Single	*Double (per person)*
Open May–Oct. Only		
2-Night Weekend Program FRI ARR/SUN DEP	$575	$575
5-Night Program SUN ARR/FRI DEP	$750	$750
10-Night Program ANY-DAY ARRIVAL	$1,990	$1,790

There is no minimum stay.

Sonesta Beach Hotel $$ FB-RH

Southampton, Bermuda 14
(800)343-7170 (Nationwide)

The Spa at Sonesta Beach is part of a famous tropical resort facility on the beautiful, tranquil island of Bermuda. It is one of the world's only spas that sits right on the ocean shore, offering its own pink sand exercise beach. A longtime favorite of honeymooners, Sonesta Beach invites romance and delivers resort luxury—of which spa pampering is a part—at an attractive price.

Those of you who don't enjoy sweating around the opposite sex will be delighted that there are separate facilities here for men and women. There are whirlpools, saunas, steam rooms, an exercise room, fitness rooms with Universal equipment, locker rooms, a beauty salon, boutique, swimming pool, spa beach, jogging trails, and a separate dining area for spa guests.

Services, all part of the spa package, include skin analysis and nutrition evaluation, Swedish massage, reflexology treatment, Rene Guinot and Geloide facials, loofah rub, manicure and pedicure, body facial, makeup consultations, aquatics, and beach hikes. The program emphasizes physical activity through a personalized schedule of exercise, relaxation, and body treatments, as well as a diet tailored to each guest's goals and condition. This may not be the right program for those of you who prefer a more regimented schedule of classes and instruction, although many prefer to move at their own pace. Fitness classes last 30 to 40 minutes and you are encouraged to alternate them with passive exercise and relaxation periods.

The entire Sonesta Beach spa staff was trained in Great Britain, and treatments are all European-styled. There are facials for specific facial skin problems, passive reducing treatments, and a full-service hairdressing salon with the latest in styling, coloring, and waving techniques from London and Paris.

In addition, all hotel guests have access to scuba diving and snorkeling equipment, mopeds, croquet, shuffleboard, glass-bottom boat rides, tennis, and an activity program to keep the kids busy while the grown-ups do their thing.

Although calorie-counting is not stressed at Sonesta Beach, a weight-reduction diet of 800 to 1,000 calories daily is preferred by many guests. Nondieters are welcome to second helpings or to order from the regular hotel menu.

All spa guests stay in deluxe rooms, with a balcony overlooking the ocean or the bay. There are a variety of spa plans from which to choose. If you're in need of a "quickie" retreat, try the Spa Refresher for three nights. The package includes accommodations; breakfast and dinner daily; unlimited use of the Finnish sauna, Turkish steam bath, and whirlpool baths; one daily exercise class; one Swedish body massage; one Rene Guinot facial; one salt-glo body rub, daily juice break; unlimited use of Universal equipment and exercycles; workout clothing; robes, towels, and locker; pools; chaise lounges; and a daily afternoon tea.

There are also four- or seven-night vacation plans that include all the above, plus three exercise classes daily, a reflexology session, and a health and beauty analysis for women or a fitness assessment for men. The seven-night plan also includes four Swedish massages.

The four- or seven-night deluxe plans offer unlimited exercise classes; private nutritional, fitness, and workout consultation and evaluation; a pedicure and manicure; shampoo, set, or blow-dry; body-toning treatment, makeup consultation for women or body-toning treatment for men; a facial skin analysis, and a skin fold test. The four-night deluxe package includes three Swedish massages and a Rene Guinot facial, while those on the seven-night plan receive five Swedish massages, three Rene Guinot facials, and a fitness chart to take home.

GUEST FEEDBACK
Sonesta Beach Hotel is a wonderful place to unwind and enjoy the beautiful Bermuda beach. The accommodations and amenities are highly rated by guests. Those of you not requiring a large spa facility with regimented fitness instruction, where accommodations are more important to you than the spa's program, will be happiest here.

Rates

Apr. 1–Apr. 30 and Jul. 1–Oct. 31	*Single*	*Double (per person)*
3-Night Spa Refresher Break	$840	$570
4-Night Deluxe Plan	$1,140–1,440	$780–1,080
7-Night Deluxe Plan	$1,995–2,520	$1,365–1,890
May 1–Jun. 30		
3-Night Spa Refresher Break	$960	$630
4-Night Deluxe Plan	$1,300–1,600	$860–1,160
7-Night Deluxe Plan	$2,275–2,800	$1,505–2,030
Nov. 1–Mar. 31		
3-Night Spa Refresher Break	$570	$435
4-Night Deluxe Plan	$780–1,080	$600–900
7-Night Deluxe Plan	$1,365–1,890	$1,050–1,575

There is no minimum stay and any-day arrival.

Sonesta Sanibel Harbour Resort $$ FB-RH

17260 Harbour Pointe Drive
Fort Myers, Florida 33908
(813)466-4000

This world-class 40,000-square-foot spa provides health, fitness, nutrition, and beauty care within a luxury resort on the sunny Gulf coast. Aerobics, weight training, body-pampering treatments, beauty services, and spa cuisine, as well as Florida's beautiful coastline all go into making this an inviting choice.

To help you get physically fit, the Spa and Fitness Center features fitness evaluations, weight-training equipment, stationary bikes, and three kinds of exercise classes, including water aerobics in an indoor pool. To ease muscle tension, there are individual whirlpool baths, steam baths, Swiss showers, and a sauna. There are separate spa facilities for men and women. Tennis buffs will appreciate the 12 lighted clay and composition courts, plus a 5,000-seat stadium, pro shop, video teaching aids, instructional programs, and teaching pro staff at the nearby Jimmy Connors U.S. Tennis Center. There are also four racquetball courts.

Both sexes can enjoy the body treatments available here. A facial, deep-cleansing back treatment, or neck-firming treatment are sure to do wonders for your mental state. These services range in price from $25 to $40. Then, too, you can pamper your body with a half-hour or hour-long massage, an herbal wrap, a loofa bath, a salt-glo rub, or a cellulite treatment, with prices from $15 to $40. The salon also offers hand and nail care for men and women, including a beard and mustache trim and makeup application or lesson.

Dining and accommodations meet the standards of a luxury resort. Jimmy's Restaurant serves up fresh seafood and specialty drinks and features live entertainment. Lodging provides all the comforts of home, plus hotel amenities. The one- and two-bedroom condominiums accommodate up to eight people and come complete with kitchen, living/dining room, cable television, and private balcony that opens to a view of San Carlos Bay and Sanibel Island.

Sonesta offers mini-day and full-day pampering plans Tuesday through Saturday and spa passes for resort guests. A mini-day runs three-and-a-half hours, costs $60, and includes a 45-minute exercise program, whirlpool bath, steam bath, herbal wrap, massage, sauna, and a shampoo and blow dry or a French manicure. A full-day plan runs five hours, costs $90, and includes 90 minutes of exercise instruction, whirlpool, steam bath, herbal wrap, Swiss shower, sauna, facial, and a shampoo and blow dry or a French manicure. Spa day passes cost $10 for one day, $15 for two days, and $30 for six days for hotel guests, which allows access to exercise rooms, lap pool, exercise classes, racquetball courts, steam room, sauna, hot- and cold-plunge pools, and whirlpools. There is also a three-night package that includes accommodations, fitness evaluation, exercise classes, loofa salt-glo rub, Swiss showers, herbal wraps, massages, facial, manicure and pedicure, shampoo and blow-dry, use of all facilities, and spa tax and gratuities.

GUEST FEEDBACK

Surveyed guests enjoyed the luxury of Sonesta and were particularly pleased with the beauty and body treatments. Tennis players found the visit especially rewarding and would definitely recommend the place to their tennis-enthusiast friends.

Rates

	Single	*Double (per person)*
3-Night Spa Package	$740	$500

There is no minimum stay and any-day arrival.

Sonoma Mission Inn & Spa $$$$ FB-RH

P.O. Box 1447
Sonoma, California 95476
(800)358-9022 (Nationwide)
(707)938-9000 (in California)

Located in the heart of California's wine country just 40 miles north of San Francisco, Sonoma Mission Inn is a 170-room world-class resort and European-style spa, situated in the romantic Valley of the Moon, where Jack London once lived. Surrounded by seven secluded acres of eucalyptus-shaded grounds, the Inn—built to resemble a California mission, complete with arcade and bell towers—attracts young, upwardly mobile people, trend-setters, and celebrities, along with "regular" folk who just want to relax in therapeutic hot springs, lose weight, and be pampered.

Considered to be one of the finest fitness and beauty facilities in the country, its spa offers a full line of body treatments, such as Swedish and Esalen-style massages, herbal wraps, and hydromassages performed with small, powerful jets in European hydrotherapy tubs, to soothe away stress and muscle fatigue. Salon services—facials, hair and scalp treatments, manicures, and pedicures—are also popular.

For spa guests, Sonoma Mission Inn offers daily scheduled classes in yoga, moderate to advanced aerobics, limbering and toning, and gentle stretching, plus morning hikes in Sonoma Valley. There are two exercise gyms equipped with the most up-to-date conditioning equipment, including Lifecycles, free weights, and Keiser CAM II weight machines. In addition, there is a co-ed bathhouse with sauna and steam rooms, indoor and outdoor whirlpools, and an outdoor exercise pool.

While visiting this historic town, you may also want to explore the landmarks, visit nearby wineries for tastings, play golf, and go horseback riding, hot-air ballooning, or picnicking in Jack London State Park. A stroll around Sonoma reveals its picturesque plaza, great shopping, and locally produced food specialities. To arrange any of these activities, you simply dial the concierge.

As a resort, Sonoma Mission Inn's restaurants have consistently received accolades from leading restaurant critics and guests. The Grille, which is open to the public, features menu favorites of wine country cuisine prepared with fresh, local products such as mesquite-grilled meat, poultry, fish, and pasta. Low-calorie selections are offered during lunch and dinner, and the wine list offers over 200 local varieties.

Big 3 Fountain serves "down home" American-style diner food in a 1950s soda fountain setting and offers cocktails and wine tasting. Also at the Fountain is the Big 3 Market which offers an assortment of premium wines for tasting and purchase, a gourmet delicatessen that provides box lunches and picnic baskets, as well as magazines, gifts, specialty food items, kitchenware, spa apparel, and logo merchandise. On Sundays, there is a lavish brunch with an array of fresh, local foods accompanied by sparkling wine. For informal dining, there's the Pool Bar which serves tropical drinks, juices, and specialty foods. The Health Bar in the spa offers a variety of fresh berry smoothies and low-calorie, no-cholesterol, 100 percent pure fruit "ice cream." Famed for its innovative gourmet meals, the spa has generated a cookbook, *Spa Food*, which guests receive as part of the package.

Guest rooms are available in twin, queen, or king size, or in suites. Each has white plantation shutters, ceiling fans, walk-in closets, and air conditioning. Rooms are decorated in peaceful earthtones and furnished with half-canopy beds, easy chairs, color TVs, and refrigerators. As in most top hotels, baths are stocked with shampoo, soap, shower cap, bath beads, moisturizers, and other niceties. Sonoma Mission Inn is also a complete conference, convention, and seminar center for small groups up to 150 people. Its clientele is usually made up of individual guests and corporate business travelers in equal parts.

There are spa vacation packages for one, two, three, and seven nights. The week-long Great Escape package includes accommodations; three spa meals daily; a fitness evaluation; nutritional consultation or hydrostatic; two aromatherapy massages and two body massages; a salt rub, herbal wrap, or two seaweed hydromassages; one European facial and a regular facial or one European facial and a makeup application; a hydrating manicure and pedicure, a hair and scalp treatment; fitness classes, five morning hikes and picnic hike; use of all the facilities; a complimentary spa robe and cookbook; and in-room movies.

If all that's too rich for your blood or your wallet, you won't feel deprived by the one-night Mini Escape that indulges you with dinner at The Grille; fitness classes and use of all facilities; choice of body massage, herbal wrap or hydromassage; choice of manicure, pedicure, haircut, or hair and scalp treatment; and a complimentary spa t-shirt and visor.

GUEST FEEDBACK

With all these amenities and luxuries, you can expect to pay accordingly. Most guests have found visits here to be rewarding in every way and have rated the program, accommodations, facilities, and meals as excellent or very good. Sonoma Mission Inn and Spa is best suited for those of you who want to mix the serious business of fitness and beauty with the luxury and comfort of a resort hotel and who don't mind sharing space with conventioneers and the general public. After all, some think the more the merrier, and it's a good way to meet not only people from other parts of the country, but the locals, too.

Rates

	Single	Double (per person)
Jan. 1–Apr. 30		
2-Night Fitness Package SUN–WED ARR/TUES–FRI DEP	$680	$530
3-Night Revitalizer SUN–TUES ARR/WED–FRI DEP	$1,350	$1,100
5-Night Deluxe SUN ARR/FRI DEP	$2,120	$1,700
May 1–Dec. 31		
2-Night Package	$746	$593
3-Night Revitalizer	$1,430	$1,155
5-Night Deluxe	$2,122	$1,700

There is no minimum stay.

Spa Concept $$ FB-RH

Le Chateau Bromont
90 Stanstead
Bromont, Quebec JOE 1LO
(514)534-2717

Located in the picturesque town of Bromont, Spa Concept is the most popular health resort in the province of Quebec and it's only 45 minutes from Montreal and 20 minutes from the U.S. border! This European-style spa offers great skiing, golf, racket sports, fitness assessments, low-calorie cuisine, and all the pampering that makes a spa visit so special.

To help get your body in shape, Spa Concept offers everything from morning walks to aqua-fitness, a fully equipped gymnasium, racquetball, tennis, aerobics, stretching exercises, Jazzercise, light gymnastics, and an indoor and an outdoor swimming pool. In addition, there is volleyball, shuffleboard, horseshoes, mountain biking, squash, and downhill and cross-country skiing. Horseback riding and water slides are available nearby.

You can do some serious relaxing or ease tired muscles in the indoor or outdoor sauna and whirlpool. Or if you've been dying to try some of the exotic massage techniques you've been hearing about—now's your chance. You can choose from Swedish, Shiatsu, Esalen, or Trager massage; aromatherapy; reflexology; polarity therapy; lymphatic drainage; and electro-puncture—all of which may sound rather strange, but are very soothing. To revitalize and beautify the outside of you, there are treatments such as body peeling, a body-firming wrap, facials, manicures and pedicures, and a hair salon. And be sure to experience one of the spa's great therapeutic baths, among which are mud, algae, or essential oil baths.

Dining here offers the opportunity to shed a few pounds and improve your eating habits, with the help of low-calorie, nutritionally balanced meals and herbal teas, which, according to the spa, can detoxify and prep your system for a new way of eating.

Catering to both men and women, Spa Concept offers a range of packages from half-day pamper or beauty programs to the all-out seven-day program. Lodging in the comfortable and luxurious accommodations at Chateau Bromont, meals, massage, a variety of beauty and salon treatments, and use of all facilities are included in all packages. The five- and seven-night programs inlcude a health profile, energy test, energy balancing, electro-puncture, and a specific number of therapeutic baths and body treatments. You choose which ones you want.

GUEST FEEDBACK
Guests return from Chateau Bromont with good reports. They cite the staff's knowledge and concern, particularly the beauty staff's, as excellent. The facilities, setting, and location are also rated highly. Cosmopolitan Montrealers know where to go for rest and rejuvenation; perhaps it's time more of us crossed the border.

Rates

	Single	*Double (per person)*
1-Night Package	C$260	C$240
2-Night Package	C$425	C$425
5-Night Package	C$660	C$625
7-Night Package	C$1,600	C$1,300

There is no minimum stay and any-day arrival. U.S. dollar prices are approximately 15 percent lower.

Spa Hotel and Mineral Springs $$ FB-RH, MS

100 North Indian Avenue
Palm Springs, California 92262
(800)854-1279 (Nationwide)
(800)472-4371 (in California)

As its name suggests, this southern California retreat combines resort activity with the therapeutic qualities of natural hot springs. Located in downtown Palm Springs, the Spa Hotel was built on the site where the Cahuilla Indians first discovered the "agua caliente" (hot water) more than 100 years ago. Bubbling to the surface at a wonderfully warm 106 degrees Fahrenheit, the waters remain the center of attention. However, a recent renovation of the facilities reflects the Spa's new emphasis on fitness and beauty.

The upgraded program now includes more aerobics and aquatics classes in the outdoor Olympic-size freshwater pool, plus classes in yoga and stress management. There is also a 12-station Paramount weight training gym, free weights, Liferower, Lifecycles, and treadmill. After a tough workout, slip on the scuffs and oversized terry towel the spa provides and head over to the eucalyptus inhalation room, sauna, or Russian steam room, where mineral water is poured onto hot lava rock creating a combination of half humidity and half steam. After a shower, why not sink into the sunken marble tubs filled with the magical water of the springs to experience pure relaxation?

While you're cooling off and waiting for a massage (Swedish, Shiatsu, or sports), have a cup of herbal tea or iced mineral water. Variations on the same theme include a dip in the pool or relaxing on the rooftop solarium. (Clothing is optional.) Afterwards, you can treat yourself to a host of treatments, such as an herbal wrap or bath where herbs are added to agua caliente mineral baths and a loofah rub or salt-glo rub. There is aromatherapy, Orthion treatment (computerized body stretch and relaxation machine), and a full-service beauty salon that provides hair and nail services, plus the Llona of Hungary Institute of Skin Care for facials, herbal waxing, scalp treatments, and makeup consultations.

A special menu, created for spa participants, consists of garden-fresh vegetables, fruits, poultry, seafood, and low-calorie, high-fiber items totaling 1,000 calories daily. A regular menu, coffee, and tea are also available at Rennick's Dining Room. The remainder of the evening can be spent enjoying a nonalcoholic cocktail while listening to the pianist in the Lobby Bar, taking an evening stroll through downtown Palm Springs (many of the shops stay open until 9 P.M.), or retiring to the privacy of your guest room. There are 230 rooms in the contemporary five-story hotel. Rattan furnishings, oversized bed, dressing area and bath, plus a balcony, color television with free cable, air-conditioning, and a morning newspaper make each room a comfortable place to retire.

The spa offers a two-night sampler and a five-night Discover the Springs package. The sampler gives guests a taste of the spa experience with use of all the facilities, plus a loofa scrub, herbal wrap, meals, and accommodations. The five-night package also includes facials, hair salon treatments, health life-style lectures, and a body composition analysis.

GUEST FEEDBACK

Most guests found their vacation to the Spa Hotel rewarding in every way and would definitely return here. They found the location, accommodations, facilities, body services, and meals to be very good or excellent, and they would recommend the place to their friends.

Rates

Jan. 1–Apr. 30 Sept. 15–Dec. 31	*Single*	*Double (per person)*
2-Night Spa Sampler	$531	$411
5-Night Discover the Springs	$1058	$758

May 1–Sept. 14

2-Night Spa Sampler	$451	$371
5-Night Discover the Springs	$858	$658

There is no minimum stay and any-day arrival.

Topnotch at Stowe $$$ FB-RH

Mountain Road
P.O. Box 1260
Stowe, Vermont 05672
(800)451-8686 (Nationwide)
(802)253-8585 (in Vermont)
(800)228-8686 (in Canada)

In the heart of Vermont's Green Mountains sits the 120-acre world-class resort that combines the best of country manor graciousness with European charm. Now the Topnotch resort also boasts its own full-service spa.

Opened in the fall of 1989, the new 22,000-square-foot complex is connected to the resort by an all-weather glass-enclosed walkway. Headed by the spa expert team of John and Ginny Lopis, whose executive credits include the programs of Doral Saturnia International Spa Resort and Canyon Ranch, the Topnotch facility is touted as "New England's finest destination spa," accommodating about 50 spa-goers.

The state-of-the-art fitness facilities include three fully equipped exercise studios, two with special floors for safe workouts and one with resistance weight-training equipment. Strength trainers can work with the David Fitness Equipment-European, which is high-tech, light, quiet, and easy to use. The studio also houses free weights, treadmills, exercycles, and StairMasters. The other two studios hold classes in low-impact aerobics, stretching and toning, yoga, posture, lower-back workouts, and one-on-one personal training sessions. The indoor pool is the site for water aerobic classes.

The spa houses ten massage rooms; separate Jacuzzis for men and women, plus one co-ed Jacuzzi with a heated hydromassage waterfall near the indoor pool; steam room, saunas, and locker room facilities; and a beauty salon for hair and nail care. Personal services include hydrotherapy, herbal wraps, salt-glo loofa scrubs, and facials.

The Topnotch program also features nutrition seminars and consultations; stress-management classes with biofeedback, guided imagery, and relaxation techniques; fitness assessments (cholesterol level, cardiovascular capacity, strength and flexibility); and life-style risk assessments and consultations. In addition, there is a library stocked with health and wellness material, evening programs on related topics, and an art studio offering classes and seminars with renowned artists.

Whether or not you are on a spa package, guests have access to the equestrian center, a cross-country ski touring center; downhill skiing; a fireside lounge; guided mountain walks, hikes, and bike rides; tennis clinics and competitions (there are ten outdoor and four indoor courts); and water volleyball, polo, and basketball.

Dining is available at two gourmet restaurants, one of which offers an exclusive spa menu and spa cooking demonstrations. The Dining Room, with its mountain view, is open for breakfast and dinner, and there's informal dining at Le Bistro.

Worn out from a full day's activities, guests can ease into the comfort of one of the 94 guest rooms, each varying slightly but all with the creature comforts. Warm, muted colors, original art works, fresh flowers, color television, air conditioning, full bath, personal library, and writing portfolio go into making Topnotch rooms cozy places to retire. There are also 15 deluxe condominiums with kitchens and seven one- and two-bedroom townhouses with fireplaces.

The seven-night spa package includes just about everything a guest would want in a fitness and beauty vacation, plus some extras. Your accommodations, meals, all fitness classes, and all personal services, such as massages, facials, hydrotherapy, and herbal wraps, are included. Also, guests have use of all facilities, including the downhill and cross-country skiing trails.

Rates

		Double
Jul. 15–Oct. 20	*Single*	*(per person)*
7-Night Spa Package	$2,280	$1,890
Oct. 21–Dec. 19		
7-Night Spa Package	$1,760	$1,450

There is no minimum stay and any-day arrival. Packages are not available December 20–31.

Tucson National Resort and Spa $$ FB-RH

8300 North Club Drive
Tucson, Arizona 85741
(800)528-4856 (Nationwide)
(602)297-2271 (in Arizona)

Standing against the backdrop of the beautiful Santa Catalina Mountains is the southwest's hot vacation spot where business and fitness pleasures do mix. After a major $20-million expansion, the resort offers health and fitness options, as well as all the makings for a smooth business conference. And while pampering indulgences are certainly at your beck and call, the emphasis is on tournament-class golfing.

More than 25 years have passed since owner William Nanini opened his internationally known golf club. Through the years, Tucson National has kept abreast of the times, and its new incarnation as a fitness resort promises to fill the needs of some often-overlooked travelers. For business executives and workaholics in need of a respite, Tucson creates an individualized program with plenty of stress-releasing service and care. Even your gym togs, robes, scuffs, and towels are provided by the resort.

The daily schedule of aerobic classes focuses more on stretching than bouncing, but there are treadmills, stationary bikes, rowing machines, free weights and a ten-station Universal weight-training gym. The spa is small and the guest-to-staff ratio is high, so although there's no formal program, help is always on hand. There's swimming in the 75-foot outdoor pool, four tennis courts, a 27-hole golf course, horseback riding, hot-air ballooning, plus some interesting shopping in the Santa Cruz Valley.

But their pure pampering treatments might make you forget about exercising, anyway. After a hectic day of business, or of working muscles you forgot you had, why not succumb to a rubdown with sea salts or grated walnuts in sesame seed oil, an herbal wrap, or the vapors of a Russian steam bath. Or drag yourself over to the Swiss shower for a 16-jet water massage which you can follow with a cold plunge. The women's locker room has steam cabinets and a recessed Roman-style whirlpool. Both locker rooms have inhalation tanks. Aromatherapy, loofa salt-glo, massages, manicures, pedicures, and hair-care services, as well as private exercise training, are also available.

If you're trying to stick to a diet, you'll find support in the meal plan that comes with the spa packages. The 1,200-calorie-per-day diet is low in sodium and cholesterol and includes entrees such as broiled swordfish, pasta primavera, and steamed vegetables for dinner. Meals are served in a restaurant overlooking the Golf Club, and you're free to order from the regular menu.

There are 171 rooms and suites in three-story wings. Rooms have king-size beds, full bath, dressing area, television, and private balcony. Casitas have wood-burning fireplaces, full kitchens, and expansive views.

The spa offers four- and six-night packages that include your accommodations, meals, massage, facial, herbal wrap or suntan session, two exercise classes, use of all spa facilities, plus your choice of one option per day: fitness evaluation, dietary analysis, salt-glo loofa, soap scrub, Scotch shower (for men), pedicure, paraffin foot or hand dip, manicure, and makeup consultation.

GUEST FEEDBACK

Most guests of the Tucson National Resort and Spa have been very pleased with its casual, unstructured environment. They took advantage of their free time and pampered themselves with loads of treatments, and did not fret about working out without a structured program.

Rates

Jan. 1–May 31	*Single*	*Double (per person)*
4-Night Package	$1,200	$927
6-Night Package	$1,800	$1,390.50
Jun. 1–Sept. 30		
4-Night Package	$840	$740
6-Night Package	$1,260	$1,110
Oct. 1–Dec. 31		
4-Night Package	$1,040	$850
6-Night Package	$1,560	$1,275

There is no minimum stay and any-day arrival.

Turnberry Isle Yacht and Country Club $$$ FB-RH

19735 Turnberry Way
P.O. Box 630578, Turnberry Isle
Miami, Florida 33163
(800)327-7028 (Nationwide)
(305)932-6200 (in Florida)

In the heart of Florida's Gold Coast is Turnberry Isle. Situated on the Intracoastal Waterway across from Miami, jet-setting executives and other "titles" retreat here to renew body and mind. Although the spa was originally designed as yet another amenity for members and visitors to the Marina, Turnberry Isle takes fitness and nutrition seriously.

Luxury is key here. With a marina for your yacht outside your window and a hot tub in your guest room, this is the place to come for romance, renewal, and privacy. The resort is set among glittering highrise condos, ritzy shops, and malls, and features world-class sports facilities, and lavish hotel accommodations.

With a maximum of ten spa guests at any given time, individual fitness and nutrition programs are designed for you, following a consultation with the medical director, nutritionist, and other spa professionals. To get your body into shape, the program begins with a walk around the five miles of waterways and golf courses; then there are four or five exercise classes daily—from nonimpact aerobics to water works—plus free weights, Nautilus equipment, Liferower, StairMaster, Lifecycles, treadmills, and a 34-course parcours. Individual instruction and exercise classes are available for an additional fee of $35. Recreational facilities include 2 swimming pools, 2 golf courses, 24 tennis courts, 3 indoor racquetball courts, and bike rentals. A spa wardrobe—warm-up suits, robes, slippers, and towels–are all provided.

To soothe your muscles, the spa offers Swiss showers, Finnish saunas, Turkish steam baths and whirlpools, and therapeutic massage. The full-service beauty salon offers everything from waxing to derma peels and regular facials. Special facial treatments and body treatments are also available. There are lympathic drainage treatments, digestive massage, cellulite treatments, and circulatory and stetch-mark treatments. Other body treatments include loofa and salt-glo rubs and herbal wraps.

Accommodations include Turnberry's 120 rooms and suites at The Marina Hotel, styled in the grand tradition of a private European hotel and nestled around the entrance to the yacht harbor. Guest rooms are spacious and lavishly decorated with vast curving terraces that provide a panoramic view of the marina. Most feature personal Jacuzzis. Deluxe suites have a parlor, bar, double Jacuzzi tub and stall shower, private solarium, and redwood hot tub. The Country Club Hotel is located within the subtropical gardens, manicured lawns, and winding waterways of the Turnberry Fairways. Mirroring the style of the Marina Hotel, the Country Club has the informal ambience of a golf retreat.

As a world-class resort, Turnberry offers diversified dining experiences. The restaurants and lounges feature formal and informal settings with scenic views of the marina, pools, golf courses, and the Atlantic Ocean. Spa cuisine is high in complex carbohydrates and fiber, low in fat, and amounts to about 900 calories per day. There is no charge for special diets, and room service is available.

Although Turnberry is a luxury resort, it still offers many affordable mini-spa packages, as well as some all-out life-style makeover packages. The seven-night Spa Nutrition & Fitness plan includes spa meals, facilities, medical exam, nutritional consultation, six massages, five personal exercise classes, two facials, six Swiss showers, four herbal wraps, a loofah salt-glo, six Vitabath treatments, and beauty salon services.

GUEST FEEDBACK
All of the guests surveyed loved Turnberry and had no complaints. They thought the structure and presentation were excellent, and for the most part, this spa vacation was a good value. They recommend sharing this private fitness vacation secret with a friend—a good friend.

Rates

Jan. 3–Apr. 15	*Single*	*Double (per person)*
4-Night Package ANY-DAY ARRIVAL	$1,737	$1,237
Apr. 16–Sept. 30	$1,162	$949
Oct. 1–Dec. 15	$1,387	$1,062
7-Night Package ANY-DAY ARRIVAL	$3,020	$2,145
Apr. 16–Sept. 30	$2,014	$1,642
Oct. 1–Dec. 15	$2,407	$1,839

There is a four-night minimum stay.

The Verandah Club $$ FB-RH

Loew's Anatole Hotel
2201 Stemmons Freeway
Dallas, Texas 75207
(214)748-1200

The Verandah Club at Loew's Anatole Hotel is a big-city spa that has the feel of a gracious mansion from the outside, but on the inside houses one of the largest and most sophisticated facilities in the country. Open to club members and hotel guests for a $12 daily fee, the Verandah's lavish spa includes modern weight and exercise rooms with all the latest equipment and a spectacular indoor pool with underwater stereo sounds.

The Verandah offers an immense variety of activities to suit all kinds of preferences—aerobic dance classes in a specially designed studio, workouts in weight and exercise rooms outfitted with state-of-the-art Nautilus and CAM II equipment, a gym with full basketball court, and even a putting green. And for jogging enthusiasts, there's an indoor track or a quarter-mile outdoor path. Plus, there are six outdoor tennis courts, eight racquetball courts, and two squash courts. The Verandah also boasts the area's most complete aquatics program in a 25-meter, six-lane indoor pool.

After a workout, relax in a whirlpool, steambath, eucalyptus sauna, or try a Verandah massage. You have a choice of co-ed or separate facilities for men and women. The salon offers a full range of beauty services, including facials, makeup sessions, hair design, color consultation, complete nail care, and year-round tanning.

Known for its fresh and creative cuisine, the Verandah has established itself as a popular dining destination. The Verandah Dining Room serves up distinctively southern cuisine, including delicious diet menus, while the cocktail lounge, poolside terrace, and Socio Grill provide casual alternatives to formal dining. In all, there are 11 restaurants and 9 lounges to choose from.

At this, the largest hotel in the southwest, there is a shopping arcade, private park, and over 1,500 guest rooms. The attractive guest rooms are extra large with suite-like sitting areas for up to five people. Rooms also have a work desk, television, and double vanity.

In addition to the fee of $12 a day, personalized fitness packages and beauty and pampering services may be purchased separately.

GUEST FEEDBACK

With so much to offer, our clients had to keep a clear focus on their goals in order to make the most of this extensive package. They were, however, very pleased with all of the options and the chance to experience them in this very modern and cheerful, yet elegant facility. Guests praised the staff, and rated the sports and spa facilities very good to excellent.

Rates

		Double
Jan. 1–Dec. 31	*Single*	*(per person)*
Per Night	$125–155	$72.50–87.50

There is no minimum stay and any-day arrival.

Joe Weider's Shape Aerobics and $$ FB-RH
Fitness Camp

Fitness Camps, Inc.
202 Main Street, Suite 11
Venice, California 90291
(800)648-CAMP (Nationwide)
(213)392-2727 (in California)

Body-builders and fitness enthusiasts are probably already familiar with publisher Joe Weider's *Shape* magazine. Now he brings this fitness life style to the general public with his specialized summer camp program that presents educational and practical aspects of aerobic training, health, and fitness. Geared to regular exercisers and fitness professionals, Weider brings together a line-up of the world's most sought-after and recognized aerobics professionals to instruct and update you on fitness education and training.

During each of the three-week sessions, the pros lead you through workshops and classes, sharing the secrets and techniques that have enabled them to reach the top of their field. In addition, each week features lectures from nutritionists, sports psychologists, and exercise physiologists. The program consists of seminars, intense training sessions, workshops, classes, nutritious meals, and entertainment.

In the past, the line-up included Kathy Smith, resident fitness correspondent for NBC's "Today Show," who presented a lecture "Flexing Your Motivational Muscle," followed by her "Fat Burning Workout;" Sheila Cluff, fitness expert, author, talk show host, and owner of The Oaks at Ojai and The Palms at Palms Springs health resorts; Brett Kelly, former competitive figure skater and professional dancer who presented his "Jammin'—The Jazz/Funk Solution;" and Petra Lansner, director of Professional Fitness Instructors Association and corporate fitness specialist, who taught the latest in aqua-aerobics. Last summer's camp sessions featured the beautiful bodies and expert knowledge of Carla Dunlap, Phil Williams, Berry de Mey, Cory Everson, Bev Francis, and Bob Paris.

In addition to the pros and lecturers, the camp has a highly trained staff of counselors and assistants who work with you to help achieve your goals. These men and women are certified aerobics instructors and have CPR and first-aid certifications and extensive backgrounds in fitness and exercise instruction. Medical personnel are also on call 24 hours a day.

Campers reside at Loyola Marymount University, the host site of the 1984 Olympic Games and just minutes from the world-famous Muscle Beach. Loyola's 128-acre, palm-tree-lined campus includes first-class contemporary housing and dining facilities, professional athletic venues, outdoor swimming pools, and Jacuzzis. The housing facilities feature two-bedroom apartments (double occupancy) with private bathroom, kitchen, and living room.

Meals are served three times per day in a private dining room with a team-training table atmosphere. The menu is designed by a nutritionist and includes wholesome, nutritious, and natural foods. The meal plan will accommodate those who are trying to lose weight, as well as those interested in learning more about nutrition.

The tuition for one week at camp covers five nights' accommodations, three meals daily, and the entire six-day training and educational program. They insure plenty of personal instruction for everyone. The AFAA Review and Primary Certification exam is offered to registered campers on Saturday of each week for an additional $60 (normally $159), but you must sign up for it when you send in your enrollment application.

GUEST FEEDBACK

Participants in this novel program have reported a truly rewarding experience. Not only did they expand their knowledge of fitness and health, they found the totally supportive environment to be very motivating. Many look forward to going again.

Rates

Camp Tuition (per week)	*Single*	*Double (per person)*
One Week	not available	$835
Two Weeks	not available	$800
Three Weeks	not available	$765

There is a five-night minimum stay. There is Tuesday arrival and Sunday departure.

The Westin Hotel Cascade Club $$ FB-RH

1300 Westhaven Drive
Vail, Colorado 81657
(303)476-7111

Vail, Colorado, is best known for its skiing, and this Westin property is no exception. Touted as the newest, largest, and most complete sports and fitness facility this side of the Rockies, the Cascade Club offers athletes—from those with competitive instincts to casual enthusiasts—a complete array of opportunities. There are four indoor and three outdoor tennis courts, two racquetball and four squash courts, jogging track, sports-medicine clinic, plus state-of-the-art weight-training equipment. And professionals will help you establish and surpass your fitness goals. In addition, hikers and skiers get full advantage of Vail's incredible terrain.

The fitness program includes a vast selection of low- and high-impact aerobic classes throughout the day, a complete line of Nautilus equipment, free weights, stationary bikes, rowing machine, cross-country ski machine, and treadmills. Soothe and relax an achy body in the thermal whirlpool and steam room or in a heated outdoor swimming pool framed by a panoramic view of Vail Valley's natural beauty. For an additional cost, you can also be evaluated, through a comprehensive questionnaire, regarding your health attitudes, habits, and specific risk factor; a cardiovascular stress test; blood pressure and pulse monitoring; body composition analysis; and a strength and flexibility test. This information is processed and individual counseling sessions are held to design personal risk-reduction programs for you to follow once you get back home. Nutritional evaluation and consultation are also available.

Relaxation and revitalization aren't neglected here either. The spa facilities, including massage rooms, invite you to release tension, breathe deeply, and simply unwind. Feeling refreshed, you will then be enticed by an icy tumbler of freshly squeezed orange juice, a host of sparkling bottled waters, or your favorite spirits at the informal lounge and restaurant.

Youngsters have Cascade Club privileges, including fitness classes, sports clinics, and competitions for all ages. Groups are broken down into 8 years and under and 9 to 14 years; teens 15 and up can use the facilities as adults. Child care at the nursery is available for children under 8 years of age.

The 344 guest rooms of the adjacent Westin Hotel are equipped with all the amenities of a first-class hotel, including central heat and air, television, telephone, sitting area, and personal care items. At mealtimes, you have a choice of restaurants offering everything from a skier's breakfast to grilled meats, chicken, and fish. There is no special diet menu. The Cascade Club offers two- and five-night packages that include accommodations, breakfast daily, total fitness assessment, individual counseling, full use of spa facilities, personal fitness program, lectures, and taxes.

GUEST FEEDBACK

Former guests to the Cascade Club rated their overall vacation experience as rewarding. Parents were particularly pleased to be able to expose their children to the joys of spa-ing, while they themselves worked out in peace. Guests also enjoyed the opportunity to examine their state of health. Most would recommend it to their friends, and many guests would return and take the family.

Rates

	Single	*Double (per person)*
Apr. 1–Dec. 15		
2-Night Program ANY-DAY ARRIVAL	$269–299	$179–199
5-Night Program SUN ARR/FRI DEP	$785	$555
	Nightly Rates Apply	No Spa Packages Offered
Dec. 16–Mar. 31		
Per Night	$195–230	$110–145

There is no minimum stay.

Wheels Country Spa $$ FB-RH

P.O. Box 507
Chatham, Ontario, Canada N7M 5K6
(519)351-1500

Just an hour's drive from Detroit, Michigan, is Wheels Country Spa, located in the Best Western Wheels Inn. Neither rain, nor sleet, nor snow will interfere with your vacation in this European-style country spa, thanks to the more than seven acres of indoor climate-controlled facilities. Add a host of revitalizing personal services and a children's program, and you get a perfect recipe for a great vacation.

The hotel also contains 16 professional conference rooms to accommodate from 10 to 700 people and a Kent Kiddie Kollege day care center—all of which make Wheels an ideal place to bring the family during business trips or for a vacation.

The fitness club features 19 racquetball courts, a bowling alley, exercise pool, tennis courts, putting green, steambaths, saunas, and whirlpools. The gym is equipped with stationary bikes, exercise machines, and free weights; plus a variety of fitness classes are held. The European-style spa offers 42 personal pampering services, including massage, reflexology, herbal wrap, loofah rubs, facials, hair and nail care, and makeup consultation and application.

Wheels Inn also caters to children with an atrium playland filled with water slides, games, Ping-Pong tables, and putting greens. In addition, there are organized activities for the kiddies.

For dieters, there is a low-calorie menu with lots of choices. Breakfast is served in the Kent Kafe. Lunch is served at the Ranchhouse in the atrium with its lush greenery and waterfalls, or in the quiet ambience of The Tree Room. The Camperdown Elm is where dinner is served and appetizers are prepared tableside. You can even pick your lobster straight from the tank. Desserts are created fresh daily with all natural ingredients in the pastry kitchen. For just plain lounging and sipping, try the Stable Lounge, the Ranch House, or the Point After Lounge in the fitness club.

Guest rooms in this 354-room hotel come with all the trappings of a first-class hotel. Some rooms even have saunas and whirlpools. Wheels offers a variety of packages, from the half-day pamper package to the five-night Super Tone-up program. The three- and five-night packages include accommodations, meals, exercise classes, herbal wraps, massages, facials, salt-glo loofah treatment, shampoo, set or blow-dry, manicure, pedicure, makeup consultation, or paraffin hand treatment. The five-night plan includes all of the above plus body composition analysis, fitness test and evaluation, and nutritional analysis.

GUEST FEEDBACK

Guest report that, in terms of the sheer range and quality of treatments for men and women, Wheels Country can't be beat. It is a great escape for the entire family, because there is something for everybody.

Some of the guests were concerned at first to learn that some of the exercise classes coincided with meal times. However, they soon came to realize that fitting in a meal was no problem at all, due to the wide selection of restaurants.

Rates

	Single or Double (per person)
3-Night Deluxe Spa Package MON OR TUES ARR/THURS OR FRI DEP	C$690
5-Night Super Tone-up Program MON ARR/SAT DEP	C$1,095

There is a three-night minimum stay. U.S. dollar prices approximately 15 percent lower.

The Woods at Killington $$ FB-RH

Rural Route 1, Box 8C, Killington Road
Killington, Vermont 05751
(800)633-0127 (Nationwide)
(802)422-3100 (in Vermont, Canada, and western U.S.)

The Killington area is perhaps best known for its famous ski center with six mountains and a wide assortment of alpine and cross-country ski trails. The Woods at Killington is also a famous ski center that offers a wide assortment of trails and year-round activities, plus a complete spa facility with Thalassotherapy and pampering services.

Fitness activities here include scenic jogging trails, biking, exercise classes, weight training with Eagle (by CYBEX) Equipment, and free weights. In addition, there is canoeing, fishing, golf, hanggliding, hiking, horseback riding, hot-air ballooning, hunting (for deer, moose, bear, and fowl in season), nature walks, sailing, sleighriding, snowmobiling, snowshoeing, swimming, tennis, water skiing, and wind surfing. Aqua-aerobics and nutritional analysis are also available.

After a day on the slopes or wandering through nature trails let The Woods pamper your body with its assortment of bodily delights. Besides Swedish massage, The Woods offers Thalassotherapy underwater massage, aromatherapy, para Fango packs (a mixture of mud and paraffin heated to 116 degrees Fahrenheit and applied as a local heat pack), herbal wraps, salt-glo loofa rubs, a dry sauna, and a steam room.

For your dining pleasure, there is Puzant's, a gourmet restaurant that serves up delicious and nutritionally sound spa cuisine. Lodging is up to par with comfortable accommodations and amenities of a first-class resort. A spa wardrobe is also provided during your stay.

Special spa plans are available for resident and local guests, designed particularly to educate guests in the many facets of health and fitness. The ideal combination of therapy treatments, exercise, and low-cal cuisine creates a total spa vacation experience. Plans include massage, fitness classes, weekly lectures and demonstrations, plus the use of the spa facilities.

GUEST FEEDBACK

Surveyed guests were pleased with their stay and found that most of their needs were met. Skiers reaped the most benefits by taking advantage of the slopes and the spa. However, all were pleased with the food, body pampering, and level of staff concern. Most would recommend it to their friends.

Rates

	Single or Double (per person)
Per Night	$65–150

There is no minimum stay and any-day arrival. Nightly rates apply, but spa packages are available upon request.

World of Fitness $ FB-RH, WL

P.O. Box 981
St. George, Utah 84771
(801)628-9201

This low-cost, time-tested program takes place in the colorful Canyon Country of southwestern Utah, and specializes in weight loss and behavior modification. Catering to all ages and levels of adult fitness, World of Fitness has a program that meets all of your weight-loss needs.

Walking and hiking are a major portion of the program, with excursions to Zion National Park, Snow Canyon, Bryce Canyon, Pinevalley Mountain, the Joshua Tree Forest, Red Cliffs, and Oak Grove. Depending on your level of fitness, this daily exercise runs between 3 and 12 miles, and the resort suggests guests prepare for their visit by walking three to six times per week for 30 to 60 minutes at a time. Guests are divided into three levels of fitness groups, and a program is designed for each group. Low-impact aerobics, swimnastics, slow stretch, and body conditioning are offered, as well as a gym with Nautilus and Polaris exercise equipment, Lifecycles, Stair-Masters, and free weights. There is a 75-foot indoor/outdoor swimming pool, sauna, and Jacuzzi, plus a lounge with a big-screen television and video games; tanning beds; and full-service beauty salon.

The 60-minute Lifestyle Change Workshops offers real-world survival techniques to insure permanent success. They cover subjects such as resetting your fat thermostat, dispelling the dieting/yo-yo mentality, correcting distorted body image, cooking demonstrations, shopping excursions, and food management. The menu here is based on the proven Pritikin Plan. Depending upon your test in appraisal, your diet of three delicious, high-fiber meals will be between 800 and 1,200 calories per day. In the evenings, there is usually musical entertainment or an educational activity. And after a rewarding and challenging day, guests retire to the comfort of the St. George Hilton Inn. Lodging is available in private, double, and triple accommodations.

World of Fitness runs one-week packages that include transportation from the airport to the Hilton, your accommodations, three meals daily; all fitness classes, lifestyle change workshops, and seminars; daily walks and hikes; health appraisal before and after your stay; full use of facility; evening activities; and personal progress evaluation and counseling. For an additional cost, guests can receive a sports massage; manicures and pedicures; blood chemistry profile and consultation; and private lessons in tennis, racquetball, weight training, and race-walking. Golf and a hiker/long-distance walker programs are also available. Movies and shopping are within walking distance.

GUEST FEEDBACK
Former guests had rewarding vacations with the World of Fitness program. They cited it as a well-structured program with lots of free time built in and of good value. Many would return and recommend it to friends.

Rates

	Single	Double (per person)	Triple (per person)
7-Night Program	$699	$499	$475

There is Sunday arrival and Sunday departure.

LUXURY SPAS

Cal-a-Vie $$$$ LUX, FB-SC

2249 Somerset Road
Vista, California 92084
(619)945-2055

This posh facility is a haven for the overworked, overweight, and overstressed. Nestled into a canyon on 125 tranquil acres of rolling hills in North San Diego County, its tiled peach-colored cottages spill down the hillside like a secluded Mediterranean village. Cal-a-Vie combines the concepts of European body and skin care treatments with the forward approach of American fitness and nutrition.

Before beginning the program, the 24 guests (mostly women) undergo a computerized fitness evaluation that measures flexibility, body fat, blood pressure, and basal metabolism. To begin with, the fitness program features top-of-the-line exercise equipment such as Dynavit bicycles, Keiser CAM II air-resistance weights, and a Berkeley Medical Research Co. computer that measures body fat and prints out a precise weight-loss prescription for each guest. Hiking, stretching, calisthenics, yoga, Tai Chi, tennis, golf, and jogging are all offered to get you moving.

Cal-a-Vie's program consists of some work and some pampering each day. Soothing massage, natural plant and sea extracts, and aromatic restorative oils are an integral component of each of the beauty treatments. Utilizing sophisticated European techniques of Thalassotherapy, hydrotherapy, and aromatherapy, there are beauty treatments for every part of the body. Swedish and Shiatsu massage and other bodywork techniques calm, yet invigorate, while the Thalassotherapy (including a seaweed wrap) helps rebalance body chemistry, stimulate body function, and assist in elimination of toxins within the skin. The spa's exclusive body- and skin-enhancing treatment, Body Glow, is a full body-slough that prepares you for aromatherapy massage and the other beauty treatments you'll receive. Treatments such as an aromatherapy massage, foot reflexology, facials, manicures, and pedicures leave no area of your body neglected.

Plants, herbs, and flowers grown on the premises are used for beauty treatments, as well as for food, dieting here (on 800 to 1,200 calories per day including two snacks) is an indulgence. The spa's nutritional philosophy follows the prevailing attitude of health and nutrition experts—a low-fat, low-sodium diet consisting of complex carbohydrates in the form of whole grains, pasta and legumes, fresh fruit and vegetables, poultry, and fish (excluding shellfish). However, Cal-a-Vie has its own forward approach to balancing and revitalizing the body with the culinary talents of chef Michel Stroot whose "cuisine fraiche" has won him respect throughout the industry. For example, each salad contains between 12 and 20 ingredients, and frequently one or two of them are colorful, edible flowers such as nasturtiums. Breakfast might be a whole-grain hot cereal with dates and nuts or a small cantaloupe filled with low-fat cottage cheese, honey, and sunflower seeds. At midweek there is a cleansing fast diet consisting mainly of juices and totaling just a few hundred calories. Dinner is served in the elegant French Provincial dining room with fresh flowers, bone china, and crystal glasses, although folks often come to dinner in sweats.

Guests stay in terra-cotta-tiled cottages individually decorated with imported chintzes covering duvets, pillow shams and drapery in soft, romantic tones. The furnishings include oversized headboards and armoires, benches, and night tables in light and dark oak and pine. The hexagon-shaped mosaic-tiled bathrooms contribute to the understated elegance of each cottage.

The one-week program at Cal-a-Vie includes everything you'd expect of a luxury spa vacation: accommodations in your private cottage, meals and snacks, exercise program, evening lectures, airport transfers from San Diego International Airport, taxes, and gratuities. All your spa clothes and toiletries are provided. In addition, you'll receive three facials, a hair and scalp treatment, two hand and foot treatments, five massages, one Thalassotherapy and two hydrotherapy sessions, a Body-Glow treatment, one aromatherapy massage, a foot reflexology session, manicure, makeup application, and hairstyling. Catering mostly to women, Cal-a-Vie does offer special weeks for men, couples, and co-ed groups.

GUEST FEEDBACK
All guests surveyed found their vacation at this secluded haven rewarding in every way—even those who thought they'd try a less pricy spa next time. Since many of the spa's guests are regulars on the spa circuit, many are already in good shape, so the spa caters to their needs with thorough workouts. Not surprisingly, food rated excellent. As one guest put it, "I never knew 1,000 calories could taste so good!" Cal-a-Vie seems to be a place many people would share with their good friends.

Rates

	Single or Double (per person)
7-Night Package	$3,500.40
SUN ARR/SUN DEP	

There is a seven-night minimum stay.

Canyon Ranch in the Berkshires $$$ LUX, FB-SC

Kemble Street (Route 7A)
Lenox, Massachusetts 01240

(800)621-9777 (Nationwide)
(413)637-4100 (in Massachusetts)

The world-famous Canyon Ranch in Arizona recently opened a sister spa in the beautiful Berkshires, featuring fitness, nutrition, weight-management, stress-reduction, and luxury pampering programs in the Canyon Ranch tradition. Like the original, this $37-million year-round facility offers a comprehensive vacation experience focused on exercise, nutrition, and permanent life-style improvement. In addition, it is a comprehensive medical center for the prevention and treatment of stress-related illness.

The site is the 120-acre Bellefontaine estate, one of the 23 historic "great mansions" of the Berkshires. As part of the conversion, they've added a 120-room inn with guest rooms, luxury suites, and a pavillion with guest reception, lounge, and spa. Facilities at this posh new resort include a 75-foot enclosed swimming pool, indoor track; exercise and weight-training room; and men's and women's locker rooms, complete with steam sauna, inhalation rooms, and whirlpool baths. The spa also houses racquetball, squash, and basketball courts. Of course there's ample room for herbal wraps, aromatherapy, hair- and skin-care services, and therapeutic treatments such as massages. And for guest convenience, all three buildings are interconnected by glass-enclosed walkways.

Outdoor facilities are abundant amid the countryside. There are miles of trails for walking, hiking, biking, and cross-country skiing, plus an outdoor swimming pool and five tennis courts. As a guest of Canyon Ranch in the Berkshires, you will also have easy access to many famous cultural events. There's the Tanglewood Music Festival; the Jacob's Pillow, the oldest dance festival in America; The Berkshire Theatre Festival; the Lenox Art Center; and the Shakespeare Company on novelist Edith Wharton's former estate, all during the summer. The Berkshires are also the summer home of the Boston Symphony Orchestra and the Boston Pops. Within 30 minutes of the Bellefontaine property there are 20 major parks, including 85 miles of the Appalachian Trail, a wildlife sanctuary, and six downhill-skiing areas.

The majority of the 120 rooms are garden units with private patios, all furnished in New England-style furnishings. Some bedrooms are specially equipped for the disabled. Deluxe suites are also available.

Canyon Ranch in the Berkshires offers packages from a two-night weekend to a ten-night wellness program. Packages include accommodations, three meals daily, use of spa and resort facilities, fitness classes, sports services, and professional health consultations.

During July and August there is a combination of outdoor and supervised fitness training for teenagers called The Young and Restless.

GUEST FEEDBACK
Because the spa opened in late 1989, there is no feedback yet. However, now northeasterners have a Canyon Ranch to call their own. Let us know what you think.

Rates

Dec. 1–Dec. 22 and Jan. 2–May 31	*Single*	*Double (per person)*
2-Night Weekend FRI ARR/SUN DEP	$600	$500
3-Night Weekend THURS OR FRI ARR/SUN OR MON DEP	$810	$670
4-Night Package MON ARR/FRI DEP	$870	$720
7-Night Package ANY-DAY ARRIVAL	$1,660	$1,380
10-Night Package ANY-DAY ARRIVAL	$2,260	$1,870

There is no minimum stay. Rates are for standard rooms only.

Canyon Ranch Spa $$$ LUX, FB-SC

8600 East Rockcliff Road
Tucson, Arizona 85715
(800)742-9000 (Nationwide)
(800)327-9090 (in Canada)
(602)749-9000 (in Arizona)

At Canyon Ranch Spa the staff outnumbers guests two-to-one! The 60-acre ultramodern luxury spa—the first co-ed spa in the country—has consistently led the way with important innovations in health spa facilities, services, and programs.

Whether you want to lose weight, improve your racquetball game, reduce stress, quit smoking, or strengthen your body, the professional Canyon Ranch staff can help with a skillful blend of exercise, nutrition, relaxation, and personal attention.

The resort accommodates 225 guests in standard, deluxe, and luxury units that incorporate casual southwestern charm with all the amenities of a world-class resort. A handy tip for those of you who are not early risers: Put out the "do not disturb" sign before you go to bed because the maids make the rounds early.

Some specialties of the spa include an arthritis program that helps people learn to manage pain and increase flexibility, strength, and stamina; prenatal and postnatal programs; and a program for those who want to break the smoking habit once and for all. For those of you contemplating plastic surgery, you can make arrangements with a prominent Tucson surgeon to have the procedure done at a nearby medical facility and then have any follow-up consultations at the Ranch, where you can recuperate in comfort and privacy.

The historic clubhouse, with its high-beamed ceilings and massive stone fireplaces, is where the hotel operations are based, including the dining room. All meals are calorie-controlled through portion size. The menu lists prices, a suggested meal, an alternate entree, or several other dishes. A vegetarian option is also available at every meal. The menu provides a careful balance of 60 percent carbohydrate, 20 percent protein, and 20 percent fat. You can dine on such gourmet delicacies as broiled lobster tail, paella, lasagna, lamb chop Dijon, crepe Suzette, blueberry cheesecake, and carrot cake.

Spa facilities here are quite extensive. There are seven gyms for aerobics, stretching, and toning classes; a fully equipped aerobics and weight-training room; three racquetball courts and a squash court; plus men's and women's steam rooms, saunas, Jacuzzis, inhalation therapy rooms, whirlpool baths, cold-dip pools, and private sunbathing areas. Outdoors there are eight night-lit tennis courts, and four swimming pools.

Fitness options are just as extensive at Canyon Ranch. They offer 30 different indoor and outdoor co-ed and men-only classes daily, bicycling, and an exer-course with exercise stations for maximum benefits and minimum boredom. There's also hiking, jogging, golf, and horseback riding nearby.

Canyon Ranch is particularly helpful to people who want to keep their newly gained health and fitness even after they've gone home. Have a home workout designed for you by an exercise physiologist; learn new strategies for dealing with food and nutrition. Or try a behavior modification approach. There's biofeedback to monitor your response to stress, and techniques for overcoming or reducing problems such as obesity, hypertension, sleeping disorders, phobias, headaches, and circulatory or respiratory problems. Learn self-hypnosis, mind fitness training, and natural healing alternatives. Coronary-risk screening, blood tests, comprehensive medical evaluation, and cardiac stress tests are all available under the supervision of Ranch physicians.

If pampering is what you crave, Canyon Ranch comes through with an array of beauty treatments such as aromatherapy, herbal baths and wraps, massage and massage instruction workshops, and, of course, hair, skin, and nail care.

A wide variety of regular and specialty packages are available (for four, seven, or ten nights), as well as *a la carte* options. For instance, a body composition test costs $30; a session with a personal trainer costs $30 for 25 minutes or $48 for 50 minutes; private swimming lessons cost $30 for 25 minutes, $48 for 50 minutes, and $115 for five 25-minute lessons. The seven-night smoking cessation program costs $295 above the cost of a seven-night stay and includes six hours of group instruction, an additional health consultation, and two additional herbal baths and wraps. Those of you who want to lose a substantial amount of weight can participate in the 30-Plus Weight Loss Program, a two-week program for men and women who want to lose 30 pounds or more. The program provides you with insights and skills you'll need to achieve a gradual and sustainable weight loss—including how to grocery shop, cook, and order in restaurants and still remain in control. Once you're home, you can expect regularly scheduled follow-up calls from Canyon Ranch staffers to encourage you in your new way of life and to help you reach your ultimate weight-loss goals.

The basic package includes your accommodations, meals, and use of spa and resort facilities; fitness classes and sports activities; presentations by medical, fitness, nutrition, and stress-management experts; and blood pressure checks, cholesterol screening, weight and body measurement, and first aid for minor injuries. It also includes local phone calls and roundtrip transportation to Tucson Airport, plus a choice of five personal or sports services and two professional health consultations.

GUEST FEEDBACK

Guests are always pleased with their stay at Canyon Ranch. Because of the spa's popularity and size, they have learned to book reservations as far in advance as possible, as well as to make their massage and beauty treatment appointments immediately upon arrival, if not before. Some guests even fly into Tuscon Airport a day early and stay at an inexpensive hotel near the airport so that a day of vacation at the Ranch isn't lost.

Rates

		Double
Jan.–June 15 and Sept. 16–Dec. 24	*Single*	*(per person)*
4-Night Package	$1,330	$1,070
7-Night Package	$2,330	$1,190
10-Night Package	$3,230	$2,630
June 16–Sept. 15		
4-Night Package	$810	$690
7-Night Package	$1,510	$1,310
10-Night Package	$2,080	$1,790

Doral Saturnia International Spa Resort $$$$ LUX, FB-SC

8755 Northwest 36th Street
Miami, Florida 33178
(800)331-7768 (Nationwide)
(305)593-6030 (in Florida)

The clay-tiled roofs, Roman arches, and formal gardens with statuary, reflecting pools, and gushing cascades may remind you of Tuscany, but the Florida sunshine, active fitness program, and the delicious spa cuisine at the Doral Saturnia say Viva America!

The list of fitness options and facilities for the 90 male and female guests seems endless at this luxury, life-enhancement spa. For starters, check your state of health with a body composition, blood-cholesterol-level, or comprehensive blood analysis. Or, take the flexibility or sports-specific muscular strength test. To find out more, have a health risk profile, a personalized home exercise program, or a "Back Fitness and Exercise" program that teaches you proper lifting techniques, tips on posture, stretching and strengthening exercises, and other ways to alleviate and prevent back pain and injury. It costs $50 an hour. In addition, you can have one-on-one workouts from warm-up to cool-down, a personal nutrition plan, and even a color analysis where you learn to select the chromas and hues that best enhance your skin tones.

Now that your're ready to begin your fitness workouts, Doral provides two fully equipped exercise studios for aerobics, circuit-weight training, flexibility, including yoga, stretch-and-tone, posture, and lower-back strengthening; strength training using European David

Fitness Equipment which is light, quiet, and easy to use; free weights, treadmills, exercise bikes, StairMasters, and rowing machines. There are also stress-management classes using progressive relaxation techniques, biofeedback, and guided imagery. On-staff professionals who care for their 90 or so guests include a dietitian, registered nurses, massage therapists, cosmetologists, and tennis and golf trainers.

Facilities include an outdoor recreational pool with Jacuzzi and cascading falls for hydromassage, an outdoor lap pool, and an indoor exercise pool. There's also an indoor climate-controlled, banked jogging track with a sound system for walking and jogging and an outdoor exercise trail with exercise stations and lush tropical landscaping. Organized games include volleyball, baketball, aerobic golf, croquet, and Bocci (lawn bowling). There are 5 championship golf courses, 15 tennis courts, and a world-class equestrian center.

When it comes to pampering your body, Doral rolls out the red carpet. All cosmetic treatments are with Terme di Saturnia products, imported from the sister spa, Terme di Saturnia, in Tuscany, Italy. Each of the 26 massage rooms have individual sound systems; facilities for herbal wraps, Jacuzzi baths, cool dips, saunas, and sundecks are separate for men and women. There are mineral salt soaks using European hydrotherapy tubs, cascading waterfalls with sitting benches for hydromassage, two Swiss showers, and an outdoor whirlpool to soak away every ounce of tension from your body.

The Institute de Saturnia offers 20 face- and body-treatment products from Italy, plus Fango treatments, body polishing, facials, skin rejuvenation treatments, and makeup application and instruction. The Images Beauty Salon offers a full complement of beauty services including hairstyling, face design, manicures, and pedicures.

For entertainment and education, there is a reading room which offers international newspapers and a wide variety of literature, and The Theatre which provides private movie screenings, guest lectures, and demonstrations.

For your dining pleasure, Doral offers two gourmet restaurants featuring full spa menus. The Ristorante di Saturnia, informal and open on three sides, is situated at the core of Spa Centre. The Villa Montepaldi, which is formal, intimate, and glass-enclosed, is sequestered in the middle of the hotel's courtyard. For the benefit of dieters, the menu lists the calories and fat content of each item, and tableside calculators help you keep track of your intake. Adjacent to the Ristorante di Saturnia is the Alfresco Room which features a full kitchen for cooking demonstrations.

As for lodging, this may be better than a home away from home. All guest rooms are actually suites with expansive views of rolling hills and beautiful gardens. Thirty-six of the suites have living rooms;

full entertainment centers with tape deck, VCR, and unlimited videos from the hotel's library; two marble bathrooms; Jacuzzi; refrigerator stocked with mineral waters; and a dressing rooms. Add to that the fact that spa clothing is provided by Doral and dress is casual (you can stay in sweats and t-shirts for all three meals in the spa building) and you many never want to leave.

Saturnia offers *a la carte* spa services (i.e., an hour-long Doral Saturnia Massage costs $50; an herbal wrap is $30; a back facial and Fango treatment is $50; while a revitalizing mask costs $50) as well as packages ranging from four days to one week. Suite accommodations, three gourmet meals daily, plus pre-dinner non-alcholic drinks, use of spa clothing and facilities, exercise and fitness classes, health fitness assessment, and transfers to and from Miami International Airport are all included. Personal services such as massages, manicures, and pedicures are also included. With so much to offer, Saturnia attempts to tailor programs to fit specific needs. For instance, there is a six-day "Crash" Cellulitis program that includes a daily 80-minute cellulitis treatment with hydromassage, meals, use of spa facilities, exercise clothing and fitness classes, a health assessment and consultation, nutritional consultation, two hour-long body massages, shampoo and blowdry, makeup application, manicure and pedicure, thermal treatment, cellulitis mud and creme for home use, and roundtrip airport transfers. In addition, there are programs with a sports emphasis and a Chef's Kitchen spa plan where you learn the art of healthy cooking and the science of nutrition. The choice is yours.

GUEST FEEDBACK
We've interviewed many satisfied guests of Saturnia; however, they offered these tips that would have made their stays absolutely perfect: plan and schedule personal services before arriving, and because there is no sundries shop for personal-care items, bring everything you may need.

Rates

	Single	Double (per person)
Jan.–Apr. 30		
7-Night Package	$3,180	$2,575
4-Night Package	$2,015	$1,575
May 1–May 31		
7-Night Package	$2,890	$2,340
4-Night Package	$1,830	$1,430

June 1–Sept. 30

7-Night Package	$2,415	$1,840
4-Night Package	$1,440	$1,150

Oct. 1–Dec. 15

7-Night Package	$3,150	$2,370
4-Night Package	$1,890	$1,500

There is a four-night minimum stay and any-day arrival.

The Golden Door $$$$ LUX, FB-SC

P.O. Box 1567
Escondido, California 92025
(619)744-5777

Street Address:
777 Deer Springs Road
San Marcos, California 92569

This intimate retreat, where east meets west, caters primarily to prosperous, health-conscious women who have already made fitness a part of their lives. Fashioned after an authentic Japanese country inn—complete with ornamental gardens, bird sanctuaries, and a Buddhist bell that calls you to meals—Golden Door attracts those in need of quiet meditation, personal pampering, and challenging exercise regimens.

With a staff-to-guest ratio of three to one (120 employees to 39 guests) the Golden Door is one of the most expensive and exclusive spas in the United States. Guests should book reservations as early as nine months in advance, since returnees tend to monopolize reservations as far as a year in advance.

As a guest, your fitness program begins with an appointment with your own counselor to determine your fitness level. You need your doctor's OK to participate in the program, and you must be less than 30 percent overweight. With this counselor you will have daily one-on-one conferences to insure that your program is totally customized and is meeting your needs. Besides a swimming pool, exercise classes, and weight training, there is tennis and golf. All spa clothing is provided.

A typical day at Golden Door starts with a wake-up call at 6 A.M. After your morning walk you have breakfast in your room, followed by Tai Chi or pre-exercise warm-ups; Da Vinci exercises (a type of aerobic movement), or weight-training; then an herbal wrap and a manicure or pedicure. You have lunch by the pool, followed by aqua-aerobics and the Golden Door special. (This little extra will appear on your daily schedule and might include a movement assessment, splash dance, water volleyball, jazz dancing, tap dancing, rhythm weights, the making of a personalized take-home exercise cassette, walk-run continuum with special warm-ups and cool-downs, or the popular individual swim training with video feedback.) You wind down with yoga or Tai Chi, capped off by a massage in your room. After dinner, there are cooking classes taught by the Door chef, or lessons on basic nutrition, stress management, midlife crises, career changes, or other life-enchancing strategies. The day ends with a pre-bedtime dip in the hot tub and mini-massage.

At the Golden Door, Nouvelle Cuisine is the fare of the day, and menus are computerized for correct nutrient content and portion control. The spa, which is literally surrounded by citrus, avocado, and more exotic fruit trees, makes 80 percent of its own food. Poultry, seafood, whole grains, legumes, yogurt, tofu, eggs (laid by Golden Door chickens), and milk are the main sources of protein. The 1,000-calorie-per-day diet is high in fiber and low in fat, sugar, sodium, and cholesterol.

So that you can bring Golden Door's cuisine home with you, classes in regular and vegetarian cookery are offered, and recipes can be found in *The Golden Door Cookbook: The Greening of American Cuisine*, which you can purchase at the boutique.

Each of the 39 guests has her own room and private Japanese garden filled with camellias and fuchsias. Not surprisingly, Oriental decor with a Japanese flower arrangement freshens every room. Catering to women for most of the year, the Door does have annual couples-only and men-only weeks. Personal valuables are locked in a vault upon arrival, and there are no room keys. Interestingly, even during couples' weeks, rooms are single occupancy. All the programs last for seven days and include accommodations, meals, full spa program, massages, herbal wraps, service charges, and airport transfers.

GUEST FEEDBACK
Although Golden Door is one of the most expensive spas in the country, its 65-percent return rate attests to the spa's level of guest-satisfaction and its non-price-sensitive clientele. Some guests have complained about it being overpriced, "but excellent, nonetheless." If luxury and serenity are what you're after . . . go for it.

Rates

	Single	Double (per person)
7-Night Package	$3,500	$3,500
SUN ARR/SUN DEP		

The Greenhouse $$$$ LUX, FB-SC

P.O. Box 1144
Arlington, Texas 76010
(817)640-4000

Originally created by Neiman-Marcus and Charles of the Ritz, The Greenhouse offers a privileged world of luxury and beauty where over 125 specialists cater to just 39 lucky women. Now under the auspices of the international spa experts of the Edward J. Safdie Group, The Greenhouse offers women the chance to blossom with personal exercise plans and loads of pampering.

Each guest is assigned a personal facialist, hairdresser, manicurist, and masseuse for the week. A resident physiologist and nurse help plan a schedule to met your needs. Your daily schedule is placed on your morning breakfast tray each day. A leotard and terry robe await you.

Exercise classes include low-impact aerobics and aquatics. Weight-training on Universal and Nautilus equipment, plus treadmills, stationary bikes, cross-country NordicTrack, StairMaster, body-ball weights, hand weights, and elastic Thorobands all help tone the body and give you a good cardiovascular workout. Outside there is a parcours, jogging track, two tennis courts, and an outdoor pool.

Your day will be interspersed with relaxing activities, including facials, massages, a stint in the sauna, a dip in the whirlpool bath, and expert beauty care. In addition, there are discussions on stress, wellness, makeup, cosmetic surgery, plus fashion shows and feature films.

Breakfast is served to you in bed, and you'll take lunch in the skylit marble-floored atrium pool. Dinner can be dressy or casual, depending on the group. It is served in the formal dining room. On Wednesday evenings, you'll be served dinner in your room. Three meals plus snacks are served daily and meal plans range from 850 to 2,000 calories daily. There are 39 single rooms, plus two suites. Hand-embroidered linens, large dressing areas, and sunken tubs, all luxuriously feminine, make the bedrooms as much a part of the therapy as your daily massage.

The Greenhouse offers a seven-night package that includes everything—meals, snacks, individually planned exercise and trainer, daily facial and massage, manicure, pedicure, and hair treatments. One afternoon each week limousines are available for a visit to the famous Neiman-Marcus store in downtown Dallas, and a Neiman-Marcus' Greenhouse consultant will smooth your way and expedite delivery of your purchases. Limousine service to and from the Dallas/Ft. Worth Airport is also included.

If you have medical problems, including allergies or dietary restrictions, that would limit or alter participation in the regular diet, exercise, or beauty treatments, the spa requires a letter from your physician stating so. They also refuse admittance to anyone in an intoxicated or medically dependent condition. Alcoholic beverages are prohibited at The Greenhouse.

GUEST FEEDBACK
Needless to say, all guests are wonderfully pleased with their stays at The Greenhouse. They consistently rated the staff, service, and facilities as of the highest quality, would recommend it to a friend, and would return themselves. In fact, The Greenhouse boasts a 75-percent rate of repeat clientele.

Rates

	Single	*Double (per person)*
7-Night Package	$2,975	$2,950

SUN ARR/SUN DEP
There is a seven-night minimum stay.

The Kerr House $$$$ LUX, FB-SC

17777 Beaver Street
Grand Rapids, Ohio 43522
(419)832-1733

The Kerr House, which is set in a Victorian mansion listed in the National Register of Historic Places, may very well offer the most personalized care in the spa world. Director Laurie Hostetler has created a fantasy world just 30 minutes outside of Toledo, where eight lucky guests—usually women—are welcomed each week. The emphasis here is on total rejuvenation, relaxation, and more personal attention than you've probably enjoyed in years—in a very private setting. That is why Kerr House is a favorite of celebrities and public officials.

The exercise program consists of Hatha Yoga, rebounder aerobics, special exercises, and hikes along the Miami and Erie Canal towpath. Leotards, swimsuits, and robes are provided. Facilities also include a cross-country ski machine, tanning machine, mineral hot tub, sauna, whirlpool, and treatment rooms.

For your body, there is a variety of therapies from which to choose. Wraps and daily massages; European and finger facials; reflexology sessions; body brush exfoliating scrubs; hair, nail, and skin treatments; and skin analysis, makeup application, and consultation all leave you feeling refreshed and somehow replenished. In addition, there are classes in body appreciation, relaxation techniques, breathing, and stretching. Evenings bring something unique each night—from astrological readings to handwriting analyses.

Cuisine at The Kerr House is all natural, containing little or no white flour, refined sugar, salt, red meat, additives, preservatives, or dyes. Breakfast is served to you in bed . . . yes, in bed! You take lunch in a charming cafe, while dinner is in a formal dining room complete with antique linens, stemware, and china. To add to the mood you'll be serenaded by the beautiful sounds of a harpsichord.

Built in 1880, The Kerr House has been completely renovated and refitted for the purpose it now serves. All four floors are lavishly furnished with Victorian antiques and memorabilia. The guest rooms have antique bureaus, high-backed carved beds, stained glass windows, and fireplaces. Although The Kerr House specializes in pampering women, it does offer special weeks just for couples and for men. If you care to, you can book the entire house for your family or group of friends.

The two-night weekend program is an abbreviated version of the standard week-long package which includes accommodations, meals (special diets are available), exercise classes, body treatments, massages, and ground transportation.

GUEST FEEDBACK

The intimacy of only eight guests can, at times, feel like a group encounter experience. Those guests who were only able to afford the two-night package said it was worth it just to experience the ultimate in pampering.

Rates

	Single	Double (per person)
5-Night Program	$2,550	$2,150
SUN ARR/FRI DEP.		
2-Night Weekend Package	$650	$575
FRI ARR/SUN DEP		

There is a two-night minimum stay.

La Costa Hotel and Spa $$$$ LUX, FB-RH

Costa Del Mar Road
Carlsbad, California 92008
(800)854-5000 (Nationwide)
(619)438-911 (in California)

One of the world's most luxurious spa resorts, La Costa is where
celebrities and those in the upper echelon of the world of film, entertainment, sports, finance, and the arts come to escape the glitz, glamour, and hustle of it all. Located just 90 miles south of Los Angeles and
30 minutes north of San Diego, La Costa is nestled on 1,000 rolling
acres between the Pacific Ocean and the foothills.

Medical and fitness evaluations, conducted by staff physicians,
include muscle-strength testing with Aerial computerized equipment, and testing of flexibility, pulmonary function, exercise endurance, and body composition. A blood test is also taken to determine
your cholesterol and triglyceride levels. In the nutrition center, you
can also get a computerized nutritional analysis that will give you a
breakdown of vitamin and mineral intake and your nutritional per-
centages. Specific recommendations for nutritional enhancement are
then made.

As you would expect, the facilities are extensive. There are separate saunas for men and women, rock steam baths, Swiss showers,
Roman pools, individual mineral pools, whirlpools, and solaria for
men and women. The fitness center has exercise equipment and machines for every phase of physical fitness, including free weights,
treadmills, Lifecycles, and Ariel computerized systems. Exercise
classes are held hourly and include aerobics, muscle toning, and relaxation techniques. La Costa also boasts two 18-hole championship
golf courses; 23 racquetball courts; 4 clay, 2 grass, and 17 composition tennis courts, heated swimming pools and aquatic center, plus
jogging trails and rental bikes.

Spa services are a speciality here. Your body will be warmed, soothed, soaked, massaged, oiled, cooled, perfumed, and pampered. Facials, skin analyses, massages, herbal wraps, tanning sessions, loofah rubs, and a variety of baths, including a milk bath, can be scheduled throughout the day. The La Costa Institute of Beauty is an elegantly serene full-service salon that offers makeup classes and a complete line of La Costa cosmetics. There's also a Men's salon.

La Costa offers a wide variety of dining experiences in its seven restaurants. Six are located in the two-level Clubhouse, while Pisces, noted for its romantic setting and gourmet seafood dishes, is a quarter-mile away. The premier restaurant is the Champagne Room offering gourmet continental cuisine served by tuxedo-clad waiters. Other culinary options include Italian, Argentinian, Oriental-Mexican featuring sushi and chili among other things, the Brasserie La Costa with an outdoor patio for informal dining, and The Spa Dining-Room which specializes in tasty low-sodium and low-fat meals. Calories are listed beside the entree and you decide how to "spend" your daily intake.

Entertainment includes a 180-seat theater showing first-run films and three lounges, including one with a live band and an intimate piano bar. There's also shopping within the resort.

La Costa's 482 luxury accommodations include 399 deluxe rooms with all the trimmings. Ceiling-to-floor mirrors, marble bathrooms, and a generous supply of personal-care products add to the luxury. There are also 75 one- or two-bedroom suites, each with a sitting room and twin vanities; two presidential suites and six self-contained executive homes with two to five bedrooms and three or three-and-a-half baths.

There is an array of sports packages (for golf and tennis buffs) and spa programs to choose from, such as the Center for Life Fitness plan. This seven-night personalized health plan and take-home package is an in-depth program dealing with nutrition, weight control, stress management, and communication in personal and work relationships. It also includes medical, nutritional, and fitness evaluations; and exercise classes and lectures on dining out, grocery shopping, and label reading.

The regular seven-night Fitness Program includes deluxe accommodations, meals (spa or regular), golf green's fees, weight-loss management, lectures and discussions, exercise classes, relaxation techniques, personal life-style counseling, a take-home program and follow-up, blood analysis and medical evaluation, treadmill endurance test, strength test, posture evaluation, pulmonary function screening, body composition, nutritional analysis, daily massage, herbal wraps, loofah rub, skin analysis and review, facials, and unlimited use of spa facilities. Women also receive a manicure and pedicure, private makeup session, and a shampoo and blowdry. Men receive a manicure and an oil-conditioning hair treatment.

The seven-night Original Spa Plan includes accommodations, meals (regular or spa); personalized consultation with medical director, spa counselor, and dietitian; skin analysis and review; daily massage, facial, herbal wrap, and exercise classes; a loofah rub, collagen facial, oil conditioning, orthion treatment, special facial machine treatment, manicure, and pedicure; spot-toning treatments; daily tanning session; green's fees and tennis court fees; use of facilities; and hair and makeup services. Two-night spa sampler and basic spa packages, as well as special spring and summer children's programs, are also available.

GUEST FEEDBACK

Most guests found their stay at La Costa to be rewarding in every way and would return for another week of fitness and pampering. This bustling, worldly resort attracts business and professional types who are mostly in good shape, but want to shed a few pounds and/or get their health priorities back on track. The casual spa-goer may find a stay here paradise, while the fitness-foremost-minded individual may be happier at a spa that focuses on challenging the body.

Rates

Per Night	Single	Double (per person)
7-Night Fitness Program	$460	$340
7-Night Original Spa Plan	$430	$310
2-Night Basic Spa Sampler	$250	$125

There is a two-night minimum stay.

Palm-Aire Hotel & Spa $$$ LUX, FB-RH

2501 Palm-Aire Drive North
Pompano Beach, Florida 33069
(800)327-5960 (Nationwide)

"Lifestyles of the Rich and Famous" television show chose Palm-Aire as one of the world's best spas. The rich and famous guests who've supported this opinion include Goldie Hawn, Liza Minnelli, Paul Newman, and Elizabeth Taylor. What makes Palm-Aire so special? Privacy, a personalized exercise and wellness program, and pampering with an incredible array of services. Plus, this sunlit haven sits on 1,500 acres in lush south Florida landscape, just a few minutes from a private ocean beach.

You don't, however, have to be a star to get the royal treatment. After meeting with the spa director, you are examined by the staff physician and the spa's physical fitness experts for a series of tests to measure the percentage of body fat to lean muscle mass, your flexibility, strength, and aerobic capacity. The results, along with your weight, are fed into a computer to help plan the right activities and diet for you. Three levels of water aerobics, two levels of low-impact aerobics and conditioning classes, as well as stretching, yoga, calisthenics, and routines on the sunny outdoor parcours help shape and tone the body beautiful. Nautilus and weight training pump up muscle strength, while walks along the coast or around the resort's five golf courses provide a healthy dose of Florida sunshine and fresh air. There are exercise pools and a 25-yard swimming pool. Men have a separate facility and training staff. Weight training, exercise classes, and workouts are combined with personal services such as facials, massages, and whirlpools to give the guys a complete spa experience. Midday and evening presentations give strategies everyone can use to manage stress and weight and to develop dietary habits for sound nutrition and general well-being.

Of course, the real indulgence comes with the head-to-toe pampering. The entire body will benefit from a visit to the sauna or steam room. Individual whirlpool baths with an assortment of moisturizing, soothing, and fragrant bath beads to choose from will prepare the body for a relaxing Shiatsu or Swedish massage or a reflexology session. Afterwards, treat your face to a deep cleansing and relaxing facial. Then, go for a salt-glo and/or loofa bath. For the ultimate in relaxation and enjoyment, have yourself wrapped in steaming herb-soaked linens—better known as an herbal wrap. Some other specialties here include anticellulite and hydrotherapy treatments such as a marine algae wrap; Balneo-Esthetics, which combines underwater jet massage with overall thermic and essential oils, and a marine algae body contouring mask, a two-part treatment that begins with a soak in the hydrotherapy tub, followed by an application of a body contouring mask that contains a protein complex. For a total makeover, you can also have your face made up and your hair and nails done.

Another big attraction of Palm-Aire is the gourmet cuisine. The spa dining room menu includes a full range of appetizers, entrees, salads, light snacks, and desserts. Spanish omelete, vegetable pizza, stuffed chicken, rack of lamb, fresh Maine lobster, and chocolate mocha mousse are some of the favorite calorie-controlled gourmet treats that keep guests coming back to Palm-Aire. Food preparation classes are conducted in the Spa lounge demonstration kitchen; the take-home packet includes a cookbook with spa recipes for preparation at home. Your accommodations are spacious with huge closets, a separate dressing alcove, private terrace, and an oversized bed. There are 191 superior and deluxe one- and two-bedroom accommodations, each with a private terrace and many with two bathrooms.

There is a variety of packages available to suit every whim. The Relaxation and Beauty Programs are chock full of personal services. The three-night package includes daily use of all facilities, including the racquetball and squash courts; three 45-minute massages, a marine algae body wrap, and hydrotherapy tub treatment; a Thalgo-mince body contour mask and hydrotherapy tub; a facial, a Frigi-Thalgo body wrap, and hydrotherapy tub; a skin analysis and cleansing; hot oil treatment and scalp massage; shampoo and set; makeup instruction, manicure, and pedicure; lectures in life-style modification, stress management, and nutrition; personal locker and daily spa wardrobe; green's fees and unlimited tennis, and roundtrip transportation from Ft. Lauderdale airport. The seven-night package includes even more goodies.

GUEST FEEDBACK
People from all walks of life have basked in the luxury of Palm-Aire. Many would return to take part in the weight-loss programs and to indulge themselves in pampering body treatments. Dieters were happiest with the menu.

Rates

		Double
Jan.–April	*Single*	*(per person)*
7-Night Full Spa Program	$2,534	$2,037
3-Night Relaxation and Beauty Program	$1,158	$945
3-Night Mini-Spa Program	$1,092	$879
May and Oct.–Dec. 15		
7-Night Full Spa Program	$2,352	$1,932
3-Night Relaxation and Beauty Program	$1,080	$900
3-Night Mini-Spa Program	$1,014	$834

June–Sept.

7-Night Full Spa Program	$2,142	$1,806
3-Night Relaxation & Beauty Program	$990	$780
3-Night-Mini Spa Program	$924	$780

There is a three-night minimum stay.

The Phoenix Fitness Resort $$$$ LUX, FB-RH

111 North Post Oak Lane
Houston, Texas 77024
(800)548-4700 (Nationwide)
(800)548-4701 (in Texas)
(713)680-1601 (in Texas)

Nestled on a 22-acre former private estate in the city of Houston, The Phoenix's grounds are shared by the Houstonian Health and Fitness Club and Houstonian Medical Center. But once on the tranquil grounds forested with beautiful trees, seasonal flowers, and flowering bushes, you will forget that you're just a short distance from city bustle and smog.

This luxury health resort caters to the body, mind, and spirit. With only 18 or so guests to attend to, the staff at The Phoenix can really focus on your individual needs—health and fitness, stress management, or even a total image makeover. Physicians are on call 24 hours a day.

Catering mostly to women (men, couples, and teenagers also visit The Phoenix during special weeks), The Phoenix is the place to go for a healthy boost to your self-image. Professionals will expose you to the benefits of exercise and sound nutrition for relieving stress. Enjoy a tightly scheduled and challenging program that utilizes Powercize—computerized machines that greet you by name and keep tabs on calories you burned while exercising.

At The Phoenix, a fitness program is prepared specifically for you based on findings from a series of tests administered upon arrival. You're given a body composition test, private consultations on your current fitness activity and life style, plus strength, flexibility, and cardiovascular evaluations. A blood analysis to determine cholesterol and triglyceride levels, a urine analysis, glucose analysis, and foot exam are all used to devise a fitness and life-style plan that you can take home. Stretch and tone classes, high-energy, but low-impact aerobics, and soothing water exercises are among the many activities scheduled at The Phoenix. David pneumatic weight-training units, stationary bikes, Universal weight-training gym, free weights, racquetball and tennis courts, an eight-lane lap pool, an indoor track, and an outdoor trail are at your disposal during your stay. In addition, there is European-style massage therapy, a whirlpool, steam room, sauna, and Swiss showers. Before leaving for home, make appointments at the beauty salon for such pampering services as a facial, makeup application and consultation, skin analysis, manicure, pedicure, and hair care.

Lectures and discussions on life-style management, fashion, eating disorders, healthy cooking, nutrition, self-defense, investments and business, entertaining, flower arranging, hypnotherapy, and art and decoration add another dimension to your spa vacation. You can also receive private consultations on fashion ideas and addictions.

The Phoenix views diet as a primary way to reward and re-energize yourself. Whether you seek to shed pounds or simply cleanse and purify your system with a healthful regimen, The Phoenix helps you reach your goals. Their 1,000-calorie-per-day meals are high in complex carbohydrates, lean protein, and minimal fats. There is no added caffeine, sugar, or salt.

Private accommodations for spa guests are located in a wing of the 300-room Houstonian Hotel. Luxury single rooms have cable television and private bath. There is also a lounge for spa guests where decaffeinated coffee and tea are always available. Your personal laundry is done daily, and the spa provides your wardrobe, including caftans which many guests wear to dinner, although jeans are acceptable, too.

The Phoenix offers a six-night Ultimate Week package that includes accommodations, three meals and snacks daily, unlimited use of all spa facilities and classes, and an in-depth medical screening, plus daily massage, beauty treatments, and lectures. There are also six-night Beauty, Fitness, and Basic packages to choose from.

GUEST FEEDBACK
Former guests found their vacations at The Phoenix rewarding in every way. They agreed unanimously that The Phoenix program's structure, presentation, and price are all right. They would return to The Phoenix themselves, and would recommend it to their friends.

Rates

	Single	Double *(per person)*
6-Night Ultimate Package	$3,200	$2,950
SUN ARR/SAT DEP		

6-Night Beauty Package SUN ARR/SAT DEP	$2,800	$2,550
6-Night Fitness Package SUN ARR/SAT DEP	$2,600	$2,350
6-Night Basic Package SUN ARR/SAT DEP	$2,000	$2,000

There is a six-night minimum stay.

Sheraton Bonaventure Hotel & Spa $$$ LUX, FB-RH

250 Racquet Club Road
Ft. Lauderdale, Florida 33326
(800)327-8090 (Nationwide)
(800)432-3063 (in Florida)
(305)389-3300 (in Florida)

Since its debut in January 1982, this luxury resort and spa has garnered a world-famous reputation for excellence. Eddie Murphy, Linda Evans, Eddie Van Halen, and the infamous Zsa Zsa Gabor have walked through its doors. You, too, can be among "the beautiful people" who come for the first-class quality and sheer quantity of services that Bonaventure offers.

Although Bonaventure is also one of the largest spa facilities in the world, don't let the crowd (guest population in the spa is about 110, co-ed) or the size intimidate you. Here you'll be treated to a total fitness and nutrition program custom-tailored to your special needs. Guests are encouraged to have a medical screening by the resident physician or nurses. A body-composition analysis and intensive training on the Keiser weight-training machines give each guest a computerized nutrition profile and an individual exercise workout routine.

Once through testing, a schedule of suggested fitness activities is posted on your locker. The ultramodern facilities include separate fitness facilities for women and men. Each has an outdoor exercise pool and sundeck; gymnasium with Paramount equipment; saunas; and steam rooms. There are individual whirlpools, hot- and cold-plunge pools, Swiss needle showers, and private massage rooms, locker areas, and siesta rooms. In addition, there is a co-ed gym and exercise pool. Three levels of aerobic conditioning are offered in a dozen different classes that range from easy stretches and energizing routines to deep-toning calisthenics. There are cardiovascular exercises for men only and body-conditioning and contouring classes just for women. Plus, the spa provides gym togs, robes, towels, and toiletries.

When it comes to pampering body treatments, Bonaventure has it all. Both men and women can indulge themselves in the pleasures of an herbal wrap, massage, salt-glo loofa scrub, and the services of a Lancome beauty center. Bonaventure also boasts a repertoire of hydrotherapy. Plus, there is a beauty salon and barber shop with a full line of hair- and nail-care services. Recreational facilities include a 51-stall equestrian center, a bowling alley, roller skating rink, 2 championship golf courses, and 23 tennis courts.

Bonaventure has its own spa dining room, so it isn't necessary to change for meals. The menu offers a wide choice of options and gives the calorie count for each item. There is also the Renaissance Seafood Grill, the informal Garden Restaurant, a poolside snack bar, and a Terrace Bar with a full range of libations, dancing, and live entertainment nightly. The Players Lounge is a combination night spot and game room with cocktails and video games.

As one would expect, the accommodations are luxurious. There are 493 guest rooms and suites in four nine-story buildings. Rooms are spacious with balconies that overlook the lake or golf course, an oversized bath and dressing area, plus all the amenities of a luxury hotel.

There are a host of two-, four-, and seven-night packages. Each includes accommodations, meals, use of all spa facilities, fitness classes, massages, herbal wraps, lectures, seminars, and demonstrations. Guests also have access to the Bonaventure Country Club, Racquet Club, Saddle Club, and Towne Center.

GUEST FEEDBACK

Many guests to the Bonaventure have consistently rated it as excellent or very good for its facilities, location (although it is not near the beach), and services. The staff, in particular, were cited as wonderful and caring. Almost all guests thought the program was well structured and well priced. A couple of guests, who visited for the day, thought it was a bargain. Both men and women would return to Bonaventure and would recommend it to their friends.

Rates

	Single	Double (per person)
Jan. 3–April 16		
2-Night Spa Sampler	$549	$439
4-Night Executive Spa Experience	$1,349	$1,075

7-Night Complete Spa Retreat	$2,250	$1,795
10-Night Lifestyle Enhancer	$3,495	$2,695

Apr. 17–May 25 and Sept. 24–Dec. 31

2-Night Spa Sampler	$495	$395
4-Night Executive Spa Experience	$1,215	$967
7-Night Complete Spa Retreat	$2,025	$1,615
10-Night Lifestyle Enhancer	$3,145	$2,425.50

May 26–Sept. 23

2-Night Spa Sampler	$380	$315
4-Night Executive Spa Experience	$796	$716
7-Night Comple Spa Retreat	$1,393	$1,253
10-Night Lifestyle Enhancer	$2,446	$1,890

There is a two-night minimum stay and any-day arrival.

WEIGHT-LOSS SPAS

The Aerobics Center Guest Lodge $$$$ WL

12230 Preston Road
Dallas, Texas 75230
(800)527-0362

The programs offered by the Aerobics Center emphasize weight-loss, nutrition, and exercise education; stress management; smoking cessation; and preventive and therapeutic medicine for total well-being. Upon completion of the program, a post-test allows you to assess your progress and plan your life-style strategies for the future. You'll receive personal attention from nine full-time physicians, plus nutritionists, exercise instructors, and even a dentist.

The main part of the program is the extensive series of medical examinations that guests receive at the Cooper Clinic. The Type I Preventive Medicine Exam, which participants of the three-night program undergo, includes your medical history, examination of the cardiopulmonary system; maximal performance treadmill exercise with multi-lead ECG monitoring; blood pressure measurements during exercise and recovery; recommendations regarding abnormal findings; exercise prescription; and test results for patient-physician consultations. Additional medical testing includes underwater weighing and skinfold tests to determine ideal body weight; blood specimen drawn for 24 different analyses, including HDL and LDL cholesterol levels; and a nutritional assessment.

The 20 participants in each 7- and 13-day aerobics program receive a Type II Preventive Medicine Exam at the Cooper Clinic, which includes all of the above, plus a psychological test; dental and oral exam; two blood analyses for 24 tests, including HDL and LDL cholesterol levels; hearing and vision tests; pulmonary function tests; urinalysis; chest x-ray; proctosigmodscopy for patients over 40; and screening for glaucoma.

Regardless of the program you choose, your days will be divided into physical activity and group discussions, seminars, and films on health-related issues. There are four scheduled exercise sessions each day. Based on your prescription, you may walk or jog on the indoor and outdoor trails; work out on the treadmill or stationary bikes; swim, play tennis, or take tone and flexibility classes or do exercises in the pool. There are indoor and outdoor tracks, two lap pools, four tennis courts, four racquetball courts, and a complete line of Nautilus equipment for weight training.

The rest of the day is spent in classes on topics such as "Preventive Medicine and You;" "Exercise Physiology, Precautions, Training and Prescription;" "Nutrition: The Facts;" "Hypertension;" and "Scheduling Your New Lifestyle." Films cover topics such as caffeine, low-fat dining, and the psychology of winning. The evening hours are at your leisure with a massage, evening walk, whirlpool bath, steam room, or sauna visit at your disposal.

Three nutritious meals, low in fat, cholesterol, and sodium, and high in fiber, are served daily in the Center Table or the Colonnade Restaurant. Men are portioned 1,200 calories per day, while women have to make do on 1,000. The 30-acre Colonial setting has 32 guest rooms and 8 suites with king- or queen-sized beds and wing chairs. The Aerobics Center Guest Lodge is billed as one of the finest in Dallas.

The Center runs four-night and one- and two-week programs geared toward total well-being. The longer your stay, the more information and practice you'll have with your new life style. Each program participant receives either a Type I or Type II medical exam, accommodations, meals, complete use of the facilities, daily exercise sessions, massage, and lectures. In addition, guests receive a 350-page program workbook and *The Aerobics Program for Total Well-Being* by Dr. Kenneth Cooper, president and founder of the Center and one of the pioneers of modern aerobic exercises who has au-

thored several books on the subject. All guests also receive a program t-shirt, telephone follow-up one month after finishing the program, and a one-year subscription to the monthly *Aerobics News*,
plus the quarterly in-residence program newsletter. Guests of the
two-week program also receive a bread-making class, supermarket-
shopping class, massage demonstration, and dinner at the Colonnade Restaurant. Your health insurance may cover some of the
costs; check with your agent.

GUEST FEEDBACK
People who visited the Center were serious about their health, losing
weight, and improving the quality of their lives. They found that the
facilities and education offered by the Center really armed them to
meet their goals. Guests also rated the extensive medical examinations and individual medical attention as a very rewarding experience. The staff and facilities rated very high. Many guests would
return, perhaps for a longer stay, and they would definitely recommend it to friends.

Rates

	Single	*Double* *(per person)*
4-Night Aerobics Wellness Weekend WED ARR/SUN DEP	$1,461–1,652	$1,309–1,372
7-Night Aerobics Program for Total Well-Being SUN ARR/SUN DEP	$2,695–3,073	$2,429–2,583
13-Night Aerobics Program for Total Well-Being SUN ARR/SAT DEP	$3,895–4,597	$3,401–3,687

There is a four-night minimum stay.

Bermuda Inn Fitness and Reducing Resort $ WL, FB-SC

43019 Sierra Highway
Lancaster, California 93534
(800)328-3276 (in California)
(805)942-1493 (in California)

In the sun-drenched desert sits this casual weight-loss retreat and one of the least expensive getaways in its class. For those with just a few hard-to-lose pounds as well as those who are severely overweight, the Bermuda Inn has undergone a complete facelift and is now more inviting than ever.

Worry and stress are prohibited at the Bermuda Inn, but movement is encouraged for the 30 co-ed guests. After your fitness level is determined by a certified instructor, choose among the 11 aerobics classes held daily or aqua-dynamics in either the indoor or outdoor pools (both are heated). In addition, there are toning-with-light-weights, "sit and fit," and dance classes. For folks who like to work out solo, there are treadmills, rowing machines, stationary bikes, and free weights. Sports activities include two lighted tennis courts (lessons are available), volleyball, basketball, badminton, croquet, and Ping-Pong. And, no matter what shape you're in, everyone can take advantage of the half-mile, lakeside walking track.

For soothing and pampering, the Bermuda Inn offers some innovative choices. In addition to Swedish massage and reflexology sessions, guests can have an acumassage or use the vibrosauna and the suntanning bed. The full-service salon offers facials, waxing, and hand- and nail-care services.

As a successful weight-loss facility, food and behavior modification are emphasized. Three calorie-controlled, low-sodium meals and two vegetable snacks are served daily, plus there is a beverage bar. You choose between 700 and 900 calories per day, with food choices such as crepes, lasagna, and quiche. Bermuda Inn's gourmet chefs create a variety of tantalizing meals with fish, lean beef, turkey, and chicken. The resort says you can lose up to a pound a day. Group behavior modification classes, which are part of the program, will teach you how to manage your life style and control your weight. Hypnotherapy and private consultations on yoga, holistic health, eating disorders, and eating patterns and habits are available by appointment and range in price from $25 to $30 per hour.

Before retiring to the guest rooms, which are available in single, double, and triple occupancy and feature private bath, air conditioning, and color television, guests can enjoy evening entertainment such as movies, board games, fashion shows, and talent shows.

As a weight-loss facility, the Bermuda Inn encourages long-term visits and does so with a very affordable price. The all-inclusive cost covers your accommodations, meals, fitness program and use of all facilities, including tennis, both pools, Jacuzzis, co-ed sauna, and lectures. Other services are modestly priced, with a 60-minute massage and reflexology session costing $40 and a 30-minute accumassage, $8.

GUEST FEEDBACK

Most people found their stay at the Bermuda Inn "rewarding in every way," so much so that they stayed longer than they had originally planned. The facilities, salon services, and meals rated excellent, and the program itself was said to be well structured and priced. All would recommend it to their friends.

Rates

	Single	*Double* *(per person)*
Per Night	$144	$99

There is no minimum stay and any-day arrival. Nightly rates apply.

The Charleston Retreat Weight Management Center $$ WL

171 Ashley Avenue
Charleston, South Carolina 29425
(800)553-7489 (Nationwide)
(803)792-2273 (in South Carolina)

If successful weight management is your goal, treat yourself to a new beginning in one of America's oldest and most beautiful cities—Charleston. The Charleston Retreat is the site of the Medical University of South Carolina's 28-day weight-management program. Developed by obesity specialists, the program's focus is on individualized weight control, exercise, and life-style change.

The natural beauty of Charleston's scenic parks and beaches provides a wonderful backdrop for the Center's pleasure/fitness program. There are regularly scheduled walks around the city's historic district and other points of interest, such as the famous homes and gardens of South Carolina's low country. An exercise physiologist will measure your present fitness level and help you develop a specially tailored exercise prescription that you can adhere to and enjoy. Several times a week guests join other University patients for monitored workouts at a nearby exercise facility with bicycle ergometers, indoor walking-jogging track, weight machines, and a 25-meter indoor pool. The Center itself offers low-impact aerobics classes and aquatic activities, plus bowling and dancing. When you leave, you'll take with you a review of your progress as well as a plan for continued exercising at home.

Upon arrival, you receive a comprehensive personal nutritional assessment based on your typical eating patterns. The registered dietician will then design a meal plan to meet your specific needs and tastes. During your stay, you select from a menu of delicious low-cal foods. Fresh seafood, vegetarian entrees, and a variety of ethnic cuisines and low-cal versions of down-home Southern meals are featured. And, you'll learn how these dishes are prepared and can take the recipes home with you. You'll also develop the nutritional knowledge and food-preparation skills—through seminars, workshops, individual counseling, plus hands-on cooking classes—that will benefit you for a lifetime. Other activities include visiting supermarkets to learn new buying strategies, and dining in Charleston restaurants to practice strategies for eating out.

A wide variety of housing options are available in the Charleston area, but they are not included in the program. Lodging rates vary during the tourist season, which runs from March through June in town and June through August for beach accommodations. Weight Management Center participants may be able to take advantge of special monthly rates. Your tuition fee does cover meals, intensive educational program, daily supervised exercise program, medical evaluation, nutritional assessment, and follow-up plan.

GUEST FEEDBACK
Guests of The Charleston Retreat were pleased with their new lifestyle changes and the program itself. They especially enjoyed the individual counsultations and the chance to visit an exciting city.

Rates

	Per Person
27-Night Program	$2,950
SUN ARR/SAT DEP	

There is a 27-night minimum stay.

Deerfield Manor $ WL, FB-SC
R. D. #1 Route 402
East Stroudsburg, Pennsylvania 18301
(717) 223-0160

This mountain retreat was voted one of the "12 Best New Spas" in the country when it opened in 1987, and it is still a good choice for spagoers. Limited to 33 co-ed guests, owner-director Frieda Eisenkraft offers personalized exercise and nutrition programs, group activities, and loads of support.

The fitness options here include daily aerobics classes and body-conditioning workouts, calisthenics, swimming exercises, yoga, and relaxation techniques. Plus, there are organized walks and a heated outdoor pool. The program also includes massages and behavior modification through group discussions on methods of weight control and exercise that you can follow when you return home.

Guests come here to lose weight, and to do so, they get to choose one of three diets: water fasting consisting of approximately 64 ounces of fresh well water daily; juice fasting on approximately 350 calories per day of freshly squeezed fruit and vegetable juices; or low-cal gourmet cuisine from an extensive calorie-controlled menu. You get to select meals according to your individual caloric requirements. Lodging is in designer-decorated rooms with deluxe bathrooms and individually controlled air conditioning. Rooms are quaint with an air of country elegance—bed ruffles, canopies, and rocking chairs.

During your free time, there's plenty to do. You can browse in the book and music libraries, view films from the video library, attend low-cal cooking classes, or socialize in one of the three informal lounges. Nearby there are indoor and outdoor tennis courts, antique markets, three summer theaters, golf courses, ice and roller skating rinks, horseback riding, and several discos and night clubs. You can even paddle down the Delaware River in a canoe.

The seven-night program includes your accommodations, choice of diets, body toning and exercise classes, yoga, and a half-hour massage.

GUEST FEEDBACK

Many satisfied clients have been to Deerfield. Most found their stay rewarding and enjoyed the unstructured environment. They do, however, recommend driving or renting a car for the vacation because of all the nearby attractions. Most really enjoyed the loads of free time they had to simply unwind and get in touch with themselves.

Rates

		Double
Apr. 29–Oct. 30	*Single*	*(per person)*
7-Night Program	$715–810	$595–675

SUN ARR/SUN DEP

There is a two-night minimum stay. The spa is closed from November through April.

Duke University Diet and Fitness $$$ WL
Center

804 West Trinity Avenue
Durham, North Carolina 27701
(919)684-6331

On the campus of Duke University, this world-famous center takes long-term weight loss very seriously, offering proven strategies for success through total life-style changes. This medically supervised program includes extensive medical, behavioral, nutritional, and fitness components, as well as some relaxation activities. In addition, you will have access to other departments and specialty clinics at Duke University Medical Center.

Upon arrival at the center, the 100 spa participants can receive a detailed health assessment based on their medical history, a physical exam, and a series of tests designed to identify health problems. Exercise, always a part of good health, is encouraged. There is a modified floor aerobics class in the gym, as well as an aquatics class in the pool. In addition, there are stationary bikes and a jogging track, plus all the campus facilities.

Behavior modification is an integral part of this program, which is designed to promote self-management through understanding. To this end, group discussions, workshops, and seminars are held to help guests become more aware of eating and exercise patterns and their relationship to your personality and life style. Individual therapy, available upon request and for an additional cost, is encouraged for participants to explore the emotional aspects of overeating and other difficulties in controlling their weight. The behavioral component emphasizes the importance of long-term commitment to change and realistic expectations about your progress. Much of the day is spent in these classes.

Nutrition, as well, plays an important role in weight loss and management, and Duke plays it up. The center attempts to establish and reinforce a pattern of eating appropriate and nutritious food at regularly scheduled mealtimes. To reinforce this, there are a series of lectures and seminars that give you the nutritional knowledge and awareness to make good choices. A calorie count is given for each menu selection, which may include a breakfast of an omelete florentine with a slice of whole wheat bread and a teaspoon of margarine. For lunch, 200 calories will feed you a stir fry of vegetables and shrimp, plus peaches and vanilla yogurt for dessert. A sample dinner entree may include roast barbecued pork with caraway cabbage, green peas, and a baked apple for dessert. There are alternative selections for each meal.

To help you with cooking at home, the chefs at the center have created a 289-page manual that you can purchase during your stay.

Packages run in two- and four-week programs, but do not include accommodations. The program fee does include three meals daily, initial laboratory fees, treadmill testing, educational classes, and full use of the facilities. And, because it is a medically supervised program, your health insurance may cover some of the costs.

GUEST FEEDBACK
Guests of the center found Duke's active and beautiful campus a most enjoyable and interesting place to take a rewarding "health holiday." Although the odds are they won't need to, they would make a return visit for this intensive program.

Rates

	Single
2-Week Package	$2,600
4-Week Package	$3,300

There is a two-week minimum stay.

Evergreen Manor $ WL, MS

P.O. Box 1154
Hot Springs National Park, Arkansas
(501)262-2344

This rustic estate, located near the therapeutic waters of Hot Springs, welcomes guests anxious to renew their health, lose weight, and even quit smoking. Many guests report dramatic reductions in blood pressure and heart rate. In many cases, too, guests report a substantial improvement in diabetic conditions, hypoglycemia, and ulcers due to the healthful diet and relaxing, albeit intensive, program administered here.

The week-long program focuses on proper rest, detoxification through a supervised fast, and bathing in the 100-degree (Fahrenheit) waters of the hot springs. Each guest is given a consultation to determine the best way to reduce his or her weight. Yoga, thermal baths, stress reduction, iridology, deficiency testing and evaluation, facials, and massages are part of the program; guests can also rent bikes for the miles of trails through the park. Other options include a therapeutic massage, colonic, and additional facials, manicures, and pedicures. For physical activity, there are stationary bikes and a trampoline; there's also an indoor pool and a lake nearby.

To help guests detox their bodies and shed pounds, the spa serves three vegetarian meals daily, consisting mainly of raw fruits and vegetables and all the spring water you want. Accommodating a maximum of 12 men and women, there are seven bedrooms in the manor house with a mixture of old and new furnishings and shared baths.

The program runs for one, two, three, and four weeks and includes your accommodations, meals, juices, fasting, consultation, evaluation, lectures, thermal bath, massage, facial, and exercise classes and equipment.

GUEST FEEDBACK

Former guests had favorable reviews of Evergreen Manor, citing the staff's personal attention as a real plus. They all considered it a very restful place to de-stress and shed pounds, and were glad that exercise wasn't the center of activity. They enjoyed their space and lots of free time to simply unwind.

Rates

	Single	Double (per person)
Jan. 1–Mar. 31		
7-Night Program	$795	$595
14-Night Program	$1,295	$1,050
21-Night Program	$1,795	$1,425
Apr. 1–Dec. 31		
7-Night Program	$895	$695
14-Night Program	$1,450	$1,250
21-Night Program	$2,095	$1,650

There is a two-night minimum stay. All programs are Sunday arrival to Sunday departure. Special discounts are available for four-week stays.

Green Mountain at Fox Run $$ WL, FB-SC

Box 164 Fox Lane
Ludlow, Vermont 05149
(802)228-8885

This secluded life-style-management center caters exclusively to women who are serious about losing anywhere from 20 to 200 pounds. Not technically a spa, but rather an educational and exercise facility, women from 50 states and 30 foreign countries have sought the guidance of director Thelma Wayler in their weight-loss efforts.

According to a follow-up study of Green Mountain's guests, an astounding 54 percent of the program's graduates lost weight and managed either to keep it off or reduce further, even five years after their stay. The program that Wayler created more than 16 years ago is based on the no-nonsense premise of behavior modification and education—that motivated and informed women will make the changes necessary to promote health and well-being. Most of Green Mountain's guests range in age from 20 to 40. About a third are extremely overweight, about a third are close to normal, and the rest fall somewhere in between.

Medically supervised by nutritionists, exercise physiologists, and behaviorists, guests begin to examine the many complex facets and issues of their weight problems. Then, they devise and practice strategies for dealing with them. There's some physical work involved, as well. After a healthy complex-carbohydrate-loaded breakfast in the dining room, guests get revved up with a brisk, hour-long walk. Discussions and workshops on the latest in nutrition, exercise, and behavioral information are interspersed with exercise sessions featuring popular dance movements, aerobics, light weights, and body-conditioning techniques. Cross-country skiing and snowshoeing in the crisp Vermont air are also available in season. In addition, there is a sauna, outdoor bikes, a swimming pool, and golfing. To ease muscles, you can also have a Swedish massage, facial, or stint in the sauna.

At mealtimes, you'll soon learn that food is not an enemy. In fact, you will be required to eat three meals a day—a salad plate, a pita bread sandwich, cottage cheese and fruit, and moussaka for dinner, for instance—consisting of between 1,000 and 1,200 total calories. You'll also get to nibble pizza, ice cream, peanuts, and pancakes. There are no waiters in the dining room. During the daily cooking class, the nutritionist-chef introduces you to the basics of healthy cooking and even helps you transform your favorite recipes to meet your health and dietary needs, while maintaining their treasured flavors. You'll also get to visit local restaurants to practice ordering foods that are low in sodium, sugar, fat, cholesterol, and calories.

Accommodations are homey, albeit Spartan. Guests supply their own towels, wash cloths, and toiletries and make their own beds. (A maid does change the linens and clean the room once a week). You also do your own laundry—so don't forget the Woolite—or pay to have it done in town (which is costly and a hassle). A maximum of 65 women are accommodated in the 26 single, double, and duplex (accommodating four people) rooms. All have their own baths.

The medically supervised program runs on one-, two-, three-, and four-week schedules. If you are referred by your personal physician for treatment of high blood pressure or other weight-related health problems, your health insurance plan may cover some of the costs. Health insurance forms consistent with eligibility will be completed. Green Mountain tuition fees may be tax deductible under the heading "Health Institute Fees." Green Mountain requests that guests bring with them a letter of approval from their doctor, medical history, and the results of a recent physical examination. However, if medical care or special evaluation are necessary, referral will be made by the staff doctor. Smoking is allowed in designated areas at Green Mountain, but the use of alcohol is not.

Your tuition covers just about everything: accommodations, meals, comprehensive weight and health life-style program, all instructional classes, use of all facilities, individual and group counseling sessions, airport or bus station transfers, taxes, and gratuities.

GUEST FEEDBACK
Surveyed guests find themselves among the many satisfied and trimmer alumnae of Green Mountain. They found their experience very rewarding, well-priced, and informative, and would recommend it to a friend who might be severely overweight.

Rates

	Single	Double (per person)
6-Night Program SUN ARR/SAT DEP	$1,500	$1,230
13-Night Program SUN ARR/SAT DEP	$3,200	$2,600–2,900
27-Night Program SUN ARR/SAT DEP	$5,500	$4,100–4,800

There is a six-night minimum stay.

Green Valley Health Resort and Spa $$ WL, FB-RH
1515 West Canyon View Drive
St. George, Utah 84770

(800)237-1068 (Nationwide)
(800)654-7760 (in Utah)

This luxury resort spa, located in Utah's canyon country, focuses on eating to lose—from 10 to 100 pounds. A medically supervised weight-loss facility about two hours from the glamour of Las Vegas, Green Valley offers a relaxed, yet intensive five-part weight-loss and fitness program.

The fitness part of the program is as varied as they come. Workout enthusiasts can participate in aerobics, aquatics, cycling, and swimming. Personal exercise training is conducted by the exercise director Michael Onstad, a former dancer and well-known teacher of dancers, athletes, and martial artists. Training sessions are designed for rebalancing and reshaping the body, emphasizing correct posture and body mechanics, and using slow exercises and breathing techniques to increase your sense of power. Additional exercise training is conducted by Roy Fitzell, former director of dance at the University of California, Irvine. There are 15 outdoor and 4 indoor tennis courts, volleyball, shuffleboard, lawn chess, and basketball. For those guests (15 to 20) who prefer the great outdoors to a gym, there are hiking expeditions on the trails and past the caverns and waters of Zion National Park, Snow Canyon State Park, Pine Valley Mountain, and the Virgin River Narros. Other outings might include hiking or riding horseback to ancient Indian petroglyphs and archaeological digs; an excursion to the North Rim of the Grand Canyon; fishing in the waters of the desert; or bathing in the mineral springs and pools of Pah Temple. Special aerobic tennis training from the staff of the Vic Braden Tennis College is provided, and a putting green next door is available. Private tennis lessons and group and private golf lessons can be arranged.

Green Valley's Oasis Spa offers a host of body and beauty services. Relax your mind and create a new image of the way your body looks and feels with a powdered-pearl body rub and bath treatment in which the body is submerged in mineral water, herbal tinctures, or flower extractions, and then gently rubbed with tiny crystalline particles and powdered pearls. As a finishing touch the body is sprayed with a fine oil mist, leaving you feeling soft and glowing, relaxed yet invigorated. A unique combination of massage styles to improve circulation of both blood and lymph, facials, and hand and foot reflexology massages are also available.

Training sessions in makeup artistry, skin care for a daily regimen, color therapy, and tension-attention control, and individual workshops in ward-robing teach you to make the best of your new look. Topics include planning a wardrobe tailored for your life style, power dressing, finding the perfect fit and evaluating your wardrobe needs.

Of course, food is an important element of the program. Meals are prepared and served in the dining room. The spa menus, including all sauces and seasonings, are created from scratch by Green Valley chef Howard Gifford, author of *Gifford Gourmet Delites* cookbook. Fresh fruits, vegetables, and herbs substitute for high-sugar, high-fat foods. Guests are invited to watch the chef prepare meals and he will provide recipes to all. He also teaches cooking classes and takes guests shopping with him. He even shows how to order from any menu and still avoid fats and sugar. For breakfast, try whole wheat pancakes with raspberry compote or maple syrup and turkey or ham; lunch may be a tasty chicken a la king with toast points, brown rice pilaf, and honeydew melon. For dinner, begin with a salad followed by Swiss steak in sauce, mashed potatoes, and fresh steamed broccoli, topped with banana-pineapple pudding. Plus, there are snacks in your room.

All accommodations are private luxury condominiums or shared units with private rooms and bath. All units have kitchens, living rooms, and balconies. Some even have a private Jacuzzi on the sun deck.

Green Valley runs six-night packages that include your accommodations, meals, and snacks; personalized program with classes on nutrition, fitness, and stress; exercise classes; five half-hour massages, facial, makeover, and manicure.

GUEST FEEDBACK
Guests were delighted with their stay at Green Valley, citing the warm and supportive staff as a major highlight. They were also impressed by the beauty and natural wonders of the area. They thought Green Valley was well priced and structured and all would return.

Rates

	Single	Double (per person)
6-Night Program	$1,195	$1,095
SUN ARR/SAT DEP		

There is a six-night minimum stay.

Hilton Head Health Institute $$ WL
P.O. Box 7138
Hilton Head Island, South Carolina 29938
(803)785-7292

At one of the world's premier resorts you can reap the benefits of a medically supervised weight-control program designed for increased fitness, enhanced mental and physical stamina, and reduced hypertension. Dr. Peter Miller is executive director of this health education center, and from his program of behavior modification, sound nutrition, and serious exercise have come such bestselling books as *The Hilton Head Metabolism Diet* and *The Hilton Head Executive Stamina Program*.

Behavior modification techniques are taught and emphasized on a daily basis so that the Institute's 40 or so guests learn how to maintain new habit patterns. Clients are encouraged to practice them step-by-step during their stay. The behavior modification process involves evaluating your current health habits, setting goals for change, developing a personal behavior change plan, overcoming self-defeating thought patterns, dealing more effectively with external influences on habits, and developing positive alternatives to old habit patterns.

Each participant receives a medical screening that includes physical exam, lab tests, and a review of his or her medical history. A stress electrocardiogram may also be required to determine a safe level of physical activity. In addition, the program's physician meets with each guest to review and discuss the evaluation.

Physical activity is central to the Institute's programs and is considered essential for permanent health maintenance. An individualized fitness plan is developed for each guest who is then encouraged to proceed at his or her own pace. Typical exercise classes include activities such as walking, dancing, training with weights, calisthenics, and aquatics. Biking, swimming, tennis, and golf are also available to complement the basic fitness program.

Meals are based on a sound, healthy, and well-balanced nutritional plan, the principles of which are moderate protein, high complex carbohydrates, low fat, low sodium, and low cholesterol. Guests work with the staff to plan a healthy nutritional program that they can continue once they leave. There are also small group seminars and demonstrations so that you learn the nutritional concepts that help you to make choices that promote good health. You also learn to prepare tasty, nutritional meals, as well as techniques for dealing with business luncheons, holidays, restaurant dining, and travel.

The Hilton Head Health Institute is located at The Cottages in Shipyard Plantation. Guests have lodging in spacious, completely furnished condominium-style villas within walking distance of the Institute, beach, tennis courts, swimming pools, and biking and walking paths. Guests may share a villa with another client, but each has his or her private bedroom and bath. Single-occupancy accommodations are also available.

The Institute offers two comprehensive programs: the Weight Control Program and the Executive Health Program. Both are designed around the concept that good health is dependent on the establishment of a sensible life style. All programs are carefully supervised and include a prescribed diet, exercise regimen, and a combination of workshops and seminars on health education, nutrition, self-management, and habit control. They also include two areas of instruction, one for bulemics and one for those who want to stop smoking. Another key element of the Institute's long-term success is its yearlong follow-up program. Participants can call staff members whenever they need consultation. Special refresher courses are offered to graduates throughout the year to reinforce changes and prevent backsliding. A newsletter is also sent to former participants to keep them informed of the latest developments in relevant health fields at the Institute.

GUEST FEEDBACK
Former guests were quite pleased with their stay at the Institute, coming away from the experience with a renewed sense of confidence concerning their life style, and feeling refreshed by the relaxed atmosphere and natural beauty. They would return, if the need arose, and would recommend it to friends who would benefit from the experience.

Rates

	Single	*Double* *(per person)*
13-Night Program SUN ARR/SAT DEP	$2,700	$2,700
27-Night Program SUN ARR/SAT DEP	$4,200	$4,200

Living Springs Retreat $ WL, NA

Route 3, Bryant Pond Road
Putnam Valley, New York 10579
(914)526-2800

Welcoming people of all religions, Living Springs is a 68-acre Seventh Day Adventist retreat located in the foothills of the Berkshire Mountains. At this cheerful, homey, nonprofit center, the emphasis is on health education and behavior modification. And it tends to attract an older crowd.

With health promotion as its main theme, guests leave with life-enhancing strategies for improved consciousness, self-control, and self-awareness. The retreat offers intensive programs in stress control, weight management, heart rehabilitation, disease prevention, life-style improvement, cooking and nutrition, natural remedies, and smoking cessation.

To supplement the educational programs, there are exercise classes, stationary bikes, hydrotherapy, and a sauna. In addition, the retreat offers cross-country skiing and biking.

In the dining room overlooking the lake, you can enjoy sound nutrition with a wide variety of natural foods in a strict vegetarian menu. No red meat or dairy products are served. There are four single and four double guest rooms for a maximum of 12 guests. Upon request, Living Springs will match up single guests who want to take advantage of the double room rate.

Living Springs offers weekend, 7-, and 21-day programs. The weekend program includes accommodations only, while the week package covers accommodations, three vegetarian meals daily, use of facilities, exercise classes, massage, hydrotherapy, lectures, and cooking classes. The 21-day Conditioning Program provides a comprehensive approach to the treatment and prevention of chronic diseases such as heart disease, hypertension, diabetes and hypoglycemia, cancer, digestive disorders, and others. Participants in this program are supervised by a medical doctor on staff. Fortunately, too, many insurance companies will reimburse up to 50 percent of the cost of this program. All guests of Living Springs must first go through medical screening before being accepted into any of its programs.

GUEST FEEDBACK

We try to provide all the inside information we can when helping people select their spa vacations. Therefore, we make sure they know that Living Springs Retreat is a wonderful, moderately priced weight-control spa for people who are *serious* about their health, and who are looking for a way to add value to their vacation by giving themselves the gift of health. Rather than concentrating on exercise and fitness classes, this spa tends to focus more on health information. There are always some guests who comment on what they perceive to be the religious tone of the retreat. Others not only do not mind it, but they enjoy it. Depending on your current state of health and awareness, however, Living Springs could save your life.

Occasionally, we hear from our younger guests (ages 20–35), who naturally are less concerned with their state of health than older guests, that they felt discussions dwelled too much on disease, which they did not want to think about. We, therefore, recommend that you keep that in mind when selecting your spa.

Rates

	Single	*Double (per person)*
2-Night Program FRI ARR/SUN DEP	$80–100	$43–53
7-Night Program SUN ARR/SUN DEP	$679	$539

There is no minimum stay.

National Institute of Fitness $ WL,FB-SC

202 North Snow Canyon Road
P.O. Box H, Ivins, Utah 84738
(801)628-3317
(801)628-4338

Having overcome serious weight problems themselves, owner and founder Dr. Marcus Sorenson, director Vicki Sorenson, and general manager Jay Cooper know how to produce the same results for their guests. Depending on how much weight you need to lose and how long you stay, you may lose anywhere from 6 to 100 pounds. The Institute offers beautiful natural surroundings, unusual geodesic dome architecture, and an excellent fitness and weight-loss program—all at very inviting rates.

Obviously, physical fitness is the focus of the weight-loss program here. Your days will be spent walking and cycling in and around Snow Canyon, a prime attraction of Color Country where majestic canyon walls of red sandstone cradle the lava flows from the ancient Triassic period. In addition, you have stretching, toning, and body-contouring classes, swimnastics in the indoor heated pool, racquetball, tennis, and a mini-trampoline to play on. You'll also enjoy weight-training equipment and a cardiovascular training area with motorized treadmills and computerized exercise bicycles. Adjacent to the pool is the hydroswirl pool, which is similar to a Jacuzzi.

On the first day each guest is given a personal fitness evaluation, which includes tests of blood pressure, body composition, flexibility, and strength and your current weight. A cardiovascular endurance test is also used to evaluate your fitness level and to determine which group level you'll work in.

Regularly scheduled classes on weight control, nutrition, and fitness are an important part of the NIF program. Guests receive expert instruction on techniques that will help them maintain their slimmer bodies once they return home. The nutrition program is a low-fat, low-salt, and low-sugar diet consisting of three meals per day. Many of the guests experience dramatic reductions in blood pressure and heart rates during their stay. Lung volumes increase, muscles strengthen and tone, and joints become more flexible. In many cases, there have been substantial improvements in diabetic conditions, hypoglycemia, and ulcers due to the healthful diet and relaxing atmosphere of the NIF program. There are also classes in exercise physiology, high-fiber nutrition, the set point method of weight control, and stress management, and there's a registered nurse on staff.

All of the facilities, including accommodations, are housed in unique geodesic domes set against the red rock country. Modern, clean, and comfortable accommodations are available in single, double, triple, and quad. The spa accepts about 48 men and women per week. There are one-, two-, three-, and four-week programs that include just about everything NIF has to offer. Guests will need to send a medical release form from their doctor with their final payment, and may also want to bring a hobby or couple of good sagas to read since there is little, if any, nighttime entertainment.

GUEST FEEDBACK
Surveyed guests were all satisfied with NIF. One guest would recommend the place to a friend if he or she wanted "a great place to exercise and meet interesting people, varied in all aspects of age, religion, intelligence, and wealth." Another guest sums up the experience as "an outstanding facility that resulted in meeting all my objectives. Their staff is exceptional and 100 percent positive reinforcers." One guest wished "it were emphasized how most guests stay for longer periods than one week. To fully benefit from NIF, plan for a longer stay." The physical setting and location, facilities, meals, exercise program, and staff consistently rated excellent. But a few guests wished to share the importance of proper footwear for the many miles you will walk in red rock country.

Rates

	Single	*Double (per person)*
6-Night Program	$849	$614
13-Night Program	$1,599	$1,079

20-Night Program	$2,249	$1,504
27-Night Program	$2,799	$1,899

	Triple (per person)	Quad (per person)
6-Night Program	$494–514	$444–474
13-Night Program	$949–1,009	$789–849
20-Night Program	$1,294–1,374	$1,114–1,184
27-Night Program	$1,599–1,699	$1,399–1,499

There is a six-night minimum stay. All packages are Monday arrival and Sunday departure.

Pawling Health Manor $ WL

Box 401
Hyde Park, New York 12538
(914)889-4141

Director Joy Gross has motivated countless people through her many radio and television appearances, lectures, gourmet health food presentations, and her books, *Thin Again! Improved Fitness in 30 Days* and *The Vegetarian Child.* All told, she has created rejuvenation programs for upwards of 40,000 individuals over the past 25 years. Her health concepts combine vegetarianism and fasting with techniques of positive mental attitude and a healthy, productive life style. The bonus here is that you not only lose weight, but detoxify your body as well.

Pawling's main building is a Georgian mansion set atop a hill overlooking the Hudson River. The retreat, situated in the Mid-Hudson Valley, is close to historical sites such as Franklin D. Roosevelt Home and Library; the Vanderbilt, Ogden, and Astor estates; Vassar and Bard Colleges; Woodstock Village; the Beekman Arms Inn; Rhinebeck Village; and the Culinary Institute of America with its calorie-controlled gourmet restaurant. Facilities include solariums with showers for nude bathing, a heated pool, Jacuzzi, steam room, sauna, boutique, tennis and racquetball courts, nature trails, and an exercise area with Nautilus equipment. Massage therapy, gentle exercise classes, yoga meditation, tanning salon, and beauty services featuring Chanel products are also available.

This weight-loss spa specializes in fasting and detoxification. Dr. Robert Gross, Ph.D., is a biochemist and nutritionist who oversees and remedies any problems that might arise during a fast. Each qualifying guest's fasting regimen is determined individually, based on his or her health background and individual needs. For those who qualify, rational fasting, under supervision, allows for effective, safe weight loss, increased mental powers, better digestion, and physical rejuvenation. The Manor's fasting and low-calorie vegetarian eating regimen allows your cells to excrete toxic materials which clog your system and keep you from looking and feeling your best. Losing bloat, salt, and other toxins will dramatically improve your sense of well-being.

There are also educational programs consisting of daily workshops, discussions, and demonstrations, all designed to teach and motivate you so that weight loss and good eating habits will last a lifetime. Topics include nutrition, relaxation, exercise, detoxification, fasting, and food preparation. Pawling has also helped thousands of guests kick the smoking habit through its detoxification program.

Accommodations for guests of Pawling Manor are in the manor with either a connecting or hall bathroom; in a motel unit across the street; or in an annex, with private bath or hall bath. Meals can be served to you in your room. Televisions can be rented, and there is a big-screen television for all to view. All packages run for a week and include accommodations, three vegetarian meals and/or fast, exercise classes, use of facilities, lectures, and take-home educational materials.

GUEST FEEDBACK

Former visitors to Pawling Manor were serious about their health, particularly their diet and nutrition. Many guests come here just to experience the wonders of a supervised fast—to detox and get more spiritually attuned—in a nurturing and supportive environment. Guests praise the staff for their knowledge and concern, and rate the facilities as good.

Rates

	Single	Double (per person)
7-Night Package	$470–760	$470–760

There is a seven-night minimum stay and Sunday arrival and departure.

The Plantation Spa $$$ WL, FB-SC, NA

51-550 Kamehameha Highway
Kaawa, Hawaii 96730

(808)237-8442
(808)237-8685
(808)955-3727 (corporate offices)

Say "Aloha" to the peace and tradition of old Hawaii and the Swedish approach to health and natural living that awaits guests to this country estate. The island of Oahu's first health resort sits amid majestic volcanic mountains and the deep blue Pacific, offering a blend of Polynesian ambience and European know-how. The program here is based on the one from Sweden's renowned Halsohem-Masegarden Spa, with which The Plantation is affiliated.

Catering to only 14 guests per week, there is a very relaxed atmosphere conducive to the natural beauty that surrounds the resort. A typical day here begins with a scenic sunrise stretch and stroll along the beach. The rest of the day can be spent doing low-impact aerobics, weight training, yoga, canoeing, aquatics, or hiking. There are cooking classes, sailing, boating, and volleyball, plus weight machines, a rowing machine, and stationary bike. And the Jacuzzi sits right near a waterfall! While there are plenty of activities for those who just can't sit still, there's also plenty of time in the program to schedule your Shiatsu or Swedish massage, facial, and herbal wrap. Evenings can be spent doing arts and crafts or hula dancing.

Accommodations are in rustic cottages with eight guest rooms. Each has a private bath and is furnished with rattan chairs, double or king-size beds, and decorative Polynesian arts and crafts. There is no television, air conditioning, or telephone in the rooms. The cottages are clustered around a farm house where gourmet vegetarian meals are served. Fruits and vegetables come fresh from the spa's own garden. A European juice and broth fast are also available upon request.

Although the spa is billed as a weight-loss facility, there are no medical facilities on the premises and the spa will not accept guests with serious health, drug, or alcohol problems. The weeklong program includes accommodations, three gourmet vegetarian meals daily, exercise classes and lectures, canoe trips, hikes, cooking classes, a massage, and an herbal wrap. The Plantation Spa is 24 miles from the Honolulu International Airport and 26 miles from the Waikiki resort area. A taxi costs about $40 one way, or you can rent a car.

GUEST FEEDBACK

Guests reported having a very healthful and relaxing vacation at The Plantation Spa. They were pleased by the fitness evaluation and the individual attention they received on diet and nutrition. They were happy for the chance to de-stress in such picture-perfect natural beauty. All would return.

Rates

	Single	*Double (per person)*
6-Night Package	$1,550	$1,250

SUN ARR/SAT DEP
There is a six-night minimum stay.

Regency Health Resort $ WL, FB-SC

2000 South Ocean Drive
Hallandale, Florida 33009
(305)454-2220

Located on Florida's Gold Coast, this resort resembles a Swiss chalet and offers relaxation, fun, and weight loss. This is a place to overcome bad eating habits and learn new ways to take care of the mind, body, and spirit.

Emphasizing permanent weight loss, the spa stresses nutrition classes, counseling, and behavior modification. There are also exercise programs, including yoga; nonimpact, water, and regular aerobics; and stationary bikes to help. A walk along the oceanfront is not only good for the body, but beneficial to the mind and spirit, as well. Other relaxing activities available include swimming in the heated pool, soaking in the Jacuzzi, or sweating it out in the sauna. Massages, facials, and nail and hair care are here to soothe and beautify.

To insure weight loss, at least during your spa visit, a diet based on the principles of the "Fit for Life" philosophy is followed. It is a strict vegetarian diet, and there are no snacks or calorie counts. Juice and water fasting are also offered to those who wish to further detoxify their bodies while shedding pounds and inches. Lectures on nutrition, food preparation, and food combinations, plus wellness workshops round out the program.

Regency offers seven-night packages that include accommodations, three meals daily, all classes, counseling, exercises, use of facilities, skin care, and makeup consultation. The spa accepts between 25 and 30 guests and there's a choice of lodgings, from a motel room to a two-bedroom suite. All rooms have a private bath, color television, double beds, and a telephone. Some have an ocean view.

GUEST FEEDBACK

Many guests were pleased with their vacation at Regency and would return, although perhaps for a shorter stay. Many, too, felt the program was well structured and of good value. They would also recommend Regency to their friends, but would warn them that the food plan may be extreme, "even for a vegetarian."

Rates

	Single	*Double (per person)*
Jan. 1–Apr. 23		
7-Night Program	$845–1,240	$745–990
Apr. 24–Dec. 31		
7-Night Program	$745–945	$645–845

There is a seven-night minimum stay and any-day arrival.

Structure House $$ WL

3017 Pickett Road
Durham, North Carolina 27705
(919)688-7379

This comprehensive program is based on positive psychological treatment and strong emotional support, as well as customized exercise and diet. Under the direction of Dr. Gerard J. Mustante, a nationally recognized clinical psychologist and innovator of long-term weight control, Structure House offers over 100 weekly activities conducted in workshops, small groups, and one-on-one sessions in which guests (co-ed) work with experts to learn why they overeat and how to change the habits, stress, and life-style patterns that have contributed to their weight problems. Other psychological issues—such as assertiveness training, understanding depression, alcohol and drug abuse, improving your body image, and managing your time—are also addressed.

To get you moving, the House has stationary bikes, rowing machines, Nautilus equipment, free weights, and a trampoline. In addition, there are supervised aerobic walks, low-impact aerobics, calisthenics, and aquatics in the indoor pool. In the gym, guests can play basketball, badminton, and Ping-Pong. Individual consultations and workshops on the benefits of exercise, exercise misconceptions, and muscle-specific exercise are also held. To help you relax and unwind so that your mind is clear and open to all the new information you'll be receiving, the House offers Swedish and Trager massage, as well as polarity therapy.

Your dietary health is also emphasized. Individual consultations and workshops on nutrition, calories, and portions; menu planning; restaurant dining; and sodium and cholesterol are just a few of the topics that are addressed. The menu you'll be served is based on a low-sodium, low-cholesterol plan that uses a variety of appealing foods such as filet mignon, omelets, and stuffed potatoes. Most participants are fed a total of about 700 calories per day, but menu and calorie modifications are made by the dietitian for vegetarians and others with special needs.

Your accommodations are in one- and two-bedroom apartments. The new, modern units have sliding glass doors leading out onto a patio, washer and dryer, linens, telephone, color television, and weekly maid service.

Structure House has one-, two-, and four-week all-inclusive programs. The fees cover your accommodations, meals, and intensive training program.

GUEST FEEDBACK

Guests not only found their stay rewarding in every way, but one woman stayed 30 days longer than she had originally planned. The facilities, program, level of staff knowledge, and concern rated excellent. As one guest put it, "This program is excellent for those wishing to make changes in their life style and/or lose weight. I particularly found helpful the individual and group therapy, as well as the exercise program. Actually, the entire staff and program are outstanding."

Rates

	Single	Double (per person)
7-Night Intensive Treatment Program	$1,500	$1,350
14-Night Executive Institute Program	$2,850	$2,555
28-Night Health Training Week Program	$4,000	$3,410

There is a seven-night minimum stay. All programs are Sunday arrival and Sunday departure.

Wildwood Lifestyle Center and $$ WL
Hospital

Wildwood, Georgia 30757
(800)634-9355 (Nationwide)
(404)820-1474 (in Georgia)

A nonprofit facility operated by the Seventh Day Adventists, Wildwood specializes in natural healing and preventive care. Wildwood is nondenominational and nonsectarian. Anyone who is committed to a vegetarian diet and is in need of continuing exercise at home is accepted. Located in the mountains of northern Georgia, the Lifestyle Center attracts patients from all over the country who want to take part in this live-in program that takes a natural approach to such conditions as arthritis and obesity, smoking, diabetes, and constipation. Wildwood also includes a fully licensed hospital.

There are cleansing fasts, water therapy, a vegetarian diet, exercise, stress control, and lectures for the center's 26 guests. Lifecycles, rowing machines, and trampolines, plus 35 miles of wooded trails help guests get in shape. A steam room, sauna, Swedish massage, hydrotherapy, a lake for swimming, and lectures on health-related and spiritual topics in the informal lounge around the fireplace help relax and inform guests to make necessary life-style changes.

Each guest receives a nutritional analysis and is offered specific recommendations for diet, taking into account his or her present physical condition, nutritional requirements, and weight-loss goals. After a complete medical examination—blood chemistry profile, EKG-exercise stress test, lung function evaluation, and chest x-ray—a physician monitors your progress and prescribes a program for you.

The meal plan is based on fruits, vegetables, legumes, and grains. Three vegetarian meals are served daily. No dairy products, fish, or meat are offered. Specialties include lasagna. Food-preparation demonstrations are also held.

Accommodations are based on semiprivate lodging, but single rooms are available upon request. There are 26 mountain lodge guest rooms with twin beds and private patios. Some share a large bath and all have woodland views.

There are 6-, 16-, and 23-night programs that include your accommodations, three meals daily, medical history, physical examination, periodic consultation with a physician, use of facilities, lectures, classes, and food demonstrations. Some of the cost may be covered by your insurance plan; check with your agent. There is also a seven-day smoking cessation program.

GUEST FEEDBACK
Guests report a very peaceful and rejuvenating time in the serene ambience of this southern retreat. Many would return, if the need arose, while others thought once in a lifetime was enough.

Rates

	Single	*Double (per person)*
6-Night Program MON ARR/SUN DEP	$1,150	$1,150
16-Night Program MON ARR/WED DEP	$2,395	$2,395
23-Night Program MON ARR/WED DEP	$2,950	$2,950

There is a six-night minimum stay.

The Woods Fitness Institute $$ WL, FB-RH

P.O. Box 5
Hedgesville, West Virginia 25427
(800)248-2222 (Nationwide)
(304)754-7977 (in West Virginia)

If you're serious about changing your diet and nutrition intake, managing your weight, and shedding pounds, this "no-nonsense" program may be the one for you. Set in Sleepy Creek State Forest, a 2,000-acre wilderness region in West Virginia's historic eastern panhandle, this year-round facility (part of the Woods Resort complex) focuses on weight loss, increased fitness levels, and improved well-being through behavior modification.

The professional staff educates the 30 to 35 men and women who participate in the program on how to reduce their risk of diseases such as obesity and hypertension, diabetes, and cardiovascular illness through physical activity, a healthful diet, and other positive lifestyle changes.

To begin your fitness vacation, you will be given a total fitness assessment to help you understand your present condition. You are evaluated for your coronary risk, blood chemistry, blood pressure, lung capacity, muscle strength, body fat, over-all flexibility, and submaximal exercise level, which regulates your oxygen intake. The results of the evaluation will determine safe levels of exercise and provide you with a baseline against which you can measure your progress. There is no physician on staff, but guests over the age of 35 or with health problems are required to bring a physician's release before enrolling in the program.

With 70 miles of hiking trails, walking is the emphasis here. The Woods offers frequent walks, jogs, and hikes into scenic and historic points of interest, such as Cacapon State Park, Harper's Ferry National Historical Park, and the mineral spring baths at Berkeley Springs. Much of the walking is done on pavement, so bring appropriate footwear.

To round out your physical activity, there are stretching exercises, swimnastics, aerobic dance, a treadmill, free weights, and Universal circuit training. The resort complex features tennis (one outdoor and five indoor courts), racquetball, and handball; a gym for basketball and volleyball; indoor and outdoor pools; a sunning room; whirlpool bath; saunas; and massage rooms.

If outdoor sports are your thing, you'll appreciate the well-stocked fishing pond. Nearby you can challenge the white waters of the Shenandoah River and play golf at a Robert Trent Jones championship golf course. In winter there is ice skating on the pond and cross-country skiing.

A typical day at The Woods begins with a morning walk, followed by breakfast; then aerobics or circuit training and stretching. After lunch, there is another hike, followed by films, lectures, or group discussions on nutrition, exercise, stress management, and life-style habits. The remainder of the evening can be spent getting a little "R and R."

Information on diet, physical activities, and stress management is constantly being updated, and regularly scheduled classes on nutrition, exercise, stress management, and life-style habits, as well as videotaped aerobic instruction are offered as an integral part of the program.

Meals here are low in sodium, cholesterol, sugar, and fats. Participants eat at specifically designated tables in the main dining room with a preplanned menu consisting of about 1,000 calories per day. Salt and sugar substitutes are permitted. Dress is casual and comfortable day and night.

The Woods Inn offers a choice of accommodations. Its deluxe rustic pine rooms are completely equipped with air conditioning, private baths, color television, telephones, and sun decks. Luxury lodge rooms have all that, plus each has its own fireplace and whirlpool bath. Pinecrest cabins, nestled among the pines, are modern two-bedroom units with central air and heat and full kitchen facilities. Each cabin is fully furnished with a fireplace and sun deck, and accommodates up to six guests. A pub in the resort serves alcohol.

The Woods offers packages by the week. Each includes accommodations, meals, total fitness evaluation, full exercise program daily, and use of all facilities. Guests without serious weight problems have vacationed here as briefly as a week in order to lose four or five pounds. Others have stayed for a month or more, but the average stay is three to four weeks. The weight-loss record is held by a guest who stayed several months and lost over 100 pounds.

GUEST FEEDBACK

The majority of guests were pleased with their vacation at The Woods and would return. They thought the program was well-structured and of good value and the food was rated highly. The only major complaint was that guests were allowed to smoke on the premises, even in the fitness center.

Rates

	Single	Double (per person)
7-Night Program	$800–900	$750
14-Night Program	$1,500–1,700	$1,400
21-Night Program	$2,150–2,450	$2,000
28-Night Program	$2,750–3,150	$1,590–2,550

There is a seven-night minimum stay with Sunday arrival and departure.

NEW AGE RETREATS

Coolfont Resort $ NA, FB-SC

Berkeley Springs, West Virginia 25411
(800)888-8768 (Nationwide)
(304)258-4500 (in West Virginia)

This year-round retreat for the budget conscious is a New Age resort in a quiet valley just two hours from Washington, D.C., and Baltimore. It appeals to a wide variety of interests and offers an interesting array of recreational, cultural, and healthful activities—all with a summer-camp-for-adults ambience. Whether you want to shape up, slim down, unwind, or quit smoking, Coolfont makes health and wellness fun and exciting.

Rustic and natural, Coolfont is nestled in the foothills of the Appalachian Mountains. Clean fresh air and lots of spring water will make you feel in the mood to get fit. Then, you'll be ready to work Coolfont's Health and Swim facility, which opened in early 1989. You'll find an indoor lap pool, weight and cardiovascular training equipment, sauna, and whirlpool; seasonal sports and recreational activities include tennis, cross-country skiing, hiking, basketball, and volleyball. Golf can be played on the adjacent Robert Trent Jones course at Cacapon State Park. Massages and facials by professionally trained staff members are available for an additional charge. An hour-long body massage costs $38, while a facial is $25. Thirty minutes in the hot tub and sauna (without the benefit of a massage) costs just $4.

A typical day at Coolfont begins with a morning walk, followed by a class in gentle stretching and guided imagery. After breakfast, there's an educational seminar, followed by a body strengthening or water exercise class. And there's free time for lap swimming before lunch. The afternoon consists of a mountain walk, a light aerobics and tone-up class or circuit weight training, followed by yoga and free time. After dinner, a starlight stroll is planned, followed by an evening program. Workshops and seminars are held on such topics as "New Lifestyle Cooking," "Right Brain/Left Brain Thinking Styles," "Emotional Health and Well-Being," "Coping with Life in the Fast Lane (New Approaches to Stress Management)," and Tai Chi. In addition, the Coolfont Foundation provides programs of music, drama, and art.

The menu here follows recommendations of the American Heart Association and National Cancer Institute for a low fat, high fiber, low sodium, and low sugar diet. The calorie counts run between 1,000 and 1,200 per day for safe, effective weight loss. Meals, which are served at the Treetop House Restaurant, emphasize fresh fruits and vegetables, whole grains, lean poultry, and fish. Typical entrees include snapper in parchment, lasagna, and lentil stew.

There are cozy, rustic accommodations in the manor house, Woodland House Lodge, and chalets. Some of the accommodations have a fireplace and a porch (where you can sleep!).

Coolfont offers an outstanding smoking-cessation program, as well as weight-loss, stress-management, and massage workshops. The five-night Health Retreat offers the chance to learn and practice sensible, workable approaches to weight control, physical fitness, and stress reduction. Included in the package are your accommodations, meals, use of all facilities, program activities, and gratuities. A Fitness Weekend is the first step to achieving your personal best. This two-night package includes your lodging, meals, program activities, and gratuities. If you're interested in learning the ancient art of massage, try this unique weekend workshop designed just for couples. Under the direction of Scott and Jane Simmons, you'll learn Swedish massage techniques to soothe tired muscles, reduce muscular tension, and relax and invigorate the body. The weekend includes ten hours of classroom instruction, meals, lodging, and gratuities. For an additional $50, couples can stay in romantic Hillside Hideaway which features an in-room whirlpool.

GUEST FEEDBACK

Guests consistently rated the accommodations, meals, and physical location as very good or excellent. One guest who had reservations about the exercise facilities and program was pleasantly surprised by Coolfont's program. She writes, "I especially enjoyed the intensive exercise program. I was afraid it was going to be too laid back, but it was a good variety of physical workouts." All of the guests surveyed would return to Coolfont, if only to participate in the highly rated "Breathe-Free" smoking cessation program.

Rates

	Single	Double (per person)
2-Night Massage Workshop FRI ARR/SUN DEP	$210–270	$190–250
3-Night Fitness Weekend THURS ARR/SUN DEP	$345–395	$285–335
5-Night Health Retreat SUN ARR/FRI DEP	$575–625	$475–525
6-Night Health Retreat SUN ARR/SAT DEP	$670–720	$550–600

There is a two-night minimum stay.

Hippocrates Health Institute $$ NA, WL

1443 Palmdale Court
West Palm Beach, Florida 33411
(407)471-8876

This New Age spa, which makes its home in a spacious *hacienda* on a ten-acre subtropical estate in southern Florida, is America's original alternative health center and the pioneer of all-natural, unprocessed nutrition based on the concept of living foods. Today Hippocrates continues to update its restorative health program through research and experimentation.

As one of 15 to 20 participants in the very regimented Hippocrates Health Encounter, you perform stress-free exercises and follow a carefully balanced diet of organically grown fruits and vegetables. To further enhance your health, massages, facials, daily health lectures, and personal counseling sessions are added, and a certified health consultant monitors your state of health.

Specifically, the five-phase plan involves gentle stretching, strengthening exercises, deep breathing, and low-impact aerobics daily; deep-cleansing facials and massage to release energy blocks in your neck, shoulders, arms, legs, and spine, and to cleanse and normalize bodily fluids; deep relaxation techniques for healing, creativity, and inspiration; personalized health counseling sessions with a doctor and counselor who will organize a personal program for you to take home; and the famous "live food" diet. Facilities include an Olympic pool, stationary bikes, weight training and jogging. An ocean beach, boating, and tennis courts are nearby, and there is a doctor and a psychologist on staff.

The diet here encourages a nutritional life style that embraces an all-natural way of eating. This enzyme-rich, living foods program, according to Hippocrates Health Institute, is essential to the revitalization of every part of the system. The raw foods cleanse and detoxify the digestive tract, enabling the body to utilize healthful nutrients more fully. You will also learn and practice how to sprout and grow greens for home use.

Fresh wheatgrass juice is taken daily to rid your system of dangerous toxins, and the all-raw diet eliminates all meat and dairy products, as well as cooked foods, which the Institute attributes to the production of all types of degenerative diseases.

Hippocrates offers a variety of unique accommodations. There is one room with a private, enclosed garden and dressing room, another that overlooks the pond, and another with a sunken Roman tub; another room has a private balcony, tropical gardens, and a whirlpool. There are also four apartments housed in tropical greenery and lake cottages with a living room, separate bedroom, and bathroom.

Lodging is made suitably comfortable, especially since Hippocrates specializes in three-week sessions that entail "super nutrition," regular exercise, relaxation, and detoxification. The Health Encounter gives you actual hands-on experience in implementing this program upon returning home. A shorter course is also available. Packages include accommodations, meals, massage, facials, medical exam, blood monitoring, chiropractic examination, psychological examination, lectures, classes, and excursions to the beach, local museums, and health-food store. Evening concerts and a dinner at a local restaurant are also included.

For the serious health-conscious spa-goer who wants to make a substantial change in life style and diet, Hippocrates is a winner. Over a period of 30 years, three million people throughout the world have learned about the Hippocrates life style by reading the 22 different titles published in seven languages. *The Hippocrates Diet and Health Program* explains the principles involved in this super-nutritious, vitamin- and enzyme-rich diet. Plus, the health center has a worldwide alumni membership.

GUEST FEEDBACK
Former guests of the Institute were committed to a change in life style and chose this small retreat because of its intensive program and highly individualized and structured program. Guests found their stay highly rewarding and would return.

Rates

	Single	Double (per person)
6-Night Package	$1,375–1,791	$842–1,271
13-Night Package	$2,640–3,404	$1,616–2,440
20-Night Package	$3,300–4,300	$2,020–3,050

There is a six-night minimum stay. All packages have Sunday arrival and Saturday departure.

Lady Diane's Health and Fitness Resort $ NA

5 Kent Avenue
Montego Bay, Jamaica 14

No longer in business.

For a healthful, leisurely vacation beneath the Caribbean sun, Lady Diane's is an attractive, affordable choice. This modest, informal hotel is just steps away from the beach, but far from the frantic tourist areas of Montego Bay. This is the place to relax, enjoy good, healthful cuisine, and detoxify your body.

The highly unstructured program here features two yoga and meditation sessions daily in an open-air garden pavillion. There are beach walks, water sports, and an Olympic-size pool. There are also free weights and bicycles for guests to use on their own. Occasionaly the spa will have talks by yoga masters and physiologists, and upon request, a clairvoyant will hold court. The spa does offer such bodily treats as aromatherapy using essences from some of the many tropical flowers that abound in Jamaica; there's also Shiatsu massage, a ginger compress for detoxification, and loofah scrubs.

Lady Diane's tropical setting also enhances its menu. Gourmet macrobiotic (no dairy) and vegetarian cuisine with tropical touches and a Jamaican flair gives guests a high-fiber/low-cholesterol diet. Jamaican specialties include saltfish and ackee and cho-cho. Meals are served family-style at large communal tables in the dining room or on the deck. Fresh fish is bought directly from the fishermen and spring water is used for cooking and drinking. Box lunches are made upon request for beachcombers.

There are 17 large, airy rooms in the main house, plus motel-like garden units for families. All are air conditioned and have a private bath. Simply furnished with touches of tropical decor, they have queen- or king-size beds. There are no telephones, televisions, or radios in the rooms.

There are three- and seven-night packages, and day rates for folks who don't wish to take the spa package. The all-inclusive packages are complete with accommodations, meals, massage, yoga, exercise session, ginger compress, skin brushing, glass-bottom boat ride, and airport transfers from Montego Bay Airport just two miles away.

GUEST FEEDBACK
Many guests fell in love with Lady Diane's, praising the kind and supportive staff of Jamaicans. They describe the place as more of a holistic retreat than a spa since facilities are limited. However, guests say that that is just what they wanted—a place to relax and de-stress. For those who wanted more action, Montego Bay is close by. Travelers

here should know, too, that they will need to exchange U.S. currency into Jamaican dollars, since that is the only legal tender in the country.

Rates

	Single	Double (per person)
3-Night Package	$330	$255
7-Night Package	$770	$595

There is no minimum stay and any-day arrival.

Maharishi Ayur-Veda Health Center $$$$ NA

679 George Hill Road
P.O. Box 344
Lancaster, Massachusetts 01523
(617)365-4549

Guests here bask in the radiance of the country's largest meditating community. Located on 200 acres of one of Massachusetts' finest estates, the center teaches a 5,000-year-old system of natural health care from India which emphasizes disease prevention and health preservation based on your specific body type. Located on the campus of Maharishi International University, the medical center welcomes those who have undergone traditional medical treatment and who want to try the Ayurveda approach, as well as those who simply want to quit smoking, lose weight, kick caffeine or sleeping pills, or ease hypertension.

To make it easy for meditators and Sidhas from around the country to participate in this program, Maharishi has designed an "out-of-town" guest program. Your visit begins with a personal evaluation by a specially trained Maharishi Ayur-Veda doctor. He or she determines your constitutional type and prescribes a personalized health care program for you. The evaluation includes recommendations for diet, exercises, herbs, daily and seasonal routines, and educational materials on Maharishi Ayur-Veda.

Programs at Maharishi include the Rejuvenation, a program designed by a doctor that features massage therapy with specific herb oils suitable to your body type, heat treatments with herbal steam, and a gentle laxative. All aspects of the program are gentle, natural, and extremely relaxing, designed to help eliminate toxins in the body.

The Neuromuscular/Neurorespiratory Integration classes are movement- and breath-education sessions, prescribed by a doctor. Through certain exercises, guests learn more efficient and effective ways of moving and develop a deeper understanding of the connection between the neuromuscular and neurorespiratory systems. These sessions explore the use of posture and breath awareness for a more flexible and balanced physiology.

The Maharishi Gandharv Ved Program employs your sense of hearing, using sounds and specific rhythms for a relaxing and nourishing effect on the system and relief of stress. The program offers broad and specific applications for restoring balance in specific areas of the body. Also using the sense of hearing is the Primordial Sound Program. According to Maharishi Ayur-Veda belief, the whole body can be seen as primordial sounds or vibrations of Natural Law. The sounds have been chosen by Maharishi Ayur-Veda experts and all originate from the Veda. Specific sounds (or vibrations) are prescribed for different body types as well as different types of disorders.

More familiar are the aromatherapy sessions where the sense of smell is employed to create balance in the body. In addition to these programs, there is a series of lectures, discussions, tapes, and literature designed to educate guests on areas such as diet, daily and seasonal routines, basic principles of cooking, and the latest Maharishi Ayur-Veda knowledge. Other programs are optional, or come with the Royal package, such as the Transcendental Meditation (TM) program, psychophysiological techniques for experiencing the transformation of consciousness into matter and simultaneously eliminating the basis of stress; and the Blissfully Thin weight-loss program.

The menu here is a light vegetarian diet served in the formal dining room, or in your own room. There are 14 bedrooms with several suites. All have a look of luxury with large beds and chairs. Some guests share a bath.

The Lancaster facility (there are other Maharishi Ayur-Veda Health Centers around the country) offers a seven-night deluxe package that includes accommodations, meals, medical evaluation, the rejuvenation, neuromuscular/neurorespiratory integration classes, programs, summary review, educational classes, tapes and materials and extended practice of the TM and TM-Sidhi program (a mental technique for stress management). The seven-night Royal package includes all of the above plus airport transfers from Logan Airport, the Marma/Aroma program, room service, and a selection of complimentary Maharishi Ayur-Veda products.

GUEST FEEDBACK
People who visited the center were prepared for the New Age teachings of this specialized retreat. They were particularly pleased with

the amount of care and contact they received from their assigned personal physician. Most were very rewarded by their experience.

Rates

	Single	*Double (per person)*
7-Night Deluxe Package	$2,200–3,100	$2,200–3,100
SAT ARR/SAT DEP		
7-Night Royal Program	$4,000–4,300	$4,000–4,300
SAT ARR/SAT DEP		

There is a seven-night minimum stay.

Northern Pines Health Resort $ NA

Route 85, RR Box 279
Raymond, Maine 04071
(207)655-7624

Seekers of "wellness" will enjoy this lakeside holistic resort. Located in the Sebago Lake region of southern Maine, you'll find the lodge and lakeside log cabins to reflect the warmth and hospitality you will receive here. And the 80 acres of pine forests, rolling hills, and mile-long waterfront offer the perfect place to unwind, shape up, slim down, and get pampered and "centered."

Owners Pat and Marlee Coughlan limit the guest list to 30 in summer and 16 in winter, so you are sure to receive plenty of attention and help in reaching your fitness goals. There are four different daily exercise programs to choose from, and you can participate as much or as little as you like—which many guests have appreciated, saying that it took the pressure off them to "perform." Fitness classes such as stretching, aerobics, body conditioning and, of course, yoga are only part of the activities roster. Add to that walking, hiking, jogging, swimming, and cross-country skiing.

When you want to be out on the lake there are row boats, sailboats, pedal boats, and canoes available for you to use. For another kind of water experience, try out the indoor or outdoor hot tubs, sauna, or flotation tank. And if your idea of a good time is more on the sedentary side, you can peruse the library or putter in the organic garden.

Pampering services, such as facials, massage, salt rubs, hair treatments, reflexology treatments, and polarity therapy, are particular favorites here.

But what makes this New Age spa special are the study sessions and special programs held on various aspects of natural health and personal development, such as acupuncture, astrology, numerology, and visualization.

Special outings to Freeport, Portland, the Coast, the White Mountains, and the Saco River are occasionally planned, depending on the interests of your fellow guests.

The cuisine here is naturally low calorie and well balanced, using whole foods and no preservatives or chemical additives. Although there are no calorie restrictions in this vegetarian diet, fish and eggs are served, and meals are high in complex carbohydrates and fiber, moderate in protein, and have no added sugar, salt, or fat. Cooking classes are regularly featured, and if you feel like helping out in the kitchen at mealtimes, don't hesitate to ask! Supervised fasting—which is said to help change your behavior patterns with regard to food, smoking, alcohol, and general attitude—is another alternative.

Accommodations are rustic and range from lakeside log cabins of yesteryear (some with fireplaces) to modern cottages and cabins, comfortably furnished in Maine decor. Guests in lakefront log cabins share modern bathroon facilities while guests in the hillside and Yurt rooms share a bath with one other room. Cedar and Pine rooms have private bathrooms.

Northern Pines, which is closed from March 20 to May 20, offers weekend, midweek, and week-long packages that include accommodations, three meals daily, yoga, fitness and study classes, massage, use of all facilities, and evening programs such as videos and storytelling. A bonus for parents visiting Northern Pines is that the Coughlan's also own Kingsley Pines Children's Camp located just two miles away. This co-educational facility operates from late June to mid-August and caters to children ages 7 to 15.

GUEST FEEDBACK

Former guests usually can't say enough about their stay at Northern Pines. One gentlemen called the staff, facilities, services, and homey atmosphere "impeccable!" All surveyed guests felt Northern Pines offered great value. (One guest even thought it was a bargain.) They also enjoyed the fact that the well-structured program still allowed them to participate as much or as little as they chose.

Rates

Jan. 27–March 19, May 21–June 30, and Sept. 1–Oct. 15	*Single*	*Double (per person)*
2-Night Weekend Program FRI ARR/SUN DEP	$200–260	$150–210
4-Night Midweek Program MON ARR/FRI DEP	$365–475	$265–375
7-Night Weekly Program ANY-DAY ARRIVAL	$615–800	$465–650
July 1–Aug. 31		
2-Night Weekend Program FRI ARR/SUN DEP	$237–300	$187–250
4-Night Midweek Program MON ARR/FRI DEP	$432–535	$332–435
7-Night Weekly Program ANY-DAY ARRIVAL	$730–915	$580–765

The spa is closed from March 20 to May 20.

SPAS ABROAD

AUSTRIA

Baden Bei Wien

The charming little town of Baden bei Wien near Vienna and the curative powers of its 96-degree sulphur springs have drawn visitors for centuries. Today, a casino, theater, and opera, plus Old World sightseeing add to its appeal. At the height of its popularity in the nineteenth century, when the entire Imperial Court moved here each summer, Baden hosted king and composer, diplomat and painter. Beethoven completed his Ninth Symphony here; Mozart, Schubert, and Johann Strauss also composed here.

Grand Hotel Sauerhof zu $
Rauhenstein

A-2500 Baden bei Wien
WeilburgstraBe 11-13
(800)223-5652 (Nationwide)
(212)593-2988 (in New York)

From Vienna, it only takes half an hour to reach the sleepy and cheerful spa of Baden at the Grand Hotel. The spa at Baden combines Old World elegance and comfort with modern facilities and therapeutic treatments. It also has its own private sulphur spring, as well as a sparkling indoor swimming pool, solarium, sauna, and two private tennis courts.

All of the available spa treatments are on individual request and under medical supervision. The hotel administers Kneipp therapy, massages, sulfur baths, and mud packs. Revitalization and cell therapy, which have been approved by the Austrian Ministry of Health, are also available.

Weight-watchers can request low-calorie meals, at no extra cost, and these menus are arranged on an individual basis. There are 87 rooms and suites in a variety of price ranges, but all of them come with a private bath, hair dryer, radio, color television, direct-dial telephone, and minibar.

The hotel offers a six-night package that includes your accommodations, two meals daily, sauna sessions, and use of facilities. The sulfur baths, mud packs, massages, and Kneipp cures are extra.

GUEST FEEDBACK
People lucky enough to visit the town and hotel have returned with a new sense of self, refreshed and culturally enriched. Given the opportunity, they'd do it again and would share the experience with a friend.

Rates

	Single	Double (per person)
6-Night Package	$473–522	$369–393.50

There is a six-night minimum stay and any-day arrival.

Kitzbühel

The fun never ceases at this Alpine resort. A world-famous ski resort in winter, "Kitz" also offers international tennis tournaments, golf, hiking, and swimming in summer, plus great year-round hotels, restaurants, cafes, pubs, and casino action. Travelers also come to Kitzbühel for the curative bogs, associated with treatments for rheumatic diseases and inflammations in the joints.

Hotel Schloss Lebenberg $$$$

A-6370 Kitzbuhel
Lebenbergstrasse 17
0-053 56-43 01
0-5356-4405 (FAX to the hotel)

The first-class Hotel Schloss Lebenberg is an old castle in the Tyrolean mountains. Once the host of earls and dukes, the hotel now offers patrons a friendly atmosphere, excellent cuisine, tennis, an ice skating rink, and all sorts of diversions such as horse-drawn-coach rides and daily bridge games.

In the hotel is Polly's Vital-Center, which offers special slimming and regeneration programs and color therapy to help you control your appetite, as well as a host of beauty and pampering treatments. Blood-pressure adjustment, rheumatism and gout, cardiovascular disorders, weight reduction, muscle spasm (fibrositis), nonsevere allergic conditions, acne, skin care, cellulite, and metabolic adjustment are some of the areas covered by the programs offered here.

A variety of techniques are used to burn fat. For instance, there is the Sauna-Wrap Cure. After a consultation and complete medical examination, herb extracts are applied to problem areas and massaged in. These act to stimulate blood circulation and help get rid of extra fluids in the tissues (edema) while encouraging your metabolism. The bandages, soaked in astringent lotion, work to tighten tissue, and at the same time, to reform your figure by applying different amounts of pressure to different areas. This is followed by a visit to the sauna and a vibration massage. There is also a Suction-Pulsate Massage, which is carried out underwater with little glass suction cups, and an interference massage which uses electrical frequencies to stimulate the nervous system and blood and lymph circulation, while loosening tense muscles and strengthening the contraction of weakened muscle, easing aches, and accelerating the re-absorption of edema.

A variety of baths for beauty and health are also administered. These include a Moor Bath for rheumatism, common feminine illnesses, and blood circulation problems; the Sulfur Bath for stress relief and skin diseases; the Oxygen Bath which stimulates and accelerates blood circulation through micromassage; and the Stanger Bath which relieves neuralgia, rheumatism, and arthritis. Loofa scrubs, aromatherapy, hydrotherapy, body masks and wraps, and water aerobics are also part of the program.

At certain times of the year, guests at Hotel Schloss Lebenberg can also participate in Dr. Federanko's inexpensive and popular fitness program of gymnastics, running, hiking, and swimming.

The hotel has 200 guest rooms, a restaurant, and a bar, plus a whirlpool, indoor swimming pool, sauna, Turkish bath, and fitness room. There is even a kindergarten for the tykes.

The variety of packages available include your accommodations at the hotel; two or three meals daily, depending on the program you choose; use of facilities; beauty treatments; medical examination; and exercise sessions. Aslan and thymus treatments are available at an extra charge. There is also a Gerovital package.

GUEST FEEDBACK
People have come from near and far to take advantage of the programs offered here, particularly the cellulite treatments. Many of them said this was a "vacation of a lifetime," and given the chance, they would do it again.

Rates

7-Night Programs	Single	Double (per person)
Polly's Vital-Center Slimming and Regeneration Program	$950–1,076	$829–953
Polly's Special Beauty Week	$808–933	$689–812
Polly's Special Treatment for Men	$763–889	$643–768
Dr. Federanko's Program	$531–654	$425–549

Micheldorf

Carinthia, the lovely southern lake district of Austria, has a reputation for great hiking trails, wonderful swimming, and delicious regional cooking. You can enjoy them all and much more in Micheldorf.

Aganthenhof $

A-9322 Micheldorf
Karnten, Austria
0043-4268-2015

This is a kind of New Age resort with an Austrian accent. This 435-acre holiday farm offers a natural paradise where, depending on the season, you can play tennis, go horseback riding, swim, ice skate, and hike through the snow.

Agathenhof, which has a nudist path for those who want to take a hike in the buff, also offers seminars on such unusual subjects as dowsing and water divining, astrology, self-hypnosis, and geomancy (divination by random figures formed when a handful of earth is on the ground, or by lines drawn at random). The farm has also gained a reputation as a resort for biological health cures, offering help to people with weight problems, stomach ailments, complaints of the heart and circulatory system, migraines, asthma, and painful joints.

The medically supervised treatments offered include pine needle baths in wooden tubs, Kneipp applications, medicinal massages and baths, and the Revitorgan cure—modified fresh cell therapy. In addition, the farm offers a line of natural cosmetics and a host of therapeutic beauty treatments.

Early morning exercises in the forest pavillion or in the main building, plus tennis, swimming in the lake or in the pool (April through October), nature walks through the Kneipp gardens, and other excursions make for invigorating physical activity.

Weight-reducing food, special diets, and Carinthian natural cooking comprise the nutritional aspect of the program. A breakfast buffet of fruit and vegetable juices from the farm, vegetarian cooking, an extensive section of honey from the farm's own bees, natural wines, an herbal tea bar, and farm-fresh spring water make up the menu. Food is cooked only with organically grown produce. Medically supervised fasting is also available. Your accommodations are either in log cabins (biologically built) with a shower, toilet, telephone, and French balcony, or a guest room in the main building.

The resort offers a variety of two-week health plans, including Fasting and Beauty Packages. The Health Package includes your accommodations, three meals daily, exercise sessions, pine needle baths with body brush massages, sauna, spa bathrobe, biorhythm chart, herbal pillow, and taxes. Beauty services, also available *a la carte*, include facial treatments (cleansing, peeling, ozone, pressing, refining, ampule, massage, mask, day cream, makeup); facial applications (active substance ampule application to improve skin moisture and build up deposit substances); breast modelings to firm up tissue (brushing to stimulate circulation, cleansing, peeling, ozone, mini-massage with firming cream, nutritional mask, ampule applications); back treatment; body treatments; body-brush massage pedicure with herbal foot bath and foot massage; manicure; and aromatherapy.

GUEST FEEDBACK

Guests of this Austrian retreat, mostly couples, were delighted and dazzled by the offerings. They found the facilities and staff to meet high American standards. Given the opportunity, they would travel again to this remarkable facility.

	Single	Double (per person)
14-Night Health Package	$1,249–1,351	$1,136–1,238

There is any-day arrival.

Villach

Halfway between Venice and Vienna, the delightful town of Warmbad Villach has drawn visitors to its thermal waters since the days of the Celts and Roman legions. Today, travelers come from all over Europe and the United States to visit the Warmbad Spa Center. Here you can reap the benefits of the water's full strength by swimming in the hot springs and inhaling its healing vapors. The rejuvenation program at the Center includes therapeutic and underwater exercises, massages, fango packs, Kneipp hydrotherapy, herbal packs, slimming meals, and beauty treatments.

Josefinehof Hotel Im Park $

9504 Warmbad Villach
(011)(43)4242-25-531

A first-class spa resort named after Napoleon's wife, the Josefinehof has its own thermal spring and a "Long-Evity" Center (the only one of its kind in Europe), where you can participate in a highly personalized fitness and weight-loss program. The elegant hotel, located in a private park, also has special programs for blood pressure problems and diabetes.

The hotel offers a week-long thermal-cure package and a longevity program. Both include your accommodations, meals, use of all facilities, medical examination, thermal cure treatments (average of ten per week) or longevity training sessions, and personalized nutrition schedule.

GUEST FEEDBACK
This spa claims to be the only longevity center in Europe. Former guests have returned home very satisfied, commenting that it is one of the few places where you really re-learn health habits. They also like the fact that the center and hotel are run by a fairly young couple—a medical doctor who runs the program and his wife who runs the hotel and kitchen. Guests cite the very individualized program as a major draw.

Rates

	Single	Double (per person)
7-Night Thermal Cure	$715–838	$669–762
7-Night Longevity Program	$800–933	$754–857

There is any-day arrival.

FRANCE

Evian-Les-Bains

Snow-capped Mont Blanc towers above Lake Geneva; together, the mountain and lake contribute to the charming city of Evian and its exceptionally mild climate, making it conducive to rest and relaxation and the sports and fitness activities offered here. Cachat, the legendary spring that put Evian on the map, has drawn health-seekers since the eighteenth century.

Royal Hotel $$

74500 Evian Les Bains
France
(800)223-6800 (also in Canada)
00-223-6800 (in Canada)

You can enjoy direct access to the Institut Mieux-Vivre (Better Living Institute) from the palatial Royal Hotel. Its exquisite floral frescoes, luxurious furnishings, and commanding position on the south bank of Lake Geneva have enchanted the cream of international society from the day it opened in 1909. Now beautifully renovated as part of the Royal Club Evian complex, the hotel offers true world-class amenities and services.

The Institut Mieux-Vivre inside the Royal Hotel is a calm, sophisticated retreat with ultramodern equipment and guidance by doctors, dieticians, physical therapists, beauticians, and hydrotherapy specialists. The program in Evian begins with a medical exam to determine the specific treatments most suitable for you. During your stay, you may undergo treatments such as ozone and oxygen baths, ionization, laser sessions, hydromassage baths, and Evian water mist treatments. In addition, there is an aquatic gymnastic pool, exercise equipment, a Vita track through the park, and a weight room. The Institute also offers a wonderful assortment of beauty services—from algae sheathing (a body mud pack) to cryotherapy fresh-cell treatments—all of which leave you feeling healthy, refreshed, and beautiful.

The Royal Hotel offers its own diversions. For example, at the putting green in the hotel's private 27-acre park, you can videotape your swing and get expert instruction to help you improve your game. If you prefer, you can avail yourself of the same professional services at the Royal Tennis Club. On the lake, you can sail, windsurf, or water ski. Other sports options include archery, horseback riding, hiking, biking, and cross-country or Alpine skiing in winter. Each spring the Royal Club welcomes Mstislav Rostropovich to conduct concerts during the International Music Festival of Evian, and you can always try your luck at Evian's world-famous Casino Royal.

Dieters needn't worry about putting on extra pounds by indulging in rich French food. La Rotonde serves up delicious meals that never go over the 1,500-calorie-per-day limit. Other culinary options include La Toque Royale at the casino; Le Chalet du Golf; Le Cafe Royal under the frescos of Gustave Jaulmes and on a terrace; and The Swimming Pool Barbecue with broiled meats and a large buffet of *hors d'oeuvres*. The guest rooms and suites, which are spacious and soothing, are decorated with period furniture. Their terraces open onto the lake or the park.

The Institute offers week-long packages that include accommodations and meals. The Dietetic Program includes an interview with the dietician, dietetic conference, cooking course, and personalized diet plan. The Better Living Programs include exercise sessions, balneotherapy, and choice of hydrotherapy, hydromassage, algae bath, hydrogen, ozone and oxygen baths, facial rehydration, Evian mineral water atomizer, body treatments, tax, and service.

GUEST FEEDBACK

As European spa picks go, Evian is a popular one among surveyed guests. Perhaps it is because Evian is easy to reach, with several high-speed trains leaving Paris every day. Plus, you can drive to Evian from many other exciting destinations, such as the French Riviera, Zurich, Geneva, and Vienna. Guests found their vacations here well worth the trip. The facilities, treatments, and food rated very good or excellent. Plus, there were lots of other diversions to make them want to return—or at least recommend it to good friends.

Rates

	Single	Double (per person)
7-Night Better Living Program	$1,342–2,182	$1,129–1,595
7-Night Super Better Living Program	$1,448–2,289	$1,236–1,701
7-Night Dietetic Program	$1,347–2,327	$1,099–1,642

There is a seven-night minimum stay.

GERMANY

Baden-Baden

Europe's summer capital for over 150 years, Baden-Baden offers cosmopolitan culture while retaining Old World charm, elegance, luxury, and service. In the dark woodlands of the Black Forest, you can enjoy more than 20 thermal springs, heavy with sodium chloride, all radioactive, their ionized mineral water bubbling up from a depth of 6,500 feet. They are the hottest springs in Europe, with Hell Spring at a sweltering 155 degrees. You'll also enjoy golf, tennis, skeet shooting, hunting, fishing, jogging, hiking, horseback riding, or cross-country skiing through the pines. From taverns and monasteries offering local wines to the excitement of watching the thoroughbreds during Racing Week at Iffezheim, to the theater, concerts, and glamour of one of the most famous casinos in the world, Baden-Baden remains the reigning queen of European spas.

Brenner's Park $$$

An der Lichtentaler Allee
Schillerstrasse 6
D-7570 Baden-Baden/Black Forest
Germany
011 49 7221 3530; 07221 353 353 (FAX)
(800)223-6800 (also in Canada)
(212)838-3110 (collect in New York State)
(800)323-7500 (Nationwide)
(312)953-0505 (in Chicago)

A member of the Leading Hotels of the World and Preferred Hotels
Worldwide, Brenner's Park is almost synonymous with Baden-Baden.
The hotel offers richly appointed accommodations, superb gourmet
cuisine (including low-calorie delights), and since joining forces with
the Lancaster Beauty Farm, world-class fitness facilities. Your program will include daily water exercises in the Roman-style swimming
pool with heated marble benches and daily exercise classes in the park
or in the fitness room. Plus there are yoga classes, gymnastics, nature
walks, sightseeing tours into the Black Forest where lunch will be
served, and a host of beauty treatments.

The Lancaster Beauty Farm coordinates whole-body treatments
for both women and men. Programs usually include lymph drainage,
body massage, and a mud pack. In addition, it offers foot reflexology;
cellulite and bust treatments; face, bust, and hand modeling; and an
intense facial that includes cleansing, peeling, eyebrow shaping, dye-
ing of lashes and eyebrows, massage or lymph-drainage, mask, eye
mask, neck pack, and makeup application. Manicures, pedicures, and
hairdressing at the Romischer Salon are also available.

Situated at a large private park facing the renowned Lichtentaler Allee and the River Oos which divides the town proper on its
right bank from the pleasure grounds and resort area for visitors on
its left bank, the Brenner complex also houses the Schwarzwald
Clinic in Villa Stephanie. Specializing in internal diseases, the clinic
provides an extensive internal diagnosis and various fields of therapeutic treatments, particularly physical and balneotherapies. It also
has a kitchen managed by trained dietitians.

The Farm's reducing diet is based on the nouvelle cuisine of its
neighbor, France. The 1,000-calories-per-day diet consists of 40 percent complex carbohydrates, 30 percent protein, and 30 percent fat.
Breakfast can be served in your room, or you can take in the
Schwarzwald-Stube, which is smaller and less formal than the main
hotel restaurant.

Guest rooms at Brenner's are well appointed with fresh flowers, chocolates, and wine waiting for you when you arrive. There is also a minibar with refrigerator, a silent valet for your clothes, sachets, long-handled shoehorns, a purse-sized sewing kit, plus the usual five-star complimentary bath and cosmetic goodies. Rooms have floor-to-ceiling French doors opening onto terraces with striped awnings to roll up or down, depending on how you feel about sun or shade; writing desks; down pillows and comforters; and contemporary- or antique-style furniture. Bathrooms are spacious. All the amenities are provided, along with courtesy, service, and efficiency, as well as the pink roses that grace your breakfast tray and the linen mat changed daily for you to step on when you get out of bed.

Brenner's Park Hotel, in conjunction with the Lancaster Beauty Farm, offers seven-day packages that include your accommodations, meals, welcome cocktail, three facials, two face lymph drainages, two body massages, two brush massages/body packs, a medical pedicure, a manicure, a makeup consultation and treatment, six water exercise classes, and six gymnastic sessions, plus two relaxing exercise sessions, sports activities, use of facilities, tax, and service.

GUEST FEEDBACK

Many visitors have not only found their experiences rewarding, but have returned year after year to "take the waters" of this famous town. Facilities, services, and food all rated very highly. Clearly, many people consider this an outstanding destination.

Rates

	Single	Double (per person)
7-Night Package	$1,904	$1,554
SUN ARR/SUN DEP		

St. Blasien

Villa Christiana Clinic $$$$

Mnzenschwander Strasse 32
(011)(49)7672-48010
(800)648-7398 (Nationwide)

In the Alb River Valley just 45 minutes from Zurich, Switzerland, you can experience the magic of the Black Forest and renew your health and vigor at this medically supervised facility located in the little town of St. Blasien. The environs of St. Blasien are world famous. For centuries people have made health pilgrimages to this sheltered valley, renowned for its pure air and breathtaking scenery. On daily hikes (or in winter, during cross-country ski trips), you will have plenty of opportunity to take in nature's beauty.

The Christiana staff consists of a physician, behaviorist, nutritionists, physical education experts, and physiotherapists—all English-speaking—who work with you on a personalized medical program. Your treatment may include hydrotherapy, massage therapy, physiotherapy, acupuncture, foot reflexology, colon therapy, gymnastics, and herbal wraps, as well as homeopathic applications—a system of natural preparations from plant, mineral, and sometimes animal sources—in addition to traditional medicinal therapies to promote health and prevent illness. With only ten guests at a time, the licensed staff personally supervises every aspect of your program, from initial medical evaluation to classes on stress relief, mind and body healing, and weight control. Villa Christiana also offers programs to help you end addictions to tobacco and/or alcohol.

With the beauty of the Black Forest surrounding you, you'll find it a joy to participate in the sports activities, such as cycling, swimming, horseback riding, hiking, and cross-country or downhill skiing. Or stay indoors and go for the jazz dance and stretching classes. By the way, you won't find television here, so in your free time, you might try an art class, folklore lessons, sightseeing, or enjoy live chamber music concerts in Christiana's "Bach" Hall.

The clinic offers a six-night program that includes your accommodations, three meals daily, lab and diagnostic testing, comprehensive physical check-up and daily physician consultations, aerobics and body-toning classes in the gym, two massages, daily steam bath, daily exercise clothing, daily hikes into the Black Forest, limousine service to and from Zurich airport, lectures, concerts, and sightseeing walks. Deluxe and suite accommodations are available at an extra cost.

GUEST FEEDBACK
People who were serious about changing the way they live found this facility to be well worth the expense of time and money. They particularly praised the staff for its knowledge and concern, and guests found their stays restful, comfortable, and pleasant.

Rates

	Single	*Double* *(per person)*
6-Night Program	$2,500	$2,100
SUN ARR/SAT DEP		

WIEDEMANN INTERNATIONAL HEALTH CENTERS

More than 30 years ago, Dr. Fritz Wiedemann developed a nature-cure method that has gained wide acceptance and application. His comprehensive therapies employ state-of-the-art medical knowledge and natural remedies to counteract the effects of premature aging and to cure or significantly improve cardiovascular, respiratory, digestive, and metabolic disorders and rheumatic and immunologically induced diseases.

Each patient receives an extensive medical evaluation consisting of blood and urine samples; ECG tests; pulmonary function test for respiratory problems; x-rays of the heart and lungs, spinal column, joints, and/or paranasal sinuses, if necessary; sonogram of the liver, gall bladder, kidneys, and pancreas; and endoscopy screening of the alimentary canal, if requested. The Wiedemann cure utilizes a host of progressive therapies based on regeneration. The success of the Wiedemann cure is based on the individual or combination of serum, cell thymus, neutral, and ozone-oxygen therapy; acupuncture; procaine therapy; chelation (infusion treatment for removing arterial deposits); physiotherapy (including hydrotherapy), massage, electromassage, ion-ozone dry-gas bath, lymphatic drainage, reflexology, irradiation, ultra-sound and cryotherapy (ice treatment for acute injuries); and a supervised diet or fast.

Fitness and sports play an important part in health, so the Centers offer programs specifically structured for your needs. Gymnastics and training equipment; aquatics in an indoor, open-air pool; bowling; cycling; table tennis; rowing; sailing; and golf nearby are some of the offerings to be found at the Centers. Dr. Wiedemann also knows that your total well-being is connected to your external appearance. Therefore, the Wiedemann cure includes an integral cosmetic program. This can include, for instance, morning brush massages, herbal baths with subsequent body packs, massages or lymphatic drainage, and sauna and solarium visits. Facials and facial exercises and nail and hair treatments help you to achieve internal peace and harmony and a glowing new look.

The Wiedemann Centers have luxurious rooms with private bath, bar, and color television, and all prepare calorie-controlled cuisine for those who require it. There are four Wiedemann Health Center locations to chose from.

Ambach, Germany $$$$

One of the most beautiful lakes between Munich and the Alps, Lake Starnberg attracted Dr. Wiedemann to establish his first Health Center here. Elegant accommodations in exclusive Bavarian-style apartments or deluxe suites, plus private beach, indoor and outdoor swimming pools, billiard room, bowling alley, and complete spa facilities grace the Center. In addition to entertainment at the Center itself, you can enjoy cultural events in Munich, winter and water sports, golf on four lakeside courses, cycling excursions, and sightseeing tours to the famous Pfaffenwinkel churches and monasteries, and even "Fruhswchoppen" (lunchtime drinking) and barbecue parties.

Meersburg, Germany $$$$

Located at the center of a park above the delightful town of Meersburg, near the borders of Austria, Liechtenstein, and Switzerland, this Wiedemann Center offers spectacular views of the Alps and the mild, healthy climate of Lake Constance. Specializing in the "fasting cure," the Meersburg Center promises results in three weeks.

Meran, Italy $$$$

A 100-year tradition of health cures for emperors and kings makes this city in the Dolomites an ideal location for a Wiedemann Health Center. Along with Meran's superb sunny climate, medicinal springs, and charming southern Tyrolean landscape, your stay at the Hotel Adria includes comfortable accommodations, tennis, miniature golf, a nearby riding school, and excellent regional and international cuisine. (The chef will meet your individual dietary needs.)

Gran Canaria, Spain $$$$

All year long you can bathe in the warm Atlantic Ocean waters off the Canary Island coast and enjoy sculpted dunes, gorgeous mountains, and the nightlife of Las Palmas. Located in the Hotel Rey Carlos at the center of Playa del Ingles, the Wiedemann Center offers superb golf at "Parque Playa Golf" and charming bungalow accommodations surrounded by subtropical gardens, some with a nudist terrace, private sauna, and swimming pool.

All of the centers offer 7-, 10-, and 14-night programs. For each, your accommodations, meals, medical check-up, laboratory screening, immune status report, stress EKG, spirometry, physical therapy (such as massages and fitness activities), medical baths, regenerating therapy (including serum therapy, thymus extract, and ozone-therapy), facials, manicure, pedicure, and entertainment are included.

GUEST FEEDBACK

Surveyed guests visited Wiedemann Centers in all four locations, and all reported a very rewarding experience. Older clients were particularly pleased with the intensity of the medical examinations and the remedies that accompanied each diagnosis. Some guests have repeated the experience, shunning traditional methods of healing.

Rates

	Single	*Double (per person)*
7-Night Program	$2,640	$2,500
10-Night Program	$3,600	$3,400
14-Night Program	$4,680	$4,400

GREAT BRITAIN

Grayshott Hall $$$$

Grayshott, Nr. Hindhead
Surrey, GU26 6JJ
England
(042873) 4331
(042873) 5463 (FAX)

This splendid 80-room Victorian mansion still maintains the poetic grandeur of its former owner, Alfred Lord Tennyson. Less than an hour from London and the Channel ports, Grayshott offers you the opportunity to revitalize yourself through a comprehensive, individual fitness plan in a wholly modern health resort facility.

After a consultation with a member of the professional staff to determine your goals, you begin your program for optimum health and beauty. The state-of-the-art gym houses exercise and circuit training weight machines; a variety of daily aerobics, yoga, and dance classes aid in getting you fit and trim. The glass-enclosed heated pool gives you a spectacular garden view as you take private swimming lessons or participate in water exercise classes. If you prefer the outdoors, you won't find a more beautiful setting than the gentle Surrey countryside. And Grayshott's own 47 acres house a par-3 golf course, year-round tennis court, grass badminton court, and a full-size croquet pitch.

Pampering for men and women has become an art form here, with exotic treatments such as cathiodermie (deep facial cleansing), aromatherapy, and reflexology as the order of the day. You can also receive Thalgo Body Mask, Clarins Bust Treatment, Decleor anti-cellulite treatment, and a host of hair, nail and salon services. There's also a Jacuzzi and solarium.

Grayshott has two dining rooms: one is for dieters and the other offers buffet luncheons and formal dinners for conventional eaters. Fresh fruits and vegetables from Grayshott's own gardens and prime local produce augment the first-class, nutritious cuisine. Menus include dishes such as trout mousse, fillet of salmon with Hollandaise sauce, and breast of duck with passion fruit. No alcohol is served.

Their seven-night plan includes your accommodations (with stereo color television, radio, and direct-dial telephone; some with a shower), meals, medical and diet consultations, heat treatments, hand and underwater massage, unlimited use of all facilities, evening lectures, airport transfers, and taxes.

GUEST FEEDBACK

Perhaps its location—a hop, skip, and jump from London—makes Grayshott a hot spot with people who were particularly pleased with the English-speaking staff. Guests described the physical location as secluded, tranquil, and beautiful, and rated the spa services as excellent. Many have returned; others have recommended Grayshott to their friends.

Rates

	Single	*Double* *(per person)*
7-Night Plan	$1,850–2,000	$1,500–1,650

There is any-day arrival.

HUNGARY

Blessed with an abundance of medicinal thermal waters, Hungary has proven popular with health seekers since the Romans. After the collapse of the Roman Empire, the Turks added their own version of the baths, many of which remain in their original form. Today, Hungary offers modern medical knowledge, state-of-the-art spa facilities, a wide variety of sports activities, beautiful landscapes, interesting cultural events, and historical and artistic treasures—all the ingredients for an ideal spa vacation.

Budapest

Thermal Hotel Margitsziget $

If you prefer a city atmosphere, we suggest Budapest and Margitsziget (Margaret Island) located between the Buda and Pest sides of the River Danube which divides the city. With three healing springs at its spa center, Thermal Hotel Margitsziget offers comprehensive services from medical gymnastics to mud applications and massage, as well as thermal bath and physiotherapy facilities, x-ray and EEG departments, a clinical laboratory, and dental surgery.

   Thermal Hotel, with 206 guest rooms with views of either the Danube River or of the gardens bordered by centuries-old trees and dotted with sculptures, has the most modern installation of thermal bath and physiotherapy equipment, including thermal pools, regular swimming pools (summer water temperatures average 91 to 99 degrees, while winter water temps do not fall below 78 degrees), sauna, underwater jet massage, carbon gas bath, electrotherapy, therapeutic gymnastics, massage, mud packs, and solarium. In addition, you're only ten minutes from Budapest's museums, churches, opera houses, nightclubs, shopping, and escorted excursions to the nearby countryside.

Ramada Grand Hotel Margitsziget $

Over 100 years old, the Ramada Grand Hotel encompasses all the traditional atmosphere of the last century and the modern comfort of today. Guests here have reciprocal privileges at the Thermal Hotel, which is connected by an underground tunnel.

GUEST FEEDBACK

Guests of the Margitsziget Health Resort have reported one of the most relaxing and soothing vacations of a lifetime. While accommodations were small, the treatments and services were incomparable.

Rates

The spa packages listed below include your accommodations, two meals daily, physician's examination, dental exam, treatments, thermal bath, sauna, and tax.

7-Night Package	*Single*	*Double (per person)*
Thermal Hotel Margitsziget and Ramada Grand Hotel Margitsziget	$648	$491

Special Supersaver Package

(Oct. 28–Apr. 1) 21 Nights for the Price of 14	$982–1,281	$982–1,281

There are also 14- and 21-night packages.

ISRAEL

Herzlia-on-the-Sea

Daniel Hotel and Spa $$

Herzlia-on-the-Sea, Israel 46769
052-54 4444

Nine miles from Tel Aviv on the shores of the Mediterranean Sea, this very modern and stylish retreat offers all the comforts of a top American resort. There is an executive business center with conference and banqueting facilities for up to 800 guests, an auditorium, and a shopping arcade.

To help you feel fit, the Daniel offers a wide range of physical activities and sports. There are aerobics, stretch-and-tone classes, water exercises, body conditioning, jogging, and dancing. Walkers and hikers can join the guided walks along the beach, then unwind in one of the relaxing yoga or gentle exercise classes. For the more energetic, there is a fully equipped gym featuring Nautilus weight machines, ergometers, and free weights. The first-class facilities also include an outdoor pool opened for eight months of the year, plus a heated indoor pool, tennis courts, and table tennis.

More of a beauty spa than a treatment center, the Daniel has an excellent full-service beauty salon (hairdressing and nail care), a range of heat treatments and hydrotherapies, including a panthermal cabinet, inhalations of soothing eucalyptus or mint vapors, herbal baths, and jet-hose body treatments, all administered under medical supervision. Then, there are the saunas and hot and cold whirlpool baths. If it's the right time of year, you can get a tan under the Mediterranean sun or opt for the suntanning salon any time of year. In addition, there are baths in mineral-rich Dead Sea mud and eight different kinds of massage, including reflexology and Shiatsu. Even facials are accompanied by a massage of the neck and shoulder muscles.

The Daniel also offers calorie-controlled spa cuisine at the Aquarius Spa Health Restaurant. Your specific diet program is determined by the balneological doctor. A healthy eating plan is also designed for you to follow when you return home. All total, there are seven restaurants and bars to choose from. Each of the guest rooms is centrally heated and air conditioned and has direct-dial telephone, radio, color television, and private bath.

The 13-night package includes your accommodations, meals, use of all the facilities, supervised fitness program, choice of eight beauty or body treatments (four with the five-night program), and service charges.

GUEST FEEDBACK

The Daniel is a popular spot for people who want the benefit of both a total spa vacation and cultural/religious enrichment. Guests have consistently rated the facilities up to par and the program as well structured. Many have returned and many others have recommended it to friends.

Rates

	Single	*Double (per person)*
Through Nov. 1		
5-Night Program	$1,242.50	$990
13-Night Program	$3,230.50	$2,574
Sunday arrival only.		

ITALY

Montecatini

From the time of the Romans, the great masters of the Renaissance, and the Medicis until modern times, the thermal waters at Montecatini have attracted those interested in cleansing and rejuvenating their bodies and minds. Situated in the breathtaking Tuscan Hills between Florence and Pisa, the beauty of the 17th-century buildings, set in a formal park, create a relaxing atmosphere for guests to partake of the curative waters, thermal and mud baths, and other spa facilities.

Grand Hotel e La Pace $$$

Via della Toretta 1
Montecatini, Terme, Italy
(800)223-6800
(212)838-3110 (collect in New York State and Alaska)
0572-75801

You can enjoy the waters and muds at the Grand Hotel La Pace, an international rendezvous since 1870. Underwater massage; ozonized bath; mineral, mud, and herbal baths; a sauna; algae treatment; and Jacuzzi make the trip worth it. Plus, there are body massages, facial massages, antiwrinkle treatments, and face and body peelings. Mud treatments include mud bath plus galvanic therapy, an anticellulite treatment, and an antipsoriasis treatment. Guided jogging and aerobics are offered each morning.

The hotel offers complete spa packages utilizing the area's waters and mud treatments. You can also book packages centered around the culinary and curative benefits of herbs and a seven-day shopping spree in Florence.

Grand Hotel Croce di Malta $$

Viale IV Novembre 18
51016 Montecatini, Terme, Italy
(800)233-5652
(212)593-2988 (in New York State)
0572-75871

This first-class hotel has included traditional Jewish offerings for the past 58 years. It also offers complete spa packages utilizing the fabled "waters and muds." In addition, you may choose from a variety of packages that allow you to take full advantage of the glories of Tuscany, including "Living in Tuscany," art and antiques classes and tours, theater-hopping (opera, concerts, and ballet) and golf on the brand new Montecatini course (with pro lessons free for the kids).

Both hotel packages include your accommodations, three meals daily, spa entrance fees, medical check-up, airport transfers, mud and water treatments, massage and beauty treatments (seven-night program), morning exercise program, taxes, and service.

GUEST FEEDBACK
Italy is always a favorite spa destination for many people. The culture, climate, and spa services are a constant draw, and all of the guests found their spa vacations rewarding.

Rates

	Single or Double (per person)
Grand Hotel e La Pace	
7-Night Health Is Wealth Program	$1,644–2,116
14-Night Good Earth Wisdom	$2,149–2,495
Grand Hotel Croce di Malta	
14-Night Good Earth Wisdom	$1,481–1,823
Shorter packages are also available.	

Chianciano Terme

This thermal center is less than 100 miles from Rome on the borders of Umbria and Tuscany. The town is surrounded by woods of beech, chestnut, and oak trees, sheltered by the multihued Valley d'Orcia. It is rich with history—castles, fortresses, and ramparts, many of which date back to the fifth century B.C.

Christina Newburgh's Spa Deus $$$

Via Le Piane, 35
53042 Chianciano Terme
Italy
0578-63232
64329 (FAX)

Located at the Grand Hotel "IL Club" in Chianciano, just 80 miles south of Florence, Christina Newburgh's Spa Deus offers the best of the California spa traditions coupled with European therapies and beauty treatments. The "Center for Feeling Good," Spa Deus reflects Christina's tremendous personal energy and knowledge gleaned from visits to spas around the world. Her enthusiasm for the good health of your mind, body, and spirit ensures that you receive a fine regimen of hydrotherapy treatments and a full fitness program.

You may find yourself working out with movie stars, fashion designers, models, and a variety of international guests who come to take advantage of ondapress hydrotherapy, a unique brand of hydrotherapy which is filled with essential salts and oils for better circulation, and to alleviate stress, quit smoking, and rid themselves of cellulite. The fitness director, Californian Mitchell Berkman, guides guests through a revitalizing aqua-building class in the heated Olympic-size swimming pool, or on daily nature walks through the rolling hills, art-laden churches, and monasteries of the Tuscan countryside. In addition, there is circuit weight training on David body-building equipment, workouts with Dyna-Bands, yoga, low- and nonimpact aerobics, chair aerobics, and classes that focus on target areas, such as the back and stomach.

When it comes to pampering the body, you can expect personal care in services from soothing aromatherapy (the spa's specialty) and cellulite treatments to organic facial masks (a different variety every day) made from Spa Deus' own recipes. Some of the varieties of massage include presstherapy, a passive hips and legs massage for better circulation in tough-to-trim areas. Hydrotherapy treatments use the natural waters famed for centuries in Tuscany, and you can take them in the Ondapress, a hydrotherapy tub filled with essential salts and oil; Finnish sauna; Scottish shower; or Turkish bath.

The Spa Deus offers its guests exquisite meals of natural food with lots of rich Italian flavor. Many people leave ten pounds lighter after only a week on the spa diet, which features virtually no fats, sugar, salt, alcohol, or caffeine, minimal carbohydrates, and high protein. For those who stay for more than one week, or who are not trying to lose weight, pasta and wine can be added to the meal plan. The healthy diet consists of three meals and four snacks a day, ending with a glass of warm milk with crushed cinnamon to induce sweet dreams when you retire to your comfortable guest room and over-sized bed.

The program includes your accommodations, meals, use of all facilities, daily fitness program, massage, and facial. Everything else is *a la carte* (be prepared to pay for the luxuries here).

GUEST FEEDBACK

People feel at home at Spa Deus, which has a great following among its guests. They cite the excellent personal services as a major draw, plus the cultural and natural benefits of the spa's location. It is rated as a well structured program that offers a good value.

Rates

	Single	Double *(per person)*
Per Night	$282	$235

There is no minimum stay and any-day arrival. Nightly rates apply.

Stresa

Hotel Des Iles Borromees $$$$

Corso Umberto 1
67-28049 Stresa (NO)
(800)221-2340 (Nationwide)
(212)935-9540 (in New York)
0323-32382-30431

The Centro Benessere di Stressa, at the Hotel des Iles Borromees, located on Lago Maggiore in the north of Italy, offers delightful sur-roundings and an American-style fitness program that will make you feel right at home. The team of experts who run the Centro Benessere (Wellness Center) tailor-make a program of physical ac-tivities, diet, and beauty treatments to suit your particular needs. They specialize in treating the problems of stress, senility, and being overweight.

Each guest receives a thorough medical check-up to assess level of fitness. Further testing, including breathing and lung capacity tests, help the experts design your personal treatment and diet. To get you back in shape or improve your state of being, there is a fully equipped gym with stationary bikes and weight machines, jogging trails, gymnastics, aerobics classes, and aquatic exercises. You can ease sore muscles with a sauna and whirlpool bath, a new hydro-wave pressure Jacuzzi, Turkish steam bath, and massage therapy.

When it comes to pampering and preening the body, who does it better than the Italians? The program includes foaming remineral-ization packs, herbal wraps, fango mud packs, facial cleansing, mas-sage and mask, and Turkish bath with oils. In addition, you can have a Shiatsu massage, oxygen therapy and physiotherapy for osteo-articular diseases. Beauty services run the gamut from manicures and pedicures to treatment for the eyes, neck, breasts, hair, hands, and feet. Special body treatments include Celluderm for the treat-ment of heavy cellulite; Guarana (a Brazilian plant with very active ingredients for making the skin more supple), a massage to stimulate skin elasticity; and Freezyslim for the treatment of circulatory prob-lems caused by fatigue or the retention of liquids.

After your exercise and treatment sessions at the Center, you can relax and enjoy boat excursions on the lake, tennis, golf, swimming in the indoor or heated outdoor pools, or just sit back and take in the enchanting scenery around you.

One of the Ciga Hotels, Italy's most prestigious chain, the Des Iles Borromees offers marvelous water views and comfortable accom-modations.

The Spa-Finders package includes your lodging, three meals daily, revitalizing treatments, seaweed packs, herbal wraps, facial massage and mask, body massage, fango packs, fitness classes, use of all facilities, diet and nutritional counseling, tax, and service.

GUEST FEEDBACK

Former guests have consistently given Centro Benessere good reviews. They especially enjoyed indulging in the luxurious body treatments. The medical examinations administered upon arrival also rated high, as did the facilities and staff. Many would return (some have already) when their weary souls need rest, relaxation, and coddling. They also raved about the delicious low-cal cuisine of northern Italy.

Rates

	Single	Double (per person)
7-Night Package SUN ARR/SUN DEP	$2,519	$2,112

SPAIN

Gran Canaria

Hotel Incosol $$$

Marbella, Costa Del Sol
Spain
52-773700

Bordered by the famous Andalusian "White Villages" at the foot of the Sierra Blanca Mountains and facing the Mediterranean Sea sits the Hotel Incosol resort spa. From acupuncture to yoga, you will find it all at this modern high-rise resort on the Costa del Sol.

The spa occupies one entire wing of the Incosol, and its doctors and specialists offer the latest medical equipment and expert help for physical and emotional problems. In addition, you can participate in a variety of fitness and exercise programs offered both outdoors and in a modern, well-equipped gymnasium. Water babies have three pools, all of them heated, one outdoor and two indoor, and the beach at La Cabane Club. The riding school offers pleasure and sport riding, as well as lessons. There is also tennis, golf, and squash.

The facial and beauty departments offer Kneipp treatments, mud baths, massages, collagen and Clarins fresh-cell facial treatments, electrolysis, hot face masks, neck and chin reaffirming treatments, hairdressing, manicures, and pedicures for men and women.

Low-calorie culinary specialties can be had at the El Mirador and El Jardin restaurants. Guest rooms are tastefully done and furnished with a small in-room safe, air conditioning, direct-dial telephones, and color television.

The Spa-Finders package includes your accommodations, meals, airport transfers, daily massage, medical evaluation, facial massage, fitness classes, photography/painting classes, use of all facilities, tax, and service.

GUEST FEEDBACK
People seem to gravitate toward this part of the world, partly because of the sun and surf and partly because of the extensive services offered under one roof at this resort and spa. Guests were satisfied with their vacations, finding the food and services to be very good. Some have returned and many have or would recommend it to friends.

Rates

	Single	Double (per person)
7-Night Fitness Program	$1,898	$1,520

SWITZERLAND

Montreux

Clinique La Prairie $$$$

CH-1815 Clarens-Montreux
Switzerland
021-964-3311
021-964-2565 (FAX)

This world-famous medical facility has a simple philosophy: They "do not accept the inevitability of . . . aging and disease."

A private retreat in a tranquil, secluded area, surrounded by a magnificent natural setting on the shores of Lake Geneva, Clinique La Prairie admits only 26 patients per week, but it has treated over 65,000 patients since it first opened in 1931.

Operating under strict medical supervision within federally licensed facilities, Clinique La Prairie is not a spa in the usual sense, but rather much like the classic European spas where renewal and therapeutic treatments are the rule.

It specializes in fresh-cell therapy, which stimulates the endocrine and immunological systems and helps to revitalize the natural functions of the body. Treatments such as hydromassage with hot and cold mobile showers spraying your skin with varying water pressures will leave you feeling exhilarated. An ozone shower—steam enriched with ozone and oxygen—stimulates your metabolic system, eliminating toxins and making fat burn more efficiently.

In addition to beauty treatments with its own private line of cosmetics, Clinique La Prairie offers special programs for wrinkle removal, stress reduction, and weight loss, as well as the services of an acupuncturist-osteopath.

The Spa-Finders package includes your accommodations and meals at the clinic, medical check-up and nursing care, individualized fitness program, beauty treatments, cellulite treatments (in the nine-night program only), tax, and service charges. It does not include a two-night mandatory pre-arrival stay in Montreux.

GUEST FEEDBACK
Guests of this New Age medical facility often went with specific goals in mind and most often returned feeling fully rewarded. The facilities and services here have been described as "impeccable," and guests would return without hesitation.

Rates

	Single or Double (per person)
6-Night Live Cell Therapy WED ARR/TUES DEP	$7,119
6-Night Slimming Program ANY-DAY ARRIVAL	$3,473
9-Night Weight-Reduction Program ANY-DAY ARRIVAL	$4,630

There is a six-night minimum stay.

BRAZIL

Ligia Azevedo $

Brazilian champion gymnast, author, and television hostess Ligia Azevedo now offers her total seven-day fitness program at two different locations: on the Brazilian Riviera at Buzios, just two hours north of exciting Rio de Janeiro, and on the Green Coast at Portobello, about two hours south of Rio.

Ligia's program at both locations includes lodging at a beautiful five-star hotel, where you can enjoy the beach, play tennis, and go horseback riding, fishing, boating, wind-surfing, snorkeling, and sightseeing.

Called "Health, Beauty and Trim and Slim," Ligia designed her program to help you lose weight, reduce stress, improve your appearance, and brighten your outlook.

Ligia's week-long package includes your accommodations, three meals daily (diets range from 600 to 1,500 calories per day); three hand massages; two salt-glo loofa scrubs; two hair treatments; two facials; a manicure; two acupuncture sessions; aerobics, stretching, jazz, and water exercises; guided walks; and jogging. Leisure activities included in the program are sightseeing tours, schooner rides, music and fashion shows, and roundtrip deluxe bus transfers from Rio.

GUEST FEEDBACK

Surveyed guests have participated in Ligia's program at both locations and have reported a thoroughly rewarding experience at both. They also thought the program offered was a good value for the services rendered. They would recommend the program to their friends.

Rates

	Single	Double (per person)
7-Night Program	$1,050	$700

There are set dates. Shorter stays are also available.

Spa Almanac

Various Groupings to Help You Find the Perfect Spa for You!

WHERE TO SPEND THE WEEKEND

(Spas within Driving Distance of Major Metropolitan Areas, that Offer Weekend Programs)

San Francisco

Carmel Country Spa, CA
Claremont Resort, CA
Sonoma Mission Inn, CA

Los Angeles

Bermuda Inn Fitness Reducing Resort, CA
La Costa, CA
Lakeside Health Resort, CA
Le Meridien Spa, CA
Marriott's Desert Springs Resort & Spa, CA
Murietta Hot Springs, CA
The Oaks at Ojai, CA
The Palms at Palm Springs, CA
Spa Hotel & Mineral Springs, CA
Two Bunch Palms, CA

Denver

Westin Hotel Cascade Club, CO

Houston or Dallas

Four Seasons Hotel & Resort, TX
The Verandah Club, TX

Chicago

The Fontana Spa at The Abbey on Lake Geneva, WI
The Heartland, IL
Interlaken Resort & Country Spa, WI
The Spa at Olympia Village, WI

Detroit

The Kerr House, OH
Wheel's Country Spa, Ont., Canada

Atlanta

Southwind Health Resort, GA

Tampa/St. Petersburg

Safety Harbor Spa & Fitness
    Center, FL
Sonesta Sanibel Harbour Resort, FL

Miami/Ft. Lauderdale

The Spa at The Biltmore, FL
Doral Saturnia, FL
Fountainbleu Hilton, FL
Lido Spa Hotel & Resort, FL
Palm-Aire Hotel & Spa, FL
Pier 66 Hotel & Marina, FL
Sheraton Bonaventure Hotel &
    Spa, FL
Turnberry Isle Yacht & Country
    Club, FL

Washington, D.C.

Coolfont Resort, WV
The Greenbrier, WV

Philadelphia or New York

The Spa at Bally's Casino Hotel,
    NJ
Canyon Ranch in the Berkshires,
    MA
The Evolution Spa at The Equinox
    Hotel, VT
The Spa at Great Gorge, NJ
Gurney's Inn International Health
    & Beauty Spa, NY
The Hilton at Short Hills, NJ
HRH, NY
Living Springs Retreat, NY
New Age Health Spa, NY
Norwich Inn, CT
Pawling Health Manor, NY
The Shoreham Hotel & Spa, NJ

Boston

Canyon Ranch in the Berkshires,
    MA
The Evolution Spa at The Equinox
    Hotel, VT
Northern Pines Health Resort, ME
Norwich Inn, CT

Le Pli, MA
The Woods at Killington, VT

Toronto

King Ranch Health Spa & Fitness
    Resort, Ont.
Schomberg Health Spa & Retreat,
    Ont.

Montreal

Spa Concept at Bromont, P.Q.

Vancouver

The Hills Health & Guest Ranch,
    B.C.

BEST SPAS FOR MEN

Aerobics Center Guest Lodge, TX
Canyon Ranch, AZ
Duke University Diet & Fitness
    Center, NC
Evian, France
Four Seasons Hotel & Resort, TX
Hilton Head Health Institute, SC
Joe Weider's Shape, Muscle and
    Fitness, CA
La Costa Hotel & Spa, CA
Maharishi Ayur-Veda Health
    Center, MA
National Institute of Fitness, UT
New Life Spa/Liftline Lodge, VT
Palm-Aire Hotel & Spa, FL
Pritikin Longevity Resort, FL
Rancho La Puerta, Mexico
Rocky Mountain Wellness Spa, CO
Safety Harbor Spa & Fitness
    Center, FL
Structure House, NC
Two Bunch Palms, CA
The Woods Fitness Institute, WV

SPAS FOR WOMEN ONLY

Cal-A-Vie, CA
The Golden Door, CA

The Greenhouse, TX
Green Mountain at Fox Run, VT
HRH, NY
The Kerr House, OH
Schomberg Health Spa & Retreat,
    Ont., Canada
Southwind Health Resort, GA

BEST SPAS FOR SENIOR CITIZENS

Many European Spas, Especially
    in Central and Eastern Europe

Also
Lido Spa Hotel & Resort, FL

BEST SPAS FOR FAMILIES

Most Fitness and Beauty Spas at a
    Resort or Hotel

WHERE TO FIND THE BEST FOOD

Cal-A-Vie, CA
Canyon Ranch, AZ
Doral Saturnia, FL
Evian, France
Gurney's Inn International Health
    & Beauty Spa, NY
The Kerr House, OH
La Costa Hotel & Spa, CA
New Life Spa/Liftline Lodge, VT
Sonoma Mission Inn & Spa, CA
Southwind Health Resort, GA
Stresa, Italy

THE LEAST EXPENSIVE SPAS

Most New Age Retreats and
    Mineral Spring Spas, as well as
    Spas in Eastern Europe

Also
Deerfield Manor, PA
Lido Spa Hotel & Resort, FL
National Institute of Fitness, UT

Pawling Health Manor, NY
World of Fitness, UT

WHERE TO STOP SMOKING

Canyon Ranch, AZ
Coolfont Resort, WV
Living Springs Retreat, NY
The Oaks at Ojai, CA
The Palms at Palm Springs, CA
Rocky Mountain Wellness Spa, CO
St. Blasien, Germany
Sans Souci Health Resort, OH
Wildwood Lifestyle Center &
    Hospital, GA

SPAS WHERE YOU CAN BUY REAL ESTATE

Canyon Ranch, AZ
Canyon Ranch in the Berkshires,
    MA
The Spa at French Lick Springs,
    IN
The Spa at Great Gorge, NJ
Green Valley Health Resort, UT
Gurney's Inn International Health
    & Beauty Spa, NY
La Costa Hotel & Spa, CA
Norwich Inn & Spa, CT
Olympia Village Spa, WI
Palm-Aire Hotel & Spa, FL

BEST WORKOUT SPAS

The Ashram Healthort, CA
Cal-A-Vie, CA
Canyon Ranch, AZ
Canyon Ranch in the Berkshires,
    MA
Chianciano Terme, Italy
Doral Saturnia, FL
The Golden Door, CA
The Heartland, IL
Jane Fonda's Laurel Springs
    Retreat, CA
Joe Weider's Shape, Muscle, and
    Fitness, CA
Lake Austin Resort, TX

New Life Spa/Liftline Lodge, VT
The Oaks at Ojai, CA
The Palms at Palm Springs, CA
Palm-Aire Hotel & Spa, FL
The Phoenix, TX
Rancho La Puerta, Mexico
Safety Harbor Spa & Fitness
   Center, FL
Sheraton Bonaventure Hotel &
   Spa, FL
Stresa, Italy

WORLD'S MOST FAMOUS SPAS

Aerobics Center Guest Lodge, TX
The Ashram Healthort, CA
Baden-Baden, Germany
Canyon Ranch, AZ
Clinique La Prairie, Montreux,
   Switzerland
Duke University Diet & Fitness
   Center, NC
Evian, France
The Golden Door, CA
The Greenbrier, WV
The Greenhouse, TX
Green Mountain at Fox Run, VT
Gurney's Inn International Health
   & Beauty Spa, NY
The Homestead, VA
La Costa Hotel & Spa, CA
Maharishi Ayur-Veda Health
   Center, MA
Montecatini, Italy
Norwich Inn & Spa, CT
The Oaks at Ojai, CA
Palm-Aire Hotel & Spa, FL
The Phoenix, TX
Rancho La Puerta, Mexico
Safety Harbor Spa & Fitness
   Center, FL
Sheraton Bonaventure Hotel &
   Spa, FL
Sonoma Mission Inn & Spa, CA

SPAS WITH THE MOST SCENIC LOCATIONS

Centro Benessere di Stresa, Italy
Clinique La Prairie, Switzerland

Evian, France
Gurney's Inn International Health
   & Beauty Spa, NY
Le Sport, St. Lucia
Ligia Azevedo, Brazil
Lowe's Ventana Canyon Resort,
   AZ
The Plantation Spa, HI
Rancho La Puerta, Mexico
Rocky Mountain Wellness Spa, CO

SPAS ON THE BEACH

The Spa at Bally's Casino Hotel,
   NJ
Dr. Deal's Hawaiian Fitness
   Holiday, HI
Fountainbleu Hilton, FL
Gurney's Inn International Health
   & Beauty Spa, NY
Herzlia-on-Sea, Israel
Hyatt Regency Waikoloa, HI
Incosol Hotel/Spa, Spain
La Fiesta Americana Condesa
   Vallarta, Mexico
Lady Diane's Health & Fitness
   Resort, Jamaica
Le Sport, St. Lucia
Ligia Azevedo, Brazil
Ponte Vedra Inn & Club, FL
Regency Health Resort, FL
Sans Souci Hotel, Club & Spa,
   Jamaica
Sonesta Beach Hotel, Bermuda
Sonesta Sanibel Harbour Resort, FL

ONE-OF-A-KIND SPAS

Clinique La Prairie, Switzerland
Ligia Azevedo, Brazil
Maharishi Ayur-Veda Health
   Center, MA
Micheldorf, Austria

SKI SPAS

See Spas in Colorado, Wisconsin,
   Austria, and Switzerland

Also
Evian, France
The Evolution Spa at The Equinox
  Hotel, VT
The Spa at French Lick Springs,
  IN
The Spa at Great Gorge, NJ
The Greenbrier, WV
The Heartland, IL
The Hills Health & Guest Ranch,
  B.C., Canada
King Ranch Health Spa & Fitness
  Resort, Ont., Canada
New Age Health Spa, NY
New Life Spa/Liftline Lodge, VT
Northern Pines Health Resort, ME
Schomberg Health Spa & Retreat,
  Ont., Canada
Top Notch at Stowe, VT
The Woods at Killington, VT

HIKING SPAS

The Ashram Healthort, CA
Canyon Ranch, AZ
Dr. Deal's Hawaiian Fitness
  Holiday, HI
Green Mountain at Fox Run, VT
National Institute of Fitness, UT
New Life Spa/Liftline Lodge, VT
The Oaks at Ojai, CA
The Plantation Spa, HI
Ranch La Puerta, Mexico
The Woods Fitness Institute, WV

SPAS WITH SUPREME PAMPERING

All Luxury Spas Including
  European Luxury Spas

Also
Aurora House, OH
HRH, NY
Marriott's Desert Springs Resort
  & Spa, CA
Sonesta Beach Hotel, Bermuda

SPAS WITH MOST ADVANCED PROGRAMS

Aerobics Center Guest Lodge, TX
The Ashram Healthort, CA
Brenner's Park, Baden-Baden,
  Germany
Canyon Ranch, AZ
Charleston Retreat Weight
  Management Center, SC
Clinique La Prairie, Switzerland
Duke University Diet & Fitness
  Center, NC
The Golden Door, CA
Green Mountain at Fox Run, VT
Hilton Head Health Institute, SC
Josefinehof Hotel Im Park, Villach,
  Austria
Maharishi Ayur-Veda Health
  Center, MA
National Institute of Fitness, UT
New Life Spa/Liftline Lodge, VT
The Oaks at Ojai, CA
Palm-Aire Hotel & Spa, FL
The Palms at Palm Springs, CA
Pritikin Longevity Resort, FL
Rancho La Puerto, Mexico
St. Blasien, Germany
Stresa, Italy
Structure House, NC
Wiedemann Health Centers,
  Germany, Italy, & Spain

MOST EXPERIENCED SPAS

See European Spas

Also
Aerobics Center Guest Lodge, TX
Canyon Ranch, AZ
Duke University Diet & Fitness
  Center, NC
The Golden Door, CA
Green Mountain at Fox Run, VT
The Greenbrier, WV
The Greenhouse, TX
Hilton Head Health Institute, SC
Ixtapan Resort Hotel & Spa,
  Mexico
La Costa Hotel & Spa, CA

Lido Spa Hotel & Resort, FL
National Institute of Fitness, UT
New Life Spa/Liftline Lodge, VT
The Oaks at Ojai, CA
Palm-Aire Hotel & Spa, FL
The Palms at Palm Springs, CA
Pawling Health Manor, NY
Rancho La Puerta, Mexico
Safety Harbor Spa & Fitness
  Center, FL
Sheraton Bonaventure Hotel &
  Spa, FL
Structure House, NC

SPAS IN URBAN AREAS

Aerobics Center Guest Lodge, TX
The Spa at Bally's Casino Hotel,
  NJ
The Spa at The Biltmore, FL
Claremont Resort, CA
Doral Saturnia, FL
Duke University Diet & Fitness
  Center, NC
Eurovita Spa at the Avenue Plaza
  Hotel, LA
Fountainbleu Hilton, FL
Four Seasons Hotel & Resort, TX
The Greenhouse, TX
Hilton at Short Hills, NJ
Hippocrates Health Institute, FL
Joe Weider's Shape, Muscle &
  Fitness, CA
La Costa Hotel & Spa, CA
Le Meridien Spa, CA
Le Pli, MA
Lido Spa Hotel & Resort, FL
Marriott's Camelback Inn Resort
  & Golf Club, AZ
Palm-Aire Hotel & Spa, FL
The Phoenix, AZ
Pier 66 Hotel and Marina, FL
Pritikin Longevity Resort, FL
Ramada Grand Hotel
  Margitsziget, Hungary
Regency Health Resort, FL
Safety Harbor Spa & Fitness
  Center, FL
Sheraton Bonaventure Hotel &
  Spa, FL
Structure House, NC

Thermal Hotel Margitsziget,
  Hungary
Tucson National Resort & Spa, AZ
Turnberry Isle Yacht & Country
  Club, FL
Verandah Club, TX

SPAS IN MOST INTERESTING TOURIST LOCALES

Baden-Baden, Germany
Baden Bei Wien, Austria
Carmel Country Spa, CA
Evian, France
Grayshott Hall, Great Britain
Herzlia-on-Sea, Israel
Ixtapan Resort Hotel & Spa,
  Mexico
Montecatini, Italy
Safety Harbor Spa & Fitness
  Center, FL
Wiedemann Center, Ambach,
  Germany

FASTING SPAS

Deerfield Manor, PA
Evergreen Manor, AR
Hippocrates Health Institute, FL
Micheldorf, Austria
New Age Health Spa, NY
Pawling Health Manor, NY
Regency Health Resort, FL
St. Blasien, Germany
Schomberg Health Spa & Retreat,
  Ont., Canada
Wiedemann Center, Meersburg,
  Germany

GOLF SPAS

Doral Saturnia, FL
Evian, France
Four Seasons Hotel & Resort, TX
Grayshott Hall, Great Britain
La Costa Hotel & Spa, CA
Loew's Ventana Canyon Resort,
  AZ

Marriott's Camelback Inn Resort & Golf Club, AZ
Marriott's Desert Springs Resort & Spa, CA
Montecatini, Italy
Norwich Inn & Spa, CT
Palm-Aire Hotel & Spa, FL
Sans Souci Hotel, Club & Spa, Jamaica
Sheraton Bonaventure Hotel & Spa, FL
Tucson National Resort & Spa, AZ
Turnberry Isle Yacht & Country Club, FL
Wiedemann Health Center, Gran Canaria, Spain

TENNIS SPAS

Doral Saturnia, FL
Evian, France
Green Valley Health Resort & Spa, UT
La Costa Hotel & Spa, CA
Loew's Ventana Canyon Resort, AZ
New Life Spa/Liftline Lodge, VT
Palm-Aire Hotel & Spa, FL
Rancho La Puerta, Mexico
Safety Harbor Spa & Fitness Center, FL
Sans Souci Hotel, Club & Spa, Jamaica
Sheraton Bonaventure Hotel & Spa, FL
Sonesta Sanibel Harbour Resort, FL
Tucson National Resort & Spa, AZ
Turnberry Isle Yacht & Country Club, FL

SPAS WITH MOTHER/ DAUGHTER PACKAGES

The Golden Door, CA
The Oaks at Ojai, CA
The Palms at Palm Springs, CA
Sans Souci, OH

SPAS IN GAMBLING LOCALES

Baden-Baden, Germany
Baden Bei Wien, Austria
The Spa at Bally's Casino Hotel, NJ
Budapest, Hungary
Evian, France
Incosol, Marbella, Spain
Kitzbühel, Austria
Sonesta Beach Hotel, Bermuda
Villach, Austria

VEGETARIAN SPAS

The Ashram Healthort, CA
Dr. Deal's Hawaiian Fitness Holiday, HI
Evergreen Manor, AR
Hippocrates Health Institute, FL
Living Springs Retreat, NY
Northern Pines Health Resort, ME
The Plantation Spa, HI
Regency Health Resort, FL
Schomberg Health Spa & Retreat, Ont., Canada

SPAS FOR STRESS REDUCTION

Canyon Ranch, AZ
Clinique La Prairie, Switzerland
Murietta Hot Springs Resort & Health Spa, CA
Rocky Mountain Wellness Spa, CO
St. Blasien, Germany
Southwind Health Resort, GA
Stresa, Italy

CLOTHING OPTIONAL SPAS

Micheldorf, Austria

DETOXIFICATION SPAS

Hippocrates Health Institute, FL
Micheldorf, Austria
Rocky Mountain Wellness Spa, CO
Wildwood Lifestyle Center & Hospital, GA

Beauty and Pampering Glossary

You'll find a wide variety of other beauty and pampering treatments available in the world of spas. To help you make informed decisions about which ones you'd like to experience, we've included a glossary of terms you should know before embarking on your spa experience. And in order to enjoy these treatments to the fullest and at your convenience, it's a good idea, whenever possible, to make your personal service appointments in advance or as soon as you arrive at the spa.

Acupuncture: an ancient and painless Chinese healing method of inserting needles into various parts of the body to relieve pain.

Aqua-aerobics: an aerobic workout in a body of water, using water and your own body weight as resistance.

Aromatherapy: a Shiatsu-style body massage that uses fragrant oils, Bach, or other flower essences to relax the body and stimulate the natural flow of lymph and other therapeutic benefits. This special massage treatment takes about an hour and a half. To enjoy the greatest benefits from this treatment, do not exercise immediately before or after your massage.

Aslavital: a drug developed by Dr. Ana Aslan of Romania used to reverse the effects of aging in the cardiovascular and central nervous systems.

Athletic massage: a deep massage directed at specific muscle groups and/or injured areas.

Balneotherapies or Baineotherapies: generic terms for mineral water treatments.

Biofeedback: the monitoring of body functions, such as pulse, and muscle tension with an electronic sensing device. Most often used to measure stress levels.

Body composition analysis: a method of measuring body fat, the result of which is used to design a specific program of diet and exercise best suited to your personal needs and goals.

Brush and tone: sloughing of the skin with a dry brush to remove dead skin layers and increase circulation. Lotion is usually applied following dry brushing.

Cellular therapy: an injection of living fetal lamb cells to help revitalize the body and impede the aging process.

Circuit training: a combination of aerobics and weight machines.

Dead Sea mud treatment: a very popular treatment that involves applications of mineral-rich mud imported from the Dead Sea to cleanse pores and relax muscles. The mud also eases the pain of arthritis and rheumatism. (Salt from the Dead Sea is very coarse and 37 percent higher in mineral content than other sea salt.)

Dulse scrub: a technique whereby the entire body is scrubbed vigorously with a mixture of powered dulse seaweed and oil or water; the treatment removes dead skin and enriches the skin with minerals and vitamins.

Electro-acupuncture: a technique of introducing electric current into the body through the tips of acupuncture needles.

Electrotherapy: treatments using ultra sound, short waves, infrared rays, or various forms of electricity.

Fango pack or Fango therapy: highly mineralized dehydrated mud mixed with wax or water is applied as a heat pack for soothing muscles, increasing blood flow, and sweating out toxins; it is usually applied to small sections of the body at a time.

Fast: a diet of fruit and vegetable juice or water for a determined period of time to detoxify the body and give the digestive system a rest.

Foot reflexology: an ancient Chinese healing technique that massages points on the foot to relax you physically and mentally, to stimulate the healing process in other areas of the body, and to restore an unobstructed flow of energy throughout your body.

Herbal wrap: strips of linen are soaked in herbal preparations then tightly wrapped around the body, after which the person is covered in a sheet and lies in a quiet place for a period of time.

Hydrotherapy: a generic term used for mineral baths and water therapies, some of which utilize jets and underwater massage.

Inhalation rooms: steam mixed with eucalyptus inhaled to decongest the respiratory system.

Iridology: a relatively new science that "reads" the markings of the eye to reveal the condition of body organs.

Kneipp system: highly regarded European therapies that combine hydrotherapy with herbal preparations and a diet of natural foods.

Loofah scrub: a full-body polish with a loofah sponge to exfoliate dead skin cells and improve circulation; an exhilarating way to begin or end a day's activities.

Low-impact aerobics: Aerobic dance routines in which one foot is always on the floor.

Lymph drainage: a deep but soft massage of specific areas of the body located around the lymph nodes; also used extensively for neck, head, and shoulders during facial massage.

Naturopathy: a natural healing therapy that uses plants and flowers for medicinal purposes.

Paraffin treatment: a massage with moisture cream and vitamin-enriched paraffin wax to cleanse pores and soften skin.

Nautilus: a line of weight-training equipment.

Paracourse (also called paracours and vitacourse): a trail of exercise stations for various areas of training.

Phytotherapy: a generic term used for mud packs, baths, massages, or inhalation treatments that use natural herbs or plant oils.

Polarity massage: a gentle massage technique used to unblock and release energy through gentle massage; also used to align the body.

Polarity therapy: A balancing of energy within the body through massage, meditation, exercise, and diet.

Reflexology: massage of pressure points on the hands, feet, or other body parts to unblock the flow of energy throughout the body.

Repechage massage or facial: herbal or aloe, seaweed, and finally clay or mud are used to create a combination of hardened masks for deep cleansing and moisturizing.

Rolfing: deep and sometimes painful massage technique used to re-align the skeletal structure, improve energy flow, and relieve stress caused by emotional trauma.

Roman bath: heated sea water Jacuzzi with jets, equipped with benches for seated bathing.

Salt-glo rub: entire body massage with coarse salt and fragrant oils for removal of dead skin and improved circulation.

Sauna: dry heat used to open the pores and encourage the sweating out of body impurities.

Scotch hose: a standing body massage delivered by a therapist with high-pressure hoses using hot and cold sea or fresh water.

Seaweed wrap: the body is covered in mineral-rich seaweed and then washed off to smooth and restore the skin.

Shiatsu massage: a Japanese version of Chinese acupressure massage following energy patterns or "meridians" of the body, applying pressure to specific points to restore the flow of energy and promote internal healing.

Sports massage: a deep massage for treating specific muscle groups.

Swedish massage: gentle manipulation of the body using five different movements and oils to improve circulation and foster healing by allowing body nutrients to spread more easily through the system.

Swiss showers: a full-body massage while standing under powerful jets; sometimes administered by a therapist using a hose.

Tai Chi (tai chi chuan): an ancient Oriental discipline of exercise and meditation.

Thalassotherapy: an ancient Greek therapy of water treatments that uses seawater, seaweed, and algae. Individual tubs of sea water are equipped with powerful underwater jets used for deep massage; therapist may also apply manual massage to body with hoses.

Trager body work: gentle rhythmic massage technique for releasing tension and realigning the body structure.

Vichy therapy: combination of Swiss shower treatment and salt-glo scrub or loofah scrub.

Waxing: a technique used to remove unwanted hair from the face, legs, arms, or body.

Yoga: a technique of stretching and deep breathing to promote relaxation.

Zen: a Japanese form of meditation to relieve tension and balance the body.

Index

Aerobic exercise, benefits of, 17–18
After-dinner activities, 16
Alcohol, 2
Aromatherapy, 29

Beauty treatments, 3, 25, 28–29
Behavior modification, 5
Body wraps, 29

Clothing, for spa vacation
    evening wear, 8
    for exercise, 8
    footwear, 9
    informal, 8

Etiquette
    in exercise studio, 10
    at meals, 10–11
    in pool/Jacuzzi, 10
    with roommate, 10
    tipping, 10
Exercise errors, 21
Exercise at home, tips for, 21–22

Facials, 3, 28–29
Fasting, 5
Fitness options, 3, 15–16
    aerobics, 16
    hiking, 15
    swimming, 16
    walking, 15
Food, 4–6, 31–33, 37–38
    and exercise, 22

at luxury spas, 4
at New Age spas, 5
spas with best, 37–38
at weight-loss spas, 5–6
Footwear, 9, 19

Health options
    at classic spas, 2
    at New Age spas, 5
    at spas abroad, 7–8
    at spas in hotel or resort, 4
Herbal wraps, 29
Hiking, 15, 19
    as aerobic workout, 19
    clothes for, 19
    footwear for, 19
Home cuisine, spa-style, 33–36
    herbs, 33–34
    oils, 35
    spices, 34–35
    vinegars, 35
Hydrotherapy, 6, 29

Jones, Jeanne, 4

Kneipp herbal treatments, 6, 29

Massage
    clothing for, 26–27
    lymphatic drainage, 27–28
    masseur vs. masseuse, 26
    Polarity, 28
    Reflexology, 28

Massage (*Continued*)
  Shiatsu, 5, 27
  Sports, 27
  Swedish, 26, 27
  Trager, 28
Meditation, 15
Mineral springs, 30
Mineral waters, uses of, 6, 7
Morscher, Betsy, 12
Mud baths, 30

Nutrition programs, 31–33
  and dietary recommendations, 31
  at luxury spas, 4
  at New Age spas, 5
  and weight loss, 32
  at weight-loss spas, 6

Personal-care items, 9
Pre-spa physical preparation, 16

Riley, Leni Reed, 33

Salt-glo rub, 3, 29
Smoking, 2, 4, 10
  cessation programs, 10

Spas, types of
  classic (self-contained), 2–3
  in a hotel or resort, 3
  luxury, 4
  New Age, 4–5

weight-loss, 5–6
Spa cuisine, exceptional, 37–38
  Cal-A-Vie (CA), 37
  Canyon Ranch (AZ), 37
  Doral Saturnia (FL), 37
  The Kerr House (OH), 37
  La Costa Hotel & Spa (CA), 37
  New Life Spa/Liftline Lodge (VT),
    38
  Southwind (GA), 38
Stress reduction, 5, 11–13
Stroot, Michel, 4, 37

Thalassotherapy, 3
Thermal therapy, 6
Tipping, 10
Tobacco, 2, 4, 10

Vegetarianism, 5

Walking, 15, 18–19
  aerobic, 18
  fitness, 18–19
  footwear for, 19
Weight loss/management
  at classic spas, 2
  at weight-loss spas, 6
Weight training, 20–21
  benefits of, 20
  components of, 20
  form for, 20
  free weights vs. machines, 20–21

SAFETY HARBOR SPA & FITNESS CENTER
SAFETY HARBOR, FLORIDA

$150 OFF 7-NIGHT TOTAL FITNESS PLAN

Stay must be 7 nights or longer. Only 1 coupon per person per visit. Coupon is not transferable. Only original coupons accepted, not reproductions thereof. This discount cannot be used in conjunction with any other promotional offer. Not valid with group rates or other discounts. Void where prohibited. Offer is subject to change without notice.

✂ —

STRUCTURE HOUSE
DURHAM, NORTH CAROLINA

$100 OFF PER PERSON FOR 2-WEEK PROGRAM

✂ —

FONTANA SPA AT THE ABBEY
FONTANA, WISCONSIN

25% DISCOUNT WITH MINIMUM 2-NIGHT STAY

✂ —

THE SPA AT THE BILTMORE
CORAL GABLES, FLORIDA

15% OFF 2- AND 4-NIGHT SPA PACKAGES

✂ —

THE HILTON AT SHORT HILLS
SHORT HILLS, NEW JERSEY

1 HALF-HOUR PERSONAL FITNESS EVALUATION

Must contact spa to make an appointment.

PLANTATION SPA
KA'A'AWA, OAHU, HAWAII

$250 OFF 1-WEEK STAY

This coupon may not be used in conjunction with any other discounts, certificates or promotions.

✂ —

✂ —

SONESTA SANIBEL HARBOUR RESORT
FT. MYERS, FLORIDA

1 COMPLIMENTARY 1-HOUR MASSAGE

✂ —

✂ —

GREEN VALLEY HEALTH RESORT & SPA
ST. GEORGE, UTAH

FREE AIR TRAVEL FROM ANYWHERE IN THE CONTINENTAL U.S. IN CONJUNCTION WITH A 1-WEEK MINIMUM SPA PACKAGE

Some restrictions apply. Please present this coupon when making your reservation.